More Praise for
Small Business Taxes Made Easy

"Every U.S. business owner will benefit from Rosenberg's clear, well-written explanations of complex, arcane tax concepts. You'll run your business more effectively and you'll stay out of trouble with the IRS. Buy this book."

—Shel Horowitz, author of
Principled Profit: Marketing That Puts People First
and owner of frugalmarketing.com

"Here is a book that is short on theory and long on practical, plain-spoken advice. From how to buy office supplies to how to deal with the IRS, Rosenberg taps decades of business savvy to walk readers through the minefields of new business ownership."

—Al Tompkins, author, teacher, consultant

"When I started my career as a CPA, one of the most valuable lessons I learned was to simplify and explain the basics. Eva has managed to take a complex subject and simplify it for all."

—Ken Leebow, The Incredible Internet Guy
www.incredibleinternetguy.com

"From the very beginning, this excellent book clearly sets itself apart from other tax books. As the title implies, Eva's book gives the small business person a good handle on tax issues, and the checklists make it easy to follow through on what you learn. This is a must-have book for every small business person and anyone wanting to start his or her own small business."

—Dennis Gaskill, BoogieJack.com

"Eva Rosenberg counsels new entrepreneurs that they'll need a business plan if they want to succeed. *Small Business Taxes Made Easy* should be the first step in that plan."

—Kay Bell, tax editor at Bankrate.com

Small Business Taxes Made Easy

How to Increase Your Deductions, Reduce What You Owe, and Boost Your Profits

EVA ROSENBERG

AMERICA'S TOP SMALL BUSINESS TAX EXPERT

McGraw·Hill

New York   Chicago   San Francisco   Lisbon   London   Madrid   Mexico City
Milan   New Delhi   San Juan   Seoul   Singapore   Sydney   Toronto

Library of Congress Cataloging-in-Publication Data

Rosenberg, Eva.
    Small business taxes made easy : how to increase your deductions, reduce
what you owe, and boost your profits / Eva Rosenberg.
        p.   cm.
    ISBN 0-07-144168-9
    1. Small business—Taxation—United States.   2. Small business—United
States—Planning.   3. Small business—Taxation—Law and legislation—United
States.   4. Income tax deductions—United States.   I. Title.

HD2341.R657   2004
343.7305'268—dc22   2004020224

1 2 3 4 5 6 7 8 9 0   DOC/DOC   3 2 1 0 9 8 7 6 5 4

ISBN 0-07-144168-9

McGraw-Hill books are available at special quantity discounts to use as premiums and
sales promotions, or for use in corporate training programs. For more information, please
write to the Director of Special Sales, Professional Publishing, McGraw-Hill, Two Penn
Plaza, New York, NY 10121-2298. Or contact your local bookstore.

This book is intended to be a guide to familiarize the reader with tax and business
concepts. It is not intended to provide legal or tax advice. No mere book is a substitute for
advice from your own tax professionals, who have a picture of your personal financial and
business situation. Also, at the time this book was written, all information was current. Tax
laws change quickly, so some information may be outdated by the time you read it.

This book is printed on acid-free paper.

This book is dedicated to the two people who've kept me going during the long days and longer nights of writing this book—and building my business over the years—my husband, Rick, and my right hand, Lourdes Rodriguez. You bring sunshine to my days.

CONTENTS

10 OWNERS' FRINGE BENEFITS, RETIREMENT, AND DEFERRING TAXES 181

11 ESTIMATED PAYMENTS 195

ACKNOWLEDGMENTS

This book would never have come about without my editor, Donya Dickerson. I am profoundly grateful to Donya for her vision and skill, which made this book possible—and easy.

So many people were responsible for the information that went into this volume; it's hard to thank them all. My clients, family, and friends over the years have taught me so much about business, taxes, and life. Their successes and failures are the models for the cases in this book—as are the experiences of all those who write to Ask TaxMama. I couldn't make those questions up.

My heartfelt appreciation to the artistic Serenata, whose feisty personality and inspired design talents shape the www.TaxMama.com website.

Three special people went out of their way in 2004 to guide my writing skills, encouraging me to challenge my tax creativity: my editor at *Revenue* magazine, Tom Murphy, who made so many things possible; and my editors at www.CBS .MarketWatch.com, Steven Kerch and Chris Pummer, who had faith despite my controversial subjects.

I especially want to thank Roger B. Adams, the enrolled agent in Lisbon, Portugal, who instigated the controversy about turning stock theft losses into casualty losses.

I've been privileged to get advice and input from many of the talented, passionate tax professional members of the Ask TaxMama Pro family—especially Bruce Drooks, J.D., of Canoga Park, CA; Lucie Sample, EA, and Blakely Sanford, EA, in San Diego, CA; John Balian, Esq., in Sherman Oaks, CA; Mel Kreger,

EA/LLM, of North Hollywood, CA; Doug Thorburn, EA, in Northridge, CA; Susan Legaspi, EA/CPA, and Dale Zuehls, CPA and attorney, from downtown Los Angeles, CA; publisher Jim Banks of Bozeman, MT; Jan Zobel, EA, in Oakland, CA; tax attorney Fred Daily of Incline Village, NV; David L. Mellem, EA, in Green Bay, WI; Diane Gray, EA, of Santa Monica, CA; Tom Blair of Callahan, FL; accountant Abraham Fasten of Brooklyn, NY; Fred W. Fetner Jr., of Rock Hill, SC; Jim Magno in Rockville, MD; Linda Dorfmont, EA, of El Segundo, CA; Richard Kehoe, CPA, in Kihei, HI; Joyce Ragels, EA, in Arizona . . . and countless others who inspire me or bring me laughter each day.

Special thanks to Tax Daddy, Dean Young, PC, of McDonough, GA, in memoriam—who touched my life briefly, and brought his joy and enthusiasm to the world of taxes.

Let's not forget the international cheering section—my friend and mentor, the Countess Logan Bentley Lessona of Italy; the hypnotically hilarious Dr. Bryan M. Knight of Canada; my favorite electronics guru and ham, Ian Purdie, VK2TIP, of Australia; my LaughMate Gunjan Saraf of India; my former *Monday* magazine editor Amit Malik, also in India; the meticulous Eric Lee in Singapore; and the indomitable Herby Olschewski, of South Africa and the world . . . and all the other HelpMates who brighten my days . . . and my biz-whiz kid, American Kevin Colleran, who has won every youth entrepreneurial award there is.

I especially want to thank all the folks at the IRS and the Taxpayers Advocate's office who are always so generous to me with their time and humor—both personally and on the job—Don Ogle in Texas; Tonjua Menefee, Bruce Friedland, Anthony Burke, and Nancy Mathis in Washington, D.C.; Laurie Keleman, Ted Meyer, Eric Smith, Pamela C. Williams, and Pearlie T. Wilson in Los Angeles; and Steve Jensen, retired Los Angeles District Director, who showed me how much fun the IRS could be. Thanks also to those special, dedicated folks at the IRS who actually go out of their way to help complete strangers solve their problems. They prove that a tax system can be administered fairly.

Let's not forget Pnina Bergman. Without her, I wouldn't be doing taxes today.

INTRODUCTION

A Letter from Eva Rosenberg to You, the Business Owner

Dear Entrepreneur,

(Yes, *you*. If you're starting a business, please start thinking of yourself right now as an *entrepreneur*.)

Many books on the market tell you how to organize for your business records, prepare your tax returns, even how to make decisions or choices. Some are excellent.

So why does the world need yet another book on small business taxes? Because even the best books focus primarily on the record-keeping or legal aspects of small business taxes. For your business to succeed, you must *also* see how the reporting requirements can be used to improve your business management, provide better decision-making tools, and increase your profits. And providing that information is what makes this book different.

With all the resentment and resistance toward paying taxes and toward the flood of reporting requirements, you've got to see what's in it for you. What do *you* get from your investment of time and money? It doesn't only benefit the IRS and your state and local governments.

While each chapter of this book explains tax concepts and responsibilities, it also helps you understand how you benefit from following those guidelines.

You're not in business to supply a flood of paperwork to the government. Nor are you sweating blood trying to meet your business, financial, and family obligations in order to buy your tax pro a new BMW.

You're in business to have more control of your life and time; to earn more money than you could on a job; and to build a future—and a legacy—for your family and future generations.

Otherwise, why work so hard? Just go back to your traditional nine-to-five job. Seriously, there's more to running a business than appears on the surface. Some people make it appear effortless—and they often go out of business quickly as a result. Others make it seem a gargantuan burden—and they end up hating every minute of it. They destroy their family and relationships in the process, blaming everyone else for their failures.

Then there are those people who start up, and everything goes right. Life is good. Family and social relationships remain solid, and they maintain balance in their lives. That's what I want for you.

Listening to the news, you often hear when large businesses fail. You're probably still shaking your head over the whole dot-com bust, wondering how all those businesses failed after raising millions of dollars in venture capital or through their initial public offering.

The businesses that failed went wrong in one, or all, of three ways:

1. They didn't have a realistic business plan.
2. They didn't plan for success.
3. They were run by immature and inexperienced people who simply blew all the money without looking for reasonable returns on their spending.

You're buying this book to avoid all those mistakes. Use this book to learn from others' failures and successes. Please, make a commitment to devote all the time and resources needed to make your business work.

Otherwise, put this book back on the shelf. It's not for you.

How to Use This Book

I didn't write this book to bore you, bully you, or enable your failure.

If you can't make a serious commitment to create your business plan, set up and use a proper accounting system, and be ethical in tax reporting—please don't start the business. You'll earn much more, with less effort, less stress, and less risk, with a job working for someone else. Really, you will.

Take into account how much you could earn on a job, or on the money you're investing to get this business going. Even if you borrow the money, think of how many hours of work it will take to pay it back.

Those are called "opportunity costs." It's important to understand what you're giving up to start your business. When I started my business, I knew what I was getting into. I relish the independence and the lack of office politics. I love my clients, the people I work with, and the ones I consult with. Despite being constantly behind in my workload, I rejoice in the flood of new work and fresh ideas that comes pouring in each day from friends and readers.

The two most important things I want you to know, going in:

- Love what you do.
- Don't delude yourself into thinking your goal is to pay the least amount of tax possible. Your real goal is to end up with the *highest disposable income possible*—and to be in great physical and mental health when you get there.

That's what I'd like to help you achieve.

You're about to learn how following the IRS's rules for small business owners will make you richer, happier, and less stressed.

TaxMama's warning: although I can make changes at the IRS, I can't change grammatical rules. So wherever you see URLs in this book that seem to have colons, commas, or periods as the last character, ignore that final character when typing them into your browser.

Comparing a Job and a Business

Be sure to understand these distinctions between a job and a business. People starting out on their own rarely realize just how many things they've taken for granted on a job. These are the things that just happened invisibly, in the background, taken care of by your employer's infrastructure. Even if you felt as though you were doing most of it for him or her, when you're on your own, the sidebar will show you just how many more things you'll need to oversee—things that will drain your time, patience, and resources.

Once you understand the additional demands owning a business places on you, perhaps you should know the benefits, too.

- You *do* get to control your time. So if you'd rather spend time with your friends or children during the day, you are free to work at night when it's quiet.

- If you want to take off and go somewhere, you don't have to ask permission.
- You never have to be afraid you'll lose your job again.
- If you don't like a client or customer, you are free to politely send them away. You never have to do business with anyone who doesn't treat you with respect.
- You are free to take chances and opportunities your boss might have turned away.
- Whenever you don't like what you're doing, you can change directions.
- You can do the work you love.
- You can really enjoy going to work each day.

When You Have a Traditional Job

THE *GOOD* THINGS

- Your boss ensures there's money coming in, that it gets into the bank, and that your payroll is covered.
- Your boss pays your payroll taxes, your workers' compensation insurance, your vacations, and your sick pay.
- Your boss, or staff paid by your boss, gets the customers; orders and pays for the supplies you use; and buys and sets up your computer, telephone, and the other tools you take for granted every day.
- Your boss arranges to take care of all the billing, the administrative paperwork, and all the day-to-day trivia needed to run a business. All you have to do is show up and do your job. You get your paycheck, leave, and don't have to think about things once you're off the clock.

THE *BAD* THINGS

- But what if you want to leave? You've got a doctor's appointment. Your kids have a recital. You're not feeling well. You just don't feel like working. You have to ask permission—which you sometimes don't get. Or you have to lie.
- You hate a customer or client, but you're stuck dealing with him or her if they're important to your boss.
- Don't like a business practice or policy? If you want to keep your job, you've got to do it their way.
- Your boss assigns the workload. How many times have they dumped stuff on you at the last minute that's been sitting there for weeks? Then you're stuck working overtime you hadn't anticipated.

When You Have a Business

THE *BAD* THINGS

- You have to take the time to do all those "Good Things" listed under "When You Have a Traditional Job."
- Or, you have to pay people to do all those things. Then you must generate enough extra income to cover their compensation.
- Trying to do it all yourself won't give you the time to sell and build your customer or client base.
- Or, if you do have the time, you won't have time to do the work.
- So you'll need to learn the most cost-effective use of your time. You'll want to learn what is worth doing yourself and what you should outsource or hire staff to do.
- Or, you'll need to create a solid budget and business plan to determine how much money you'll need to raise to cover your operating costs until your business starts to turn a profit.
- Please, please remember, while being in business for yourself does mean you work your own hours, it could mean you work *all* of them. Expect to put in 50 to 75 percent more hours than you worked doing the same job for someone else.

THE *GOOD* THINGS

- You can take time off whenever it suits you—no excuses or lies needed.
- You don't have to keep clients or customers who don't treat you with respect. (Or, you can charge them lots more to make it worth your while.)
- You set the policies. You never have to do anything against your morals or ethics.
- *You get to enjoy your life!*

If you're still prepared to go forward, if I can't talk you out of it—then let's get to work. You're going to do great!

Join me for your adventure in building a business.

Best wishes,
Eva Rosenberg
Your TaxMama

LIGHTEN UP

You're about to venture into dangerous and terrifying territory—the World of Taxes.

It's not as bad as you think. Get comfortable with the humor and ironies in this ever-shifting world. It will make all the onerous rules easier to bear.

Believe it or not, these quotes come to you courtesy of the Internal Revenue Service. Come back to this page any time your spirits need a boost of humor.

Taxes are what we pay for civilized society.

—Oliver Wendell Holmes Jr.,
U.S. Supreme Court Justice

The power of taxing people and their property is essential to the very existence of government.

—James Madison, U.S. President

To tax and to please, no more than to love and to be wise, is not given to men.

—Edmund Burke, eighteenth-century Irish political philosopher and British statesman

I am proud to be paying taxes in the United States. The only thing is—I could be just as proud for half the money.

—ARTHUR GODFREY, entertainer

People who complain about taxes can be divided into two classes: men and women.

—UNKNOWN

No government can exist without taxation. This money must necessarily be levied on the people; and the grand art consists of levying so as not to oppress.

—FREDERICK THE GREAT, eighteenth-century Prussian king

Like mothers, taxes are often misunderstood, but seldom forgotten.

—LORD BRAMWELL, nineteenth-century English jurist

The best measure of a man's honesty isn't his income tax return. It's the zero adjust on his bathroom scale.

—ARTHUR C. CLARKE, author

Next to being shot at and missed, nothing is really quite as satisfying as an income tax refund.

—F. J. RAYMOND, humorist

A tax loophole is something that benefits the other guy. If it benefits you, it is tax reform.

—RUSSELL B. LONG, U.S. Senator

Few of us ever test our powers of deduction, except when filling out an income tax form.

—LAURENCE J. PETER, author

The hardest thing in the world to understand is the income tax.

—ALBERT EINSTEIN, physicist

Taxation with representation ain't so hot either.

—GERALD BARZAN, humorist

Where there is an income tax, the just man will pay more and the unjust less on the same amount of income.
—PLATO

Income tax has made more liars out of the American people than golf.
—WILL ROGERS, humorist

A good tax return is like a good mystery novel. You follow the clues, make deductions, and arrive at a profitable conclusion.
—EVA ROSENBERG, TaxMama

1

SMALL BUSINESS CHECKLIST

The most exciting phrase to hear in science, the one that heralds new discoveries, is not "Eureka!"[1] but "That's funny."

—Isaac Asimov

Starting a business is really easy. Many small business owners are in business before they even realize it. Someone likes something you make or do and offers to pay for it. Then another person asks. Pretty soon, something that started out as a hobby or family meal is bringing in a stream of income, even though you never intended to be in business. This is particularly true for the millions of people starting their own personal websites. Sure, the sites might start out as personal interest pages. But as you fill them with so much good information, suddenly they are discovered by hordes of people and income starts rolling in. Oops, you're in business and didn't even know it. It is a wonderful feeling, though, isn't it?

Other times businesses are started with a clear purpose. Some people, for example, get frustrated because a type of product isn't available or because a service that should be there isn't obtainable. These smart people see the void and fill it. Sometimes, they simply start doing it for friends, like a carpool service, and a business grows from there.

Other people come up with a great idea to hit it rich and start building the business around the idea. Usually, they get so excited their friends and family get caught up in the excitement and give them money. Or, if they're really aggressive, they'll raise the money from strangers or through banks, loans, or venture capital.

---

1. *Eureka* means "I found it."

And then there are those people who really want to start a business, but don't know what business to start. If you don't have a clue but want one, read Paul and Sarah Edwards' book *The Best Home Businesses for the 21st Century: The Inside Information You Need to Know to Select a Home-Based Business That's Right for You*, published by Jeremy P. Tarcher. It will not only give you ideas, but tell you what skills and tools you need to make that business work for you.

Which of these businesses will succeed? Which will fail? Can you tell just by reading about the personalities involved and the nature of the start-up? Not really.

Three Indicators Will Predict the Success of the Business

There are three key factors that will predict the success of any business. Look at the descriptions below and see how they fit your business.

1. **How big will the business grow?** If a business stays small—such as a mom-and-pop operation—it may never make a fortune, but it can generate a nice, modest cash flow, without a fuss. If handled properly, some of these businesses will support forever—without much stress—a household in modest, happy style.

2. **Has the business developed a plan—something to map out how it is organized and when it grows, how to deal with success?** The people who have the foresight to treat their businesses as a real enterprise generally grow it properly, make excellent profits, and have something solid to pass on to their children. Or, they sell out to a larger company, for millions, when they are ready to retire or exit.

3. **Did the business owners take all the right compliance steps to learn of their tax and licensing obligations, and stay on top of them?** Too many small business owners, even those that aren't home-based, just never take the time to look into the laws and rules that regulate them. They just trip along blithely, doing what they do, and not dealing with licenses, payroll issues, or, sometimes, even filing issues, until these issues come and bite them in the derrière. Don't think I'm kidding. I've seen too many nice people come to me because they were in such trouble with the IRS (or city licensing people or sales tax departments) that they were about to lose their business—even though it was successful. Or maybe these people were in trouble precisely because their business was successful and it had finally come to the attention of the authorities.

Remember, *ignorance of the law is no excuse.* It's your responsibility to learn what your business must do—it's not the government's responsibility to tell you. On the other hand, most cities and states offer excellent free information on their websites and through local training sessions at colleges or other outreach programs. This help is often free, or costs very little. Using those resources, you'll also build a good contact network of the officials and bureaucrats who administer many of the programs. The small effort is well worth the trouble.

Let's ensure that your business is one of those that succeeds. This book will help make sure you're one of the winners. Even if you're already in business, the information you'll find here will help you. It's not too late to get it right—to protect the time and dollar investment you've already made.

So, What Do You Need to Do?

Before you get started, use the checklist in this chapter to get on track and make sure you are doing everything right. Try to follow the steps in the order they are presented. As you go along, you may think of some other things that need to be done at that particular point for your specific business or industry. Keep a stack of self-stick notes handy so you can record your thoughts when you think of them. (Did you know that Post-its came about as an error? 3M found a brilliant use for a glue that didn't stick.)

Many of the resources mentioned in this book will take you to the Internet. When I was starting my business, I had to drive fifty miles to the nearest Department of Commerce office in Los Angeles, or spend days in the little glassed-in room in the back of the Santa Ana law library, to do my tax research. Today, you can get the same answers in a few minutes using the Internet. Most of the resources are free—at least, the ones I've found for you and included in this book. If you don't have Internet access, go to your public library. Most public libraries offer free Internet access—and the librarians can be very helpful. Perhaps it's time you were reacquainted with those libraries you loved as a kid.

You don't need a computer to start a business (e.g., house-sitting or dog-walking). You don't even need Internet access. But it helps. As Chapter 6 points out, the cost of a computer and Internet access are deductible as business expenses.

You'll be coming back to the following checklist often. In fact, it may be a good idea to photocopy the pages and put them on a clipboard, so you can work with them as you go along.

The first time you read the checklist, keep your mind open. Free-associate with the ideas and treat it as a brainstorming session. Don't do anything yet—just add your notes. Then, read the list through again. Treat the second read-through the same way. Only this time, make your notes more specific. Write the names of vendors or suppliers you already know, the ones you'll be contacting to implement the steps on the checklist.

Finally, start taking the actions and check them off when they are completed. Cross off anything that doesn't apply to you, so you're not distracted.

Ready? Let's go.

The Checklist in To-Do Order

☐ Set Up an Advisory Team

Even if you're not incorporating your business, you need something similar to a board of directors. No one can run a business in a vacuum. Call upon professionals and people in your social or family circle or people in your community who've achieved success in the industries or fields you'll be servicing. You can't be expected to know everything, so don't try. Find an expert in each field to help your business succeed.

Plan to meet at least every month until the business is established. Then meet at least every quarter during the first year or two as the business develops. Meet at least once each year after that. And, be sure these people are available for you to call upon throughout the year. Expect to pay them for their time. You might even want to keep them on retainer. Questions will come up that they can answer quickly and easily, saving you time and money in the process.

Who should be on your team? Your insurance broker, business attorney, tax professional, bookkeeper (if you have one), office manager, banker, largest vendor or supplier, largest customer, at least two people who have successful businesses in your community, and your spouse. Once you start hiring employees outside the family, add a human resources expert to your team.

Where can you find these professionals? Ask people you know for recommendations. Or visit the websites of their professional organizations.

- **Enrolled agents (EAs).** For tax specialists licensed to represent taxpayers before the IRS, contact the National Association of Enrolled Agents (NAEA), www.naea.org, (202) 822-NAEA (6232).
- **Certified public accountants (CPAs).** CPAs are authorized to perform certified audits and issue financial statements. For a referral, contact the American Institute of Certified Public Accountants (AICPA), www.aicpa .org/index.htm, (888) 777-7077 or (201) 938-3750.

- **Attorneys with the American Bar Association (ABA).** For tax attorneys, business attorneys, and intangibles experts (patents and copyrights), contact the ABA, http://abanet.org, (800) 285-2221 or (312) 988-5522.
- **National Association of Tax Professionals (NATP).** You'll find a cross-section of all kinds of tax professionals here—EAs, CPAs, attorneys, and licensed tax professionals. You can use their online search function to find a local tax professional at www.natptax.com, or you can call their toll-free number, (800) 558-3402.
- **Insurance agents and brokers.** To locate insurance professionals, try the Independent Insurance Agents and Brokers of America (IIAA), www.iiaa.org, (800) 221-7917.

Incidentally, if a really big part of your business involves shipping, see if you can get your shipping company's representative on your team. People rarely think about including them, but they often have worldwide contacts. They may be able to help you find the best vendors, as well as customers, for your business. And they can even design custom packaging for you at little or no cost, if you're doing volume. For example, UPS created really beautiful packaging for Randazzo's Goodchildren Bakery Shoppe.

Get started now assembling your team; you'll need all these people to help you with the rest of this checklist.

☐ Contact Small Business Advocacy Groups

Two of the most helpful advocacy groups for small businesses have websites with invaluable information. They are the Small Business Administration (SBA) at www.sba.gov and the Service Corps of Retired Executives (SCORE) at www.score.org.

On these websites, you'll receive lots of useful information about the business climate, your industry, and general business start-up help. SCORE even provides free advisors, or coaches, to help your business follow the right paths. Bear in mind that most of the people working for SCORE come from the corporate world and have little experience with small businesses. But they have good contacts, and, if you let them guide you, they can help groom your business to grow in ways you couldn't do alone. What's the key with SCORE volunteers? Listen.

☐ Decide Your Business Focus

Focus on one or two things you do well or products or product lines you want to focus on selling or producing. If you think of many, list them so you don't forget about them. Then, select only the top one or two things you can implement most easily. Once the business is running smoothly, you can always add products or services later.

☐ Prepare a Business Plan

We'll explain why you need a business plan and show you how to create one in Chapter 2.

☐ Decide on Your Business Structure

Will you be a sole proprietor, corporation, or what? We'll help you decide in Chapter 3.

☐ Decide on the Name or Names You Will Use

How do you decide on a name? Perform some searches first. Try looking online to make sure there isn't another company with the same name already in operation. Here are some other steps to take when selecting a name:

- **Trademark your name.** If you are planning for the long-term or ever want to take your business public, this is an excellent precaution. You can do it yourself with the U.S. Patent and Trademark Office, www.uspto.gov/index .html. Before you file, even before you settle on your name, however, it may be worthwhile to run a trademark search to see if anyone is using it. A great web resource for this is http://tess2.uspto.gov/bin/gate.exe?f=tess&state=bng 1i1.1.1. Once you've decided on a name, you may submit your application online at www.uspto.gov/teas/index.html.
- **Get an Internet domain name to match your business name.** Even if you're not planning to have a website right away, buy the name now and hold on to it until you need it. Otherwise, it will be gone when you're ready. Domains are cheap. GoDaddy.com (http://godaddy.com) sells domain names for only $8.95 per year. If operating online is important to your business, your business name might depend on what's available as a domain name. The very memorable TaxMama.com was chosen after just such a search. The boring tax-related domains I wanted were no longer available. So, to our ever-lasting delight, we came up with something clever and original.
- **File fictitious name announcements in your local newspaper, if necessary.** This step will protect your name at the local level. Often, if you incor-

porate, you can skip the fictitious name filings because the corporate name is protected at the state level.

☐ Set Up a Corporation, Partnership, or LLC—If You Plan to Be One

There are several documents that you have to fill out to become a corporation, partnership, or limited liability corporation (LLC). You'll need certain of those documents in order to take several of the next steps. So save yourself some time by filling these documents out now. You could use an attorney to handle the setup for you. I've found that attorneys tend to charge about $1,500 to $2,000 to set up your entity. They provide about an hour of advice and order the kit from an outside service that creates all the documents. The law firm turns it all over to you, and you or your tax professional have to get your own federal identification number. They rarely remember to file the S-corporation election. That keeps cropping up consistently when clients come to me with their new corporations. What can you do instead? Do this. Pay your attorney for the hour of consultation about your business structure. Better yet, include your tax professional in that meeting, too. Then, use one of these two services to set up your entity. They are the same ones your attorney would use.

- **Contact AccountStreet.com.** They are owned by The Company Corporation, which is one of the oldest and largest incorporating services in the country. AccountStreet.com will give you lower prices than their main service. Their website (www.accountstreet.com) is a good source of information about business structures, or call (800) 315-9420. Tell them TaxMama sent you and get a $25 discount.
- **Hubco has the cheapest prices for entity setup.** Attorneys who prepare some of their own bylaws and articles use these folks. They service the public, too, but you'll need to take care of several aspects of the setup yourself. Call (800) 443-8177. (They are also a good source for supplies, such as corporate seals, stock certificates, etc.)

Remember, it's essential to get the guidance of your team's attorney and tax pro on this issue.

Before you start working with a partner or an investor who plans to participate actively in your business, consider reading Doug Thorburn's *Drugs, Drunks and Debits: How to Recognize Addicts and Avoid Financial Abuse* (visit his website at www.preventragedy.com). Deciding to work with a recovering addict or obvious addict is easy. You know their condition and can make your decision with your eyes open. It's the hidden addict who will destroy your business and your own emotional stability. Read the book and you'll know the signs going in, and be able to decide if you want to go forward.

☐ Open a Separate Bank Account for Your Business

Open a unique bank account for your business even if you plan to operate as a sole proprietor. Remarkably, many people overlook this fundamental business step. But it is crucial so your personal money doesn't get confused with funds from your business. If you are ever audited, having a separate account can help you gather your paperwork together quickly.

When you are picking a bank, shop around. Find a local bank willing to waive first-year fees on business accounts. Arrange to get copies of your cancelled checks. Many banks are discouraging this service, or charging for it. Pay the fee. Having those cancelled checks right at hand will save you in tough situations. Arrange for online access and downloads. Often with online banking, you'll get free accounting software. If you are given a choice, opt for Peachtree or QuickBooks, not Quicken (we'll cover this topic in detail in Chapter 4). You're welcome to establish a business savings account and/or investment account to store your profits or start-up loans until you need the money.

☐ Select an Accounting System or Software

Chapter 4 will guide you through the record-keeping process.

☐ Research the Licenses You Need and Agencies to Which You'll Be Reporting

Gather all the forms and determine what your costs will be—both initially and annually. You'll need all of this for your business plan and budget (we'll discuss this more in Chapter 2). In brief, though, here are several forms you'll probably need to fill out:

- **City or county license.** Even a home-based business may need one. Call your city, county, or parish clerk's office for more information. Bankrate.com has a resource linking to small business information in each state. See the Resources at the end of this chapter. Read your local government's business website carefully. Most localities have inexpensive licenses, around $25 to $75 per year. Be aware, however, that the Los Angeles license, based on a percentage of sales, could cost hundreds of dollars each year. And Los Angeles aggressively collects those funds.

- **IRS registration for an employer identification number (EIN).** File the Form SS-4 online yourself. You'll find a link at TaxMama.com's Resource Center. Note: If you are a sole proprietor who doesn't plan to have employees, say you will have them, just to get the identification number issued. Having that EIN will make the difference between looking like a real business and a hobby. (More about this in Chapter 2.)

Sign up with IRS's online payment system at www.eftps.gov. You can deposit your estimated tax payments, pay payroll taxes, and conduct other business tax transactions online.

☐ **Research State Taxes and Licenses**

A variety of agencies may be regulating your industry, and you should learn the details about taxes, licensing, zoning, unions, et cetera, before you start. The fastest way to get the information you need is on the Internet. Start with your state's official website. When you get to the state's home page, look for a business link. If you need information about other states, use this link to all state tax agencies: www.taxadmin.org/fta/link/forms.html. This is the website for the Federation of Tax Administrators. This link goes to their tax forms pages, but if you do a little backtracking, you'll find the tax home page of the state you are interested in.

If you don't have access to the Internet, pull out your residential telephone book. In the front, you'll find pages listing all your local and state agencies. Spend some time reading that whole section. You'd be surprised at the agencies you'll find. Some of them may even become a source of funding or contracts. Who knows? At least you'll find the key agencies that affect your industry. Be sure to call your city clerk (or local equivalent) about local licensing. For state issues, call your secretary of state's office. If they are not the ones you need to speak with, they'll tell you whom you should call.

- **State income tax registration.** This is generally necessary only if you have formed an entity other than a sole proprietorship.
- **Sales tax.** You'll need to know about sales taxes even if all your sales are online sales. Chapter 12 explains why. You must collect sales taxes if you are selling products to the end user. Some states might charge sales taxes on services. Check with your state's Department of Revenue, or its equivalent.

- **Payroll taxes.** Register with your state's payroll tax department if you plan to have employees. Your children might be employees—if they actually do the work they're supposed to do. (Chapter 9 will explain who is and isn't an employee.)
- **State licenses.** State licenses are usually required for child-care providers, cosmeticians, most professionals, contractors, those selling alcohol, anyone dealing with hazardous substances, truckers, and who knows what other industries. It's best to check before you find you're operating without a license.
- **Other.** Check to see what else your industry needs or requires. If you can't find answers online, interview people who are successful in your industry. Or, just call your state and ask them to point you to a list of your obligations. Better yet, have them mail the list to you. Save the list, and use it as a checklist. Of course, hiring a good tax professional with expertise in your industry will save you hours or even weeks of research. They already know what you must do.

☐ Research Your Costs

Find the best vendors, providing good service at fair prices. Be willing to sacrifice a bit of price to get personal service. For instance, our toll-free line is through National Comtel, a small local company at (800) 987-0100. We can call the office and speak to the same two or three people every time, even their president. No long waits on hold. No random customer service people who keep getting it wrong. I pay five cents per minute for incoming calls. Small companies are willing to negotiate, which is great, but don't make them cut their prices low enough to put them out of business. With a little bit of work, you'll be able to find good suppliers in your own neck of the woods.

One of the first things you'll need to get quotes on is insurance costs. Consider working with good business insurance brokers. They'll know where the deals are and your coverage requirements.

- **Business liability, fire, theft.** Get a combined policy. For malpractice insurance, check with your professional association for the best prices.
- **Auto.** A good local broker can find you the best rates, and you may be able to cut your rates by having one company carry several of your policies. Check several sources for better rates, but be sure that the coverage you're pricing is equivalent. Visit the American Automobile Association at www.aaa.com

to find your local automobile club or call information to get the number of a local office. They offer some of the most complete insurance coverage and great service in case of accidents. GEICO, (800) 861-8380 or www.geico.com, offers different discounts for members of organizations. I started with a Good Sam discount. Then, when I obtained a letter from my alma mater, the university discount cut my policy by another $116 for six months. Seniors taking driving classes can get another discount from most insurers. Mercury Insurance's commercials are everywhere you turn. They have good prices, but their policies do not cover other people driving your car or accessories on your car, even if you got them from the dealer.

- **Health.** You'll probably need health coverage for yourself and/or your employees. Start out small. If you can't afford to pay your employees' insurance, consider setting up a Health Savings Arrangement (HSA) plan. Find an insurance carrier in your state at www.ehealthinsurance.com. HSAs are a new program, signed into law in December 2003.

- **Workers' compensation (WC).** Find a local carrier. Some WC carriers, especially the quasi-state agencies, will pay you dividends if the fund makes money. Those dividends can reduce your net premiums by 10 percent or more per year. If you belong to an association or professional or trade organization, contact them. Some have negotiated deals for their members. I got a substantial rate reduction through one of my accounting associations. For a comprehensive list of state agencies and carriers across the country, North Carolina has an excellent resource available at www.comp.state.nc.us/ncic /pages/all50.htm. Or call your state insurance commissioner for carriers in your area.

- **Disability insurance.** If you can qualify, get covered. You'll need a source of income if you get sick or hurt and can't work for several weeks. Check with your state if you can't get covered commercially. Many states offer coverages for small business owners that are similar to employees' coverage. The cost may be higher if you're not on payroll. Another way to get coverage if you don't meet the minimum health requirements is to buy a group policy for yourself and your employees. It usually requires a minimum of three people, but there are no medical exams. If you can find a really good policy, you'll be able to live on it if—heaven forbid—you become permanently disabled.

- **Life insurance.** Work with your advisory team on life insurance. Don't go overboard, but get the coverage you need. For instance, seriously consider getting key-man insurance, which allows you to buy out partners or their heirs in case of catastrophic injury or death.

- **Other.** There may be other insurance you will need, depending on your area, your business, and your industry. Your advisory team can alert you to the right coverage.

☐ Select Facilities

Will you work from home, or buy or rent space? Whenever possible, look at the long-term picture. If you can afford to buy a place, do it. If you outgrow it, you can always rent it out or sell it. Be unconventional, if you can. Will your business work if you put it into a house or an apartment? If it will, buy one. Many law firms and professionals take over old houses and fix them up as stately offices. If buying isn't an option, be creative. Can you share space with a vendor in exchange for some service? If the service doesn't interfere too much with your time, that may be a way to fund your first office space. (Read Chapter 5 about barter income.) If you must rent, negotiate. Offer to accept a higher monthly rent than you'd like in exchange for free months each year. That helps the landlord show a high monthly rental rate in case they want to sell the building. Meanwhile, you end up paying a lower overall average rate.

The other option is to set up an office in your home, which has some excellent tax benefits. We'll discuss this in depth in Chapter 7.

☐ Make Lease Versus Buy Decision on Equipment and Vehicles

When it comes to the equipment and vehicles you'll use, your first step is deciding whether or not you want to lease or buy. For equipment that either becomes obsolete quickly or is older and more subject to breaking down, a lease may be preferable. You can deduct the lease costs. Leases will often include service contracts, which will save you some money on that score. There are also benefits to buying automobiles you need for your job. We'll cover this in more depth in Chapter 8.

☐ Arrange for Inventory

When manufacturing a product, inventory is the heart of your operation. Though you'll find suppliers around the world on the Internet, don't rely on people you've never seen at facilities you've never visited to make your main products. Legwork is critical. Inspect the facilities, and talk to their customers. Once you have prices, plug them into your business plan. Let your advisory team help you find the right sources. Oh, and be on site when they manufacture your products—or have a representative there to inspect the finished products—before shipping.

☐ Establish Supplies Accounts

Establish accounts with office supply houses, both locally and online. My company has worked with Quill (www.quillcorp.com) and Office Depot (www.officedepot .com) for decades. They both offer free overnight shipping for orders of $50 or more. Quill always includes something extra—cookies, briefcases, radios, and so on. Whenever a product is wrong or damaged, both companies take the materials back, no questions asked.

Develop a reasonable budget for the things you need, and be careful not to spend money on things you don't need. Don't get things because they're cute.

☐ Research Legal Issues

A variety of legal issues will affect your business. For instance, you'll need to know about your area's labor laws—so call your state's employment department.

- **Contract law.** Everything you sell is under contract, even if it is implied. Understand how to limit your responsibilities to your customers. The attorney on your advisory team can help.
- **Bad debts.** Customers don't always pay on time . . . or ever. Set up protections in your invoices and contracts before the problems arise.
- **Liability laws.** When you have an online presence, your business is exposed to liability in a number of ways—sometimes through actions of others. As you're beginning your business planning, please read Jonathan I. Ezor's *Clicking Through: A Survival Guide for Bringing Your Company Online*. It will give you a handle on the legal areas you'll need to address, so you can develop your legal budget. There's lots of practical information in this book—if only he'd written it before I went online.

☐ Consider Your Services Needs

Even if you decide not to hire employees initially, you'll still need help. There are many people who can assist you with their services. Get an answering service, so you're not constantly interrupted by calls. You may even need a virtual assistant. Certainly, you'll need an attorney and a tax professional, and you might need a consultant. For instance, you may not want to ship all your own products. Will you need a fulfillment house? Price out all the services you're going to need. Chapter 9 will give you a hiring set-up checklist for freelancers and will provide you with more information on paying taxes for the people who work for you.

☐ Select Communications

If there's a way to integrate your telephone, cell phone, Internet, and fax into one billing plan, do it. It's easier to get one bill from one service provider. On the other hand, it doesn't hurt to duplicate some of these services in case of trouble. For instance, my company has SBC DSL service. In case they go down, we have Earthlink's dial-up service as a backup.

☐ Start to Work on Image and Visibility

Establishing brand awareness among your clientele and in the marketplace will help you keep your customer base in the tough times. When they're devoted to your brand, you become their only choice.

- **Build your brand.** Rob Frankel's *The Revenge of Brand X* provides invaluable guidelines that you can use to cement your identity from day one.
- **Develop a presence in the marketplace.** Public relations is less costly than advertising—and more effective. Good PR will get you established as an expert in your industry. If you can't afford the cost of a public relations firm, but you're able to speak clearly and eloquently about your business, sign up for Dan Janal's PR Leads service available at www.prleads.com. Be prepared to invest a lot of time, at least initially. But if you write good responses to journalists' requests for experts, you'll be flooded with calls. Press releases also generate attention, when written well. For that, you will need an expert. Your advisory team can help you find the best person locally.
- **Consider advertising.** It's the lifeblood of a growing business. But don't shotgun your ads all over the place. Target your audience carefully and find the most effective, least expensive publications. If you're on a tight budget, Shel Horowitz's *Grassroots Marketing: Getting Noticed in a Noisy World* offers twenty-first-century tips for getting the most attention for your product or service.

☐ Take Care of Money Issues

Some businesses or industries have a really long accounts receivable lag. Some businesses require you to advance money on merchandise or services. Then, you must wait 30, 60, 90, or even 120 days to get paid. That's industry standard. Unless you have a charming and clever way to speed up the payments, you will need financing. Look into all the options available to you. In some industries, like the schmatte industry (the textile trade), "factoring" is common. Factoring is the practice of selling your accounts receivable to another company, at a slight discount. Essentially, you're paying interest on your money, in advance. The factor becomes responsible for collecting the money from your customers. Consider factoring or accounts receivable financing if you're planning to sell to any government agencies. They are notoriously slow pays—often ninety days or more.

This checklist (shown in shorter form in Figure 1.1) is probably more comprehensive than you expected from a tax book, but you'll soon find that good tax planning goes hand in hand with good business planning. Without a solid business, who needs to worry about taxes? You'll have nothing but losses (and that requires a whole different set of plans—for failure). Well, this book isn't about failing. It's designed to make you a stunning success, without too much money or stress on your part.

Checklist Resources

In this chapter, you saw a variety of resources. Here's a summary of them, so you can find them quickly and easily.

U.S. Government Resources
- **IRS.** www.irs.gov: For IRS forms and publications. Use the links on the navigation bar at the top of the page to find things quickly, or use the two search boxes to search the site or the forms and publications database.
- **Employer ID number.** www.irs.gov/businesses/small/article/0,,id=1027 67,00.html: This site explains how to fill out your SS-4 application and file for your EIN online.
- **U.S. Patent Office.** www.uspto.gov/index.html: This is the place to go for patents and trademarks.

State Resources
- **State-by-state business start-up information.** www.bankrate.com/brm /news/biz/Green/states/states_text.asp: Find out about local resources available in your state.
- **Small business information.** www.bankrate.com: This is a good resource for fundamental information on licensing and start-up tips.
- **State tax forms.** www.taxadmin.org/fta/link/forms.html: This site links to the tax agencies of all fifty states.

FIGURE 1.1 The Carry with You Checklist in To-Do Order

☐ Set up an advisory team.

    Tax advisors

    Attorneys

    Insurance agents and brokers

☐ Contact small business advocacy groups.

    Small Business Administration: www.sba.gov

    Service Corps of Retired Executives (SCORE): www.score.org

☐ Decide your business focus.

☐ Prepare a business plan.

☐ Decide on your business structure.

☐ Decide on the name or names you will use.

    Trademark the name with the U.S. Patent Office: www.uspto.gov/index.html.

    Get an Internet domain name to match your business name.

    File fictitious name announcements in your local newspaper, if necessary.

☐ Set up a corporation, partnership, or LLC–if you plan to be one.

☐ Open a separate bank account for your business.

☐ Select an accounting system or software.

☐ Research the licenses you need and the agencies to which you'll be reporting.

    City or county license

    IRS registration for an employer identification number (EIN)

    Sign up with IRS's online payment system: www.eftps.gov.

☐ Research state taxes and licenses

    State income tax registration if you are not a sole proprietorship

    Sales tax

    Register with your state's payroll tax department

    State licenses

    Other: Check to see what else your industry needs.

☐ Research your costs, especially insurance

    Business liability, fire, theft

    Auto: www.aaa.com to find your local automobile club; GEICO, (800) 861-8380, www.geico.com

    Health–for yourself and/or your employees: www.ehealthinsurance.com

    Workers' compensation (WC): www.comp.state.nc.us/ncic/pages/all50.htm

    Life

    Other–depending on your area, your business, and your industry

☐ Select facilities: will you work from home, rent space, or buy it?

FIGURE 1.1 *continued*

☐ Make a lease versus buy decision on equipment and vehicles.

☐ Arrange for inventory.

☐ Establish supplies accounts.

☐ Research legal issues.

☐ Consider your services needs.

☐ Select communications: telephone, cell phone, Internet, fax.

☐ Start to work on image and visibility.

   Brand recognition

   Public relations

   Advertising

☐ Take care of money issues.

   Loans

   Other financing

Business and Legal Resources

• **The Company Corporation.** www.AccountStreet.com, (800) 315-9420: Register your corporation, LLC, or other formal structure at much lower prices than attorneys charge.

• **Hubco.** www.inc-it-now.com, (800) 443-8177: Register your corporation, LLC, or other formal structure and handle most of it yourself, a cheap option. It is also a great source of corporate supplies, such as corporate seals, binders, and so on.

• *Clicking Through: A Survival Guide for Bringing Your Company Online* by Jonathan I. Ezor (Bloomberg Press). The best book about how Internet issues affect your business. If you read nothing else I recommend, you must read this book. Ezor provides practical information in plain English about the issues you face the minute your business opens its website.

• *The Revenge of Brand X* by Rob Frankel. www.revengeofbrandx.com: Find out how to make your company the only choice.

• *Grassroots Marketing: Getting Noticed in a Noisy World* by Shel Horowitz (Chelsea Green Publishing Company). www.frugalmarketing.com: This book will help you focus your marketing efforts to get the most attention for the least amount of money.

- **Dan Janal's PR Leads.** www.prleads.com: Janal explains how to get interviewed by the top publications in the country.
- *Drugs, Drunks and Debits: How to Recognize Addicts and Avoid Financial Abuse* by Doug Thorburn. www.preventragedy.com: This book will help you avoid going into business with hidden addicts—or do it with your eyes open and precautions in place.

Internet Resources

- **GoDaddy.** http://godaddy.com: Domain names are only $8.95. There are other designations you could choose to buy, like .biz or .org, but if you can't get the .com version of the name, choose another name. Whoever owns the .com site will get all your traffic.
- **Yahoo!.** Yahoo.com has just entered the domain name business. So if you're more comfortable with a brand name you recognize, Yahoo! is selling domains for $9.95. Naturally, they've added a whole host of website tools. Go to http://smallbusiness.yahoo.com.
- **SiteBuildIt.** Ken Evoy has built an all-inclusive online business package. It includes the website, the hosting, the domain name, mailing lists, merchant accounts, shopping cart, all the tools you need to build a website and make it pay—even if you don't have a clue about programming or Internet mysteries. It even has a built-in affiliate program to let you track and pay for referrals. For little more than the price of hosting a website, you're going to get tools I've paid thousands of dollars to use. You really can put up your own site—even without the help of your ten-year-old. Go to www.sitebuildit.com /taxmama.html.
- *Revenue* is a new magazine that covers all aspects of the affiliate marketing business model. It's all about teaching you how to get other people to sell your products and give you brand exposure, just the way Amazon.com did. This is the easiest way to build a large customer base. Go to www.revenue today.com.
- **National Comtel.** (800) 987-0100: Long-distance toll-free numbers.
- **Google.com.** This search engine will find what you need quickly. Google has the unique ability to perform subsearches. When searching for "office supplies," if you come up with 2,850,000 hits, Google can narrow that down. Scroll to the bottom of the page to the bottom search box and click on the text link to the right—"Search within results." Entering "filing cabinets" will bring the search down to only 17,900. Asking for "lateral" drops it down to 1,760. Search within again, this time for "discount," and the number drops to only 233 . . . and so on.

Office Supplies for Accounting and Taxes

- **Avery Labels.** (800) GO-AVERY, (800) 462-8379, http://avery.com.
- **Costco.** http://costco.com: Shop online or visit a warehouse nearby.
- **Image One.** (800) 462-4366, www.800imageone.com: Where the tax professionals shop.
- **Office Depot.** (800) GO DEPOT, http://officedepot.com: Shop online or visit a store nearby.
- **Quill Corporation.** (800) 982-3400, www.quillcorp.com: Great customer service.
- **Staples.** (800) 3STAPLE, http://staples.com: Shop online or visit a store nearby.
- **Viking Office Products.** (800) 711-4242, http://viking.com: For accounting forms and supplies.

2

BUSINESS PLANS YOU KNOW AND TRUST

I've been rich and I've been poor. Believe me, rich is better.

—MAE WEST

We're just starting out and already you're ready to turn the page. You're thinking, I don't need a business plan. I know what I'm doing. It's just me, basically working from notes in my back pocket.

You might just do all right playing it by ear. But why not do great?

Frankly, you're going to need a business plan if you want to succeed. You will especially need a business plan if you fail (to protect your tax deductions—I'll explain in a moment). Without a plan, you're courting failure. There are so many details to remember in a business, it's hard to keep track of them without a scorecard, especially when you're working alone. Why sabotage your chances for success? Don't be one of those people who are secretly afraid to succeed. Take the time to sit down, make a few notes, and shoot for success.

Why You Need a Business Plan

The main reason you need a business plan is that the IRS will want to see it when your tax return shows losses for the first several years.

I know. You don't plan to have losses. But even the best-laid plans sometimes go wrong. When you run losses for more than two or three years—that business plan is going to make the difference between getting to keep those deductions and having the IRS disallow them all under the hobby-loss rules.[1]

You're almost asking for an audit if your business shows a loss for more than two years out of five (or five years out of seven, if you're dealing with breeding, training, showing, or racing of horses). While the IRS really is auditing a smaller percentage of returns than they ever have (less than 0.5 percent of 2002 returns), the current audits are more targeted. The IRS's audit selection software is more apt to select returns that really do have something wrong with them—and tax returns of businesses with constant losses get audited more frequently than the average returns. In fact, of the 2.5 million 2002 tax returns with a Schedule C, more than 2.6 percent of those returns showing less than $25,000 in income were audited. That's five times the percentage of the total population of audits— and more than twice the percentage of high-income (more than $100,000) Schedule Cs.[2]

What if you know, at the outset, that it will take you five or ten years of losses, as you build up your product or your market, before you make a profit? What if you know that if you can hang on for those ten years, you're going to make millions?

The IRS doesn't know that. They have no way of knowing. But when they come along with their audit, the strongest defense you can have is your solid business plan in hand. Oh, you'll need a few more tools, as you'll see in Chapter 13, but the foundation of your audit defense will be your plan.

---

1. Straight out of the tax code—IRC §183(d) Presumption: If the gross income derived from an activity for 3 or more of the taxable years in the period of 5 consecutive taxable years which ends with the taxable year exceeds the deductions attributable to such activity (determined without regard to whether or not such activity is engaged in for profit), then, unless the Secretary establishes to the contrary, such activity shall be presumed for purposes of this chapter for such taxable year to be an activity engaged in for profit. In the case of an activity which consists in major part of the breeding, training, showing, or racing of horses, the preceding sentence shall be applied by substituting "2" for "3" and "7" for "5."

2. IRS Data Book—Table 10. Examination Coverage: Recommended and Average Recommended Additional Tax After Examination, by Size and Type of Return, Fiscal Year 2002, available at www .irs.gov/pub/irs-soi/02db10ex.xls.

General Benefits

You're clear on the tax reason for the business plan, right? What other benefits can it give you?

- **Focus.** A plan can save you lots of time. You won't be floundering, wondering what to do next.
- **Cost control.** A plan can help you keep your costs under control because you're not just shotgunning your spending. You only spend money on those things that are part of your plan.
- **Capital.** Except for small amounts, you won't get a bank loan or attract investors unless you have a business plan. Of course, you could use your credit cards . . . and with the no-interest or low-interest rate cards, that might even be a good option. But, at best, you're not going to get more than $5,000 to $50,000 that way. If you want real money—enough to fund your operation and let you fill large orders (for products or services)—you need a plan. No one will give you money if you don't understand your own business.
- **Confidence.** It's amazing the way your self-respect and confidence soar when you know what you're doing. You can look people in the eye and give them straight answers when they ask you how your business is doing.
- **Growth.** Decide up front just how large you'd like your business to be. You may as well put the correct systems in place for the future—leaving room for expansion of software, phone systems, and so on. Decide if you plan to go public, build the business just so far and sell it, leave it to your children, or turn it into a franchise or a multi-level marketing operation. You can always decide to keep it small later. But to grow, when you haven't planned for it, will cost much more down the road.

The Fine Line Between Success and Failure

Running a business was easy as long as I just had my tax practice. It was a cinch to plan out what needed to be done by what date, how many clients I had to see, by when, and so on. One of the things I've discovered since operating on the Internet is that the world is full of distractions, temptations, and opportunities. You're going to find yourself being torn in many directions. They all look like exciting opportunities. If you give in to those offers and invitations of quick money, you will slowly learn that if you had just stuck with your own business and your own plan, you'd be much further ahead.

The price of distraction is more than mere dollars. Time is also a finite commodity. My husband is too kind to point out that simply focusing on my tax practice, I'd have more evenings and most weekends free. We'd be totally out of debt—even to the point of having our mortgage paid off. Instead, because I am guilty of succumbing to those alluring temptations, I work twelve to fifteen hours each day, including most evenings and practically every weekend and holiday. (We're only nearly out of debt. The mortgage, which just dropped to a 4.375 percent fixed rate, will be paid off in just a few years—but not yet.)

Sure, I love what I do—*all* the things I do. But sometimes it would be really nice to do a bit less—quite a bit less. That's my price of success—spreading myself too thin. However, I have a plan in place that will let me gradually reduce my workload and raise my income to the point where, in another year, my time and life will be in balance again. So far, I am on target.

Is trying to do everything worth it? That's a personal decision. You'll have to decide. But let's see what happened to a few people and how they did or didn't focus.

Success

Brad Waller and his partners started ePage, www.ep.com, in 1996. The Internet was young and wild, much like the Old West, and people were trying daring things. Opportunities were everywhere. Brad and ePage just boringly focused on their business plan and deflected distractions. All of their energies went into building an online classified system for websites to use as their own. They were pioneers in income-sharing programs, like affiliate commissions (Amazon.com's came later).

Today, they have more than twenty-seven thousand merchant sites, run nearly half a million ads, and attract more than five million page views a month. They have more than three-quarters of a million visitors. It's one of the top fifteen thousand sites online, without much of an advertising budget. (They used affiliate programs instead.) During all of this, ePage never needed to get venture capital. The business has been supporting all the original founders, plus several employees, full-time, for years. Better yet, Brad's marketing efforts require that he take an annual cruise to the Bahamas and trips to Hawaii and other exotic locations. Yes, life is tough.

Too Much Success Equals Failure

Carolin Benjamin had the most charming idea for a site: www.dujour.com. It was a place where you could play games, test your knowledge, compete against other people, and win prizes. Participants registered for free. Starting in November 1996, Carolin got the idea to invite merchants who wanted exposure to donate prizes, daily, weekly, or monthly, depending on the kind of visibility they wanted. The site was an instant hit, attracting more than eighty thousand visitors a day, myself included. I loved to play there and won an elegant wooden pen and pencil set as well as other handcrafted items. Well, Carolin had the traffic and the prizes. But where was the revenue? She and her partner were too busy with their day jobs to plan how to make money.

Frankly, even with all the traffic, it was hard to find paying advertisers. Carolin maintained the site for several years, staying up most of the night to post winners, send out prize announcements, and respond to volumes of e-mail. She nearly collapsed from exhaustion. Carolin had to sell the site. Why was the workload too much? She made the same mistake many companies make—even large ones—she didn't plan for success. She had traffic but not the means or resources to respond to her members' needs—or the income to cover the costs of additional help.

Failure, Well, Almost

In Australia, Ian Purdie started putting up articles about electronics, ham radios, audio devices, and all kinds of related technical and hobby information. His site, http://electronics-tutorials.com, became so popular that universities were using his free technical articles in their courses. Ian believed that if he put high-quality information out there, people would be sensible enough to contribute funds, or tip him, to support keeping the site alive. Even small sums would be welcome. Amazon offered a payment system so Ian didn't need to incur the cost of merchant credit card accounts. His costs weren't high. Living on a pension, he could, essentially, get by.

Though users sent him many letters of high praise, few—if any—made donations. Few people used his links to buy their books or supplies, which would have let him generate commissions from their purchases. They'd buy those things—but not so he got the credit. Ian never diminished the quality of the articles he provided, despite years of frustration at the lack of financial support. Finally he just about gave up.

Why did he fail? He didn't have a business plan. Ian never arranged for a way to charge students and readers for his how-to articles. He never thought through the issue of where his income was going to come from. He just believed that people would be honorable and make contributions to support his useful site. To his credit, unlike Carolin at www.dujour.com, he didn't have to spend hours each night dealing with time-sensitive prizes and things. He could choose to add articles or not, as he saw fit. But, he didn't have any money either.

He was just about to do something violent to his computer when he got really lucky. The Google folks came along with Adsense, which provides a stream of advertising revenues. But, that's another story, for another time. Today, Ian is in clover and his business is a labor of love again.

Utter Failure

Mike was a very popular realtor in Southern California, earning a six-figure income as sales manager for a real estate brokerage, when a friend of his invited him to open a business leasing private homes and condominiums. When Mike broached the idea to me, I did my best to persuade him to do two things: (1) work out a business plan and (2) keep his day job. He could build up his new business slowly, from home, with a low overhead until it generated enough money to support him. In fact, if he'd told his boss about it, chances were, he'd have supported him, even to the point of helping him capitalize the business. No one else was making a concerted effort to tap into the San Fernando Valley market with a comprehensive service providing leasing and management for owners of single units. There was a demand for this service, not just among the homeowners, but for people looking for places to rent. Renters keep running into those bait-and switch ads, offering them attractive houses, condos, or guesthouses—then telling them they'd have to pay a fee to get the address. When they finally do get the addresses, those units are always already taken (probably always were), or don't exist.

So, with this great potential market, off he went, returning to me several months later. Mike had skipped the business plan. He also had quit his job and opened an expensive office. His overhead, before he got to take home a single dime, was more than $17,000 a month, but his income was nowhere near that. He was lucky to generate $2,000 per month. To support his business, Mike was drawing money from savings.

Mike begged me to help, so I stepped in and cut his costs by $10,000 a month, even after my fees. It turns out that although he was an expert in real estate sales, he didn't understand how the leasing business worked. Mike was still paying out of his own pocket for expenses that the homeowners should be paying. The owners paid them willingly, once we rewrote the contracts.

We doubled his sales overnight by getting some high-end brokerages to refer their low-commission home leasing business to him. In fact, one brokerage owner told his staff that they must forward all leases to Mike. If he ever saw them wasting their time with a lease they'd be fired. (You have to understand the economics. It takes about the same amount of time to find tenants as it does buyers, showing them lots and lots of houses. But where a lease commission might be $3,000, selling the same luxury home will generate more than $30,000.)

Those referrals doubled revenues, but it was too late. Mike's business was still hemorrhaging money. Even though he'd been in business less than a year, Mike had dipped so deeply into his financial reserves that within a few more months, he had to file bankruptcy. It's a real shame. He was one of the most popular members of the local board of realtors. Everyone would have been very happy to refer their leasing business to someone reliable. Had Mike started out with a budget, low overhead, and better information, he'd literally be a millionaire today.

Letting Your Ego Rule

Can you name the one person who personifies great success, but turned it into a smashing failure? Hint: Living.

Yes, Martha Stewart's company, Martha Stewart Living, Omnimedia, Inc. (NYSE MSO) almost folded after her conviction. Large blocks of television stations dropped her show. Since the show was all Martha—and she was going to jail—even if they hadn't dropped her, who was in the wings to take her place? No one.

As a result, when she was indicted, then tried, and then convicted, the MSO stock went from more than $20 a share to below $10 in April 2004.

What's the criticism here? Surely, Martha had a business plan. No one could be more focused than her. The problem is the excessive focus—on her, on Martha. Unlike most media businesses that plan to survive for the long run, everything was about Martha. She made no provisions, even after the indictment, to introduce someone else into her television show or on her radio features. There should have been someone groomed to become her replacement if she were convicted—or if she died. The MSO business plan didn't have any continuity built in.

Be sure to treat the business as an entity of its own. Why build something up that no one can step in and take over if you get sick or die? If you tie it too closely to your irreplaceable personal services, your business won't have any value to anyone else. You won't be able to sell it.

Let's Not Fail Due to Success

Are you getting the idea? Even if you're on a success track, if you don't have a business plan in place to deal with it, you're apt to fail. (Talk about a monotonous refrain!) These are the kinds of things to think about to prepare for success:

- Your ads are successful. Your phones are ringing off the hook. What do you do when the phone lines are jammed with customers wanting to give you money—but you haven't made any provisions for enough people to answer the phones?
- You get the largest order of your career. Where are you going to manufacture it? Or, where will you get the trained staff to perform all those services on short notice?
- You get the largest order of the year. You can find the staff and facilities to fulfill it. But where are you going to get the money to pay for it all, until you collect your accounts receivable from this sale?
- You introduce a new electronic product that can be downloaded from the Web. It's all automated. No sweat, right? You get a great review in *PC Magazine* and David Letterman is all over it with his jokes in his nightly routine. You get so much traffic that your website crashes. Can you bring new bandwidth online in time to save the sales? Or mirror sites?

Outline of a Plan

There are many different books, software, and websites to help you create a good business plan. Whatever you use, even if it's only a simple list, there are ten basic elements you'll need to consider (see Figure 2.1). Answer these ten questions. Use them to build your business plan using the books or tools that follow. With good planning, you are bound to succeed.

Important Things to Consider

When you sit down to develop your business plan, be sure to understand how you (and your partners) are going to be spending your time in this business. Face up to the tasks you hate to do. The simple fact is—if you hate to do something, you'll slough it off, do it poorly, or not do it at all. Don't economize by promising to do something you hate. The onerous tasks will be different for each person. Some people just dread having to sell. If you can't overcome that, delegate it. Or hire someone to do it. Others hate to do bookkeeping. If you have a mental block against it, don't torture yourself. Find someone on your team, or outside, who loves that task. Build the costs of delegation into your plan.

Sometimes, with the right team of people, it will work out perfectly. Be sure to have each person define their expectations—of themselves, of you, and of the company—so you're all going in the same direction.

FIGURE 2.1 Ten Fundamental Questions for a Business Plan

1. What kind of business will you be? (sole proprietorship, partnership, corporation)
2. What will the business do? (products, services)
3. Where will you get the money to start and fund the business until it generates income? (you, investors, loans, credit cards)
4. How much money will you need to tide you over until income is generated? (to cover operations, wages, rents, supplies)
5. How will the business generate income? (sales, rents, grants, dues)
6. When will the stream of income start? (research time, construction time, sales cycle)
7. When will you break even?
8. What contingency plans do you have to back you up if suppliers or investors fail you?
9. What contingency plans do you have to be able to fulfill orders or sales when you succeed beyond your wildest dreams?
10. What is your exit plan? (sell, go public, invite partners, shut down, give to children)

Rebalancing Your Business Plan for Tax Consequences

You're always hearing stockbrokers and investment advisors talking about rebalancing your investment portfolio. That means, once you've agreed on an investment approach, with a specific percentage of your money in various risk levels of investment, you need to review it each year. As the values of the investments change due to price fluctuations, dividends, and capital gains, one group may become worth more or less in proportion to the other groups. To keep the proportions in balance, you may have to sell some units of one group, or buy units of another.

Use the same concept with your business plan. Review it annually to make sure you're on track with your overall goals.

Then review it again to see how any tax law changes, phaseouts, or phase-ins affect your business. Particularly, look at depreciation rules—politicians like to change this area often, increasing or complicating the deductions or credits. Look at business credits. Are there new incentives in place for hiring, locations, or special industries? Expect changes in the areas of travel, meals, and gifts. Those need updating for this millennium.

What are the top three best things about having a good business plan in place?

Team Building in College

Working on my master's degree at California State University at Fullerton at night, I soon discovered that most of the courses required us to do team projects. At first, I was incensed. My grade would depend on three other people, strangers, who were also working full-time during the day. Although most of them were men, somehow, I always ended up being the group leader. That was fine with me. But, assigning tasks would be touchy. Who's going to get the bad tasks or the grunt work? Well, drawing each person out, I learned that they each had a different idea of the chump job. There was usually someone who reveled in research. (I hate that.) There was often someone who was a great typist (yes, before word processors and instant corrections) or had a secretary who was willing to type our papers. And most of them hated to write. For me, that was the easiest part of the job. They were relieved to be off the hook—I felt I was getting away with murder, sending them all out to dig up the information and present it to me. All I had to do was organize it and write it all up. Someone else was going to make it all look pretty. We each did our share of the work gladly, because we were each using our strengths. Those teams generally earned As.

Play to your strengths.

---

1. You'll spend much less time and money running your business. By not floundering and wasting time and money going in too many directions, all your investment will go toward producing profits.
2. You'll be able to take the best advantage of tax benefits available to your business, income level, or industry.
3. You'll be in good shape if you're ever audited. The IRS so rarely sees business plans for small businesses. When they see that level of organization and discipline in that area, they will believe you've carried it through into your accounting and tax areas, too.

Business Plan Books and Resources

If you're going to get tools and resources, don't go cheap. Saving yourself $50 to buy a cheaper resource may cost you much more in the time you'll spend to find the information that's probably already in the more expensive tool. Whenever possible, get the material on disk or CD so you can copy and paste or fill in forms. It will save you more time than you can imagine. Besides, magnetic media lets you click on links to resources, which will take you directly to additional information, as you need it.

Books and CDs

- *Small Business Management: An Entrepreneur's Guidebook with CD Business Plan Templates* (with CD) by Leon Megginson, Mary Jane Byrd, and William L. Megginson. Not only does this cover setting up a business plan, it guides you through marketing, budgeting, growing, and the continuity of the family business. It is a most comprehensive book.
- *Nolo's Tax Savvy for Small Business* by Frederick W. Daily. Looks at business setup and selecting a business entity from an attorney's point of view. It's an excellent companion piece to this book. You can get it from nolo.com or Amazon.com.
- *Nolo's Business Plan Pro 2004* on CD. This includes sample business plans, financial statements for thousands of industries, SBA loan documents, and links to loan sources and venture capital.
- *Nolo's How to Write a Business Plan* by Mike McKeever. This book helps you evaluate your idea's profitability, estimate your expenses, and prepare your cash flow forecasts. It offers tips about sources of funds—and where not to get them. The Nolo books are available from nolo.com.

Online Resources

- **The Small Business Administration.** www.sba.org
- **Links to business plans.** www.sba.gov/hotlist/businessplans.html
- **Center for Business Planning.** www.businessplans.org: They conduct a Moot Corp competition and post the best sample business plans online at www.businessplans.org/businessplans.html.
- *Inc.* **magazine.** www.inc.com: Their Business Plan Guide walks you through your business plan, step-by-step: www.inc.com/guides/write_biz_plan/20660 .html.
- *Entrepreneur* **magazine.** www.entrepreneur.com: A series of articles and guides, including tips from Wharton's Business Plan competition, is available at http://entrepreneur.com/Your_Business/YB_Node/0,4507,109,00.html.
- **The Small Business Advocate.** www.smallbusinessadvocate.com: Jim Blasingame's site and radio show has a wealth of articles, links, and interviews archived on the site. The "Gentleman of the Airwaves" (my title for him) is accessible for guidance if you need help.
- **CyberSchmooze at the IdeaCafe.** www.businessownersideacafe.com/cyber schmooz: Brainstorm with other business owners and have those who've "been there, done that" examine your problem through fresh eyes.

3

ENTITIES

History will be kind to me, for I intend to write it.

—Winston Churchill

To complete your business start-up and operations checklist as well as your business plan, you need to know what kind of body your business will wear. Why body? That's what *corporation* means.

> *Incorporate—1398, "to put [something] into the body or substance of [something else]," from L.L. incorporatus, pp. of incorporare "unite into one body," from L. in- "into" + corpus (gen. corporis) "body." The legal sense first recorded in Rolls of Parliament, 1461.*
>
> From the Online Etymology Dictionary, www.etymonline.com/i2etym.htm

Decisions, Decisions, Decisions

Once you get past all the setup and planning, your business will be a joy to run. You'll love what you're doing. Everything will fall right into place, and you soon won't have to stop and make decisions each time you must make a move. So far, you've been doing drudgework, getting set up, but that will change. You have one more big decision to make. And then, you'll be ready to go forth and conquer the world. (Of course, that one big decision comes only after lots more little decisions.)

What Do You Want to Be When You Grow Up?

The official term for the form—or body—of your business is *business entity*. There are two ways to decide what kind of business entity you are: decide for today or decide for the long run. Those not making plans, by default, decide only for today. But, you—you have great plans. You want a dynasty! You want a piece of that IPO (initial public offering) pie.

There's no reason not to get it. *Wired* magazine claims venture capitalists (VCs) are flush with money, chasing too few good ideas. VCs are experiencing a funding hangover—"There's 50 times too much cash: The money has to go somewhere."[1] Why not tap into that?

To get it, you've got to start out with a corporation or limited liability corporation (LLC), and you must have the right accounting team. Your advisory team can help you find the right firm to lay the foundation.

Not everyone wants the stress of venture capital oversight. You might want the freedom to succeed or fail on your own strengths. That doesn't mean you can't have investors. You may—but you can keep them at a distance with smaller LLCs or limited partnerships, composed of people you know. Before you decide, let's see what all your choices are.

First, understand that what is presented here is just an overview of your options. To fully list all your options would take volumes. Use this information as a starting point for a discussion with your advisory team. There's just enough information here to help you frame intelligent questions.

A Quick Overview of Entities

Presently, in the United States, there are only two basic types of entities—those that pay taxes and those that pass the taxes over to your personal tax return. Some entities swing either way. Once a small business decides what type of entity it is, it must stay with that decision. For some entities, like S-corporations, there are exceptions, but they may only change once every five years. Here are three of the key issues you'll need to understand before going deeper into the body of your business.

Taxation. Figure 3.1 displays your tax-paying options. As you can see, corporations are the only businesses that must pay their own taxes. Figure 3.2 supplies the

---

1. Gary Rivlin, "The Roots of Bust 2.0," *Wired* magazine, April 2004: pp. 120–125.

FIGURE 3.1 How Income Taxes Are Handled by the Entity

You Pay	They Pay	Either Way
Sole proprietorship	Corporation	Limited liability corporation
General partnership		Trusts
Limited partnership		
Limited liability partnership		
S-corporation		

tax rates. Income or losses from all other business forms are, or may be, passed on to you. You report them on your tax return and pay taxes at your highest tax bracket. These businesses are called "pass-through" entities.

Unless you're currently in the highest personal tax bracket, you're better off not forming a corporation. They are notorious for double taxation. Corporations pay tax. Then you pay tax on the dividends or wages they pay you.

Self-Employment Taxes. Chapter 11 goes into self-employment taxes in depth. For now, all you need to know is that they cost you 15.3 percent of your business profits, even if your taxable income is zero. Income from all the "You Pay" entities are subject to self-employment tax, except one—the S-corporation.

Payroll. Working officers of corporations, S-corporations, and LLCs filing as corporations are required to take a reasonable salary. Until 2004, the IRS didn't look closely at S-corporation wages unless the officer took none. But the IRS has hired an army of auditors, and the newly trained auditors are testing for reasonableness. For all the other types of entities, wages are not permitted for the owners. Owners' families may be paid, if appropriate, as Chapter 9 explains. Owners may be required to receive "guaranteed payments."[2] But those are not subject to payroll taxes.

---

2. Guaranteed payments are required when most income comes from services. The IRS requires that if one partner performs most of the services, they get a reasonable amount of income before the profits are split. This reduces the income that can be moved to children or other nonparticipating partners, who are apt to be in lower tax brackets.

FIGURE 3.2 Tax Rates

Corporations

Taxable Income Over	Not Over	Tax Rate
$0	$50,000	15%
50,000	75,000	25%
75,000	100,000	34%
100,000	335,000	39%
335,000	10,000,000	34%
10,000,000	15,000,000	35%
15,000,000	18,333,333	38%
18,333,333		35%

Qualified personal service corporation. A qualified personal service corporation is taxed at a flat rate of 35 percent on taxable income.

Personal Holding Company

Personal holding companies are subject to an additional tax on any undistributed personal holding company income. (IRS Code Sec. 541)

Year	Rate
2003–2010	15.0%
2002	38.6%

Accumulated Earnings Tax

In addition to the regular tax, a corporation may be liable for an additional tax on accumulated taxable income in excess of $250,000 ($150,000 for personal service corporations). (IRS Code Sec. 531)

Year	Rate
2005	15.0%
2004	15.0%
2003	15.0%
2002	38.6%
2001	39.1%
2000 and prior years	39.6%

None of the other entities pay tax at the federal level.

NOTE: Filing partnership returns late will result in penalties of $50 per partner per month. If you have a good enough reason for being late, do take the time to write to the IRS requesting abatement of penalties. They generally comply.

Entities, in All Their Glory

So, how do you decide? This section discusses all the major business formats with a brief explanation of how they work. Read the pros and cons carefully. There is no one perfect entity. Each one may have some advantages that are important to you. But there may be some other feature that makes it impossible for you to use. This will help you narrow down your decision.

Sole Proprietorships

This is just you, in business alone. You file your business tax return as a part of your personal tax return. Use the long version of Form 1040 and Schedule C. If you're in business with your spouse, you're really a partnership, aren't you? The IRS thinks so and prefers that you report your income that way.

Pros
- It costs nothing to set up—unless you register a fictitious name, and then it's about $50–$100 every few years.
- You have complete autonomy in business operations and decisions.
- You aren't required to keep a balanced set of books. But do it anyway.
- You are not required to have a separate bank account—but you should.

Cons
- Your profits are subject to self-employment taxes.
- Your business gets no tax benefit for medical expenses and insurance, without the complication and expense of a special plan, as described in Chapter 10.
- Without any structure, owners often get mentally lazy and don't think of their operation as a real business—so they rarely grow as they should.
- You are personally liable for everything that happens. All your assets, including your home and your savings, are at risk if you're sued.
- There is no continuity of life for the business. If you die, the business does, too.

General Partnerships (GPs)

Two or more people in business together are considered a general partnership. Income is reported on Form 1065, with Schedule K-1s issued to partners.

Pros

- They are inexpensive to set up. You may even write your own agreement. That's not a great idea, but it is a good starting point from which your attorney may prepare your partnership agreement. Even if there is no agreement, if two or more people are working together, you're automatically a partnership.
- General partnerships pay no taxes.
- Profits and losses may be split by formula, time devoted to the company, or another criteria, instead of only by ownership percentage.
- Losses are fully deductible on personal returns, unless they are real estate losses. Those face passive loss limits, which are described in Chapter 6.
- Certain partnerships can get out of filing a tax return altogether. The partnership may file an election (which is a formal announcement to the IRS) that the partners chose to report the transactions on their personal tax returns. You may do this with investment clubs, certain real estate rentals, or groups of people simply sharing expenses but not in business together.

Cons

- All the partners must be consulted for decision-making.
- If loans are required, all partners must provide their tax returns and financial statements. Many refuse because they don't really want their partners to know how rich—or poor—they are.
- Profits are generally subject to self-employment taxes.
- All partners are personally liable for everything that happens. All their assets, including homes and savings, are at risk if sued.
- All partners are liable for the acts of other partners and employees, too.
- There can be continuity of life issues. This means if your partner dies, either the partnership is over or you're saddled with an heir (spouse or child) who's in a position to make business decisions. This usually results in conflict. Avoid this by using the key-man insurance policies described in the checklist in Chapter 1.

Limited Partnerships (LPs)

Limited partnerships are coming back into vogue. In a limited partnership, the limited partners put their money in and get complete protection from any liability or lawsuit of the business. However, limited partners don't get to participate in the decision-making. There must always be at least one general partner who takes on the liability for the whole company.

Pros

- LPs are less complicated than corporations, LLCs, or LLPs.
- LPs don't pay federal taxes.
- They provide complete liability protection for all limited partners.
- Raising money from partners is easy. You don't have lots of general partners to answer to or get approval from.
- Getting loans is easier with LPs than with GPs. Only the entity's and the general partner's financial reports need to be produced for the lenders.
- Profits and losses may be split by formula, instead of only by ownership percentage. Some partners may want losses—others may not be able to use them at all.
- A benefit for the general partner in the LP is that partnership agreements may have buy-out clauses, or prohibitions against selling the partnership interest without the general partner's approval.
- Limited partners' earnings are not subject to self-employment taxes.

Cons

- LPs are more expensive to set up than GPs. You must get an attorney involved—whether it's yours or the people investing with you.
- Limited partners have no control over decisions. They could lose their investment if the general partner is inept or crooked. They won't know in enough time to do anything about it, since the general partner often doesn't keep them informed.
- Some states, such as California, charge minimum taxes.
- For the limited partners, partnership agreements may have buy-out clauses, or prohibitions against selling the partnership interest without the general partner's approval.
- Limited partners' income or losses are considered passive. Loss deductions are limited to passive income from other sources.
- General partners are fully liable if the company is sued.

Limited Liability Partnerships (LLPs)

This type of entity is usually reserved for professional groups, such as attorneys, accountants, architects, and others with special licenses—or really good political lobbyists.

Pros

- LLPs don't pay federal taxes.
- They provide complete liability protection for all limited partners.

- They provide liability protection from the acts of other partners.
- No general partner is needed.
- Profits may be split by formula, time devoted to the company, or other criteria, instead of only by ownership percentage.
- There is continuity protection so that even if a member dies, the company continues. Do set up buy-sell agreements and key-man insurance policies in case of death or disagreement.

Cons
- They are expensive to set up. All partners have a say in the issues. And being professionals, they are all experts—so they do tend to put in their two cents' worth. All this "cooperation" pushes up attorney fees.
- Some states, such as California, charge minimum taxes.
- Rules are different in each state.
- Profits are subject to self-employment taxes.

Limited Liability Corporations (LLCs)

Limited liability corporations are an interesting creation. You'll see why when you read all the features in the Pros section below. It's one of the most popular business forms with attorneys, since they can set them up easily using boilerplate forms. LLCs solve the problem of general partner liability. All partners, including managing partners, have liability protection.

Pros
- LLCs get to choose whether to report their business as a partnership, a corporation, or an S-corporation.
- One-person LLCs may report either as a corporation or on a personal Schedule C.
- LLCs may have multiple classes of ownership—this allows companies to give nonvoting shares to consultants and employees. Those members can share in profits but not decisions.
- LLCs are permitted to issue shares that may not be sold. Again, this is perfect for consultants and employees. If they leave, you may buy them out at a prearranged price or formula, whether they like it or not.
- LLCs filing as a partnership don't pay federal taxes.
- They provide complete liability protection for all members.
- No general partner, with liability exposure, is needed.
- There is no requirement for keeping minutes, thus reducing paperwork.

- Profits may be split by formula, time devoted to the company, or other criteria, instead of only by ownership percentage.
- Even if a member dies, the company continues. Remember to set up buy-sell agreements and key-man insurance policies in case of death or disagreement.
- The manager running the LLC does not need to be an owner.

Cons
- They are expensive to set up properly.
- Some states charge minimum taxes. California also charges a gross revenue tax.[3]
- Rules are different in each state.[4]
- Profits are subject to self-employment taxes if the LLC files a Schedule C or a partnership return.

Corporations (Corps)

This type of entity is still the most common large business format used in the United States. Most publicly traded companies are corporations. Some, on the smaller stock exchanges, may be LLCs.

Pros
- All shareholders, including officers, have liability protection.
- Corps may have multiple classes of stockholders. Generally, preferred shareholders get a guaranteed rate of return, but no voting power. This allows companies to give preferred shares to consultants and employees. Those members get an assured stream of income but stay out of management decisions.
- Corporate dividends to shareholders have a preferred tax rate of 15 percent if the stock is held long enough.
- Corporations receiving dividends from other corporations they own may be able to exclude up to 80 percent of those dividends.

---

3. If you're operating a small business in California, stay away from LLCs. They are usually your most expensive choice, due to all the state taxes and gross revenue fees.

4. "LLCs and LLPs—a State-by-State Tax Treatment and Overview," by attorney Bruce P. Ely, partner at Bradley Arant Rose & White LLP: www.barw.com/pdf/Sept%20LLC%20Charts%201%20&%202.pdf.

- No general partner, with liability exposure, is needed.
- Shares are easy to sell, though in small corporations the stock may have restrictions—or no market.
- Even if a member dies, the company continues. Remember to set up buy-sell agreements and key-man insurance policies in case of death or disagreement.
- Shareholders owning qualified small business stock (QSBS) for more than five years may exclude 50 percent of the capital gains on the sale.[5]
- Shareholders of QSBS may deduct up to $50,000 ($100,000 for couples) per year on losses.
- You may have unlimited shareholders.
- Anyone, anywhere on the planet may own your corporate stock, subject to any Homeland Security restrictions.

Cons
- Corporations are expensive to set up properly.
- Some states, such as California, charge minimum taxes, even when you have a loss.
- Profits are subject to double taxation. The corporation pays tax, and the shareholders pay tax on dividends issued from those already-taxed profits.
- The IRS may impose taxes for constructive dividends if you draw too much money.
- The corporation may be subject to an accumulated earnings tax if you draw too little money.
- The IRS may decide your wages are too high or too low and penalize you accordingly.
- If the corporation's income comes primarily from the services of shareholders, you may be subject to a flat tax of 35 percent as a personal service corporation.
- Undistributed income of personal holding companies may get hit with personal holding taxes.

S-Corporations (S-Corps)

S-corps have all the protections of corporations, but most of the advantages of partnerships.

---

5. TurboTax has an excellent overview of the tax benefits of qualified small business stock: www.turbotax.com/articles/taxbreaksonsmallbusinessstock.html.

Pros

- All shareholders, including officers, have liability protection.
- Corporate dividends to shareholders have a preferred tax rate of 15 percent, if the stock is held long enough.
- Corporations receiving dividends from other corporations they own may be able to exclude up to 80 percent of those dividends.
- No general partner, with liability exposure, is needed.
- Even if a member dies, the company continues. Remember to set up buy-sell agreements and key-man insurance policies in case of death or disagreement.
- You may choose to switch to a C-corporation format or back, once every five years, as long as you file Form 2553 by the fifteenth day of the third month of your fiscal year.

Cons

- Corporations are expensive to set up properly.
- Attorneys and corporate set-up paralegals rarely file the S-corporation election. You must remember to file it yourself or have your tax pro do it for you.
- When shareholders are added, all shareholders must sign the S-corporation election, Form 2553, all over again. Companies often overlook this.
- Shares are not easy to sell because there is no public market. Generally, it's wise to place restrictions on the stock to keep outsiders from owning your business.
- There are restrictions on the employee benefits of shareholders who own more than 2 percent of the business.
- Some states, such as California, charge minimum taxes, even when you have losses.
- The IRS may decide your wages are too low and penalize you accordingly.
- S-corps may only have one class of stockholders. Profits and losses are allocated by ownership percentage.
- S-corp stock is not eligible for the qualified small business stock benefits.
- Nonresidents of the United States may not own S-corp stock.
- You may have no more than seventy-five shareholders.

Whew! That's a lot of data. How can you decide what your company will be? Photocopy these last pages. Draw a line through all the things that are unacceptable to you. Highlight the items you like. This will give you a visual feel for which entities will and won't work for you. To help you out, look at Tables 3.1 and 3.2 on pages 46–49. Table 3.1 provides a side-by-side comparison of the primary tax considerations of all the entities. Table 3.2 provides a side-by-side comparison of the primary nontax considerations of all the entities.

A Brief Word About Nevada and Delaware Corporations

You've probably heard many radio ads tempting you with the virtues of the Nevada or Delaware corporations. They encourage you to set up your corporation in Nevada or in Delaware. They promise to fix your credit, get you loans without your guarantee, and other things you could never do as a small business. Sure, there are good things about them—privacy, for one. The corporate registrars of Nevada and Delaware won't reveal your identity, only the identity of your agent for service. If you're hiding out from creditors or former spouses, this may be a way to hide your assets.

Neither of these states have corporate, LLC, or partnership income taxes. They don't even require state tax returns. All you have to do is fill in a report about the current officers and agent for service—and pay them a franchise fee.

What's bad about using them? If you're not living in one of those states, you'll have to register your corporation to do business in your own state, too. Often, that will require you to reveal who you are. It will mean filing and paying your state's taxes. It will mean extra forms and registrations.

What if you follow the advice of those aggressively pushing the Nevada and Delaware corporations and you don't register in your home state? If someone doesn't want to honor any of your contracts, they don't have to and you have no standing in your state. Someone who figures out your company is not registered to do business in your state can walk away from your bills and you can't sue. Your own state, when they catch you, will charge you taxes, penalties, and interest for all the years you didn't file tax returns locally. Try getting the courts to hear your case.[6] You won't have any luck.

If you feel you must set one up, because you think "Someday I'm going to leave my state. Besides, nothing really happens in my state. It all happens on the Internet," it will cost you. To legitimately have all your transactions take place in

---

6. In order to file a lawsuit to collect bad debts, or anything, you must have legal standing in the state where you are filing the lawsuit.

Nevada or Delaware, you'll need a local address. All your mail must be delivered to that state and then forwarded to you. Not only does this cost you money, it adds about a week of time to each of your orders or banking notices. You must either have a phone number in that state or a toll-free number. Even local customers in your hometown must use that out-of-state phone number. Your bank account must be in that state. You must pay an agent for service. How much extra can you expect to pay, so you can avoid taxes in your own state? Here are some annual numbers:

Post office box ($20 per month)	$240
Postage—mail and package forwarding	$240
Agent for service	$125
Extra bank costs due to late notices[7]	$120
Toll-free phone number, or forwarding	$300
Annual franchise fee (approximate)	$100
Total cost of tax-free corporation	$1,125

If you set up in Nevada to save the annual $800 minimum fee in California (one of the more expensive states), you've just outsmarted yourself. You've spent $300+ more than the taxes would have been. If you're in a less expensive state, as far as corporations go, seeing how high the costs can run may make you think twice—the inconveniences generally outweigh the benefits.

What About Nonprofits?

If you want to get attention and raise money quickly, a nonprofit organization is a great structure. The right cause will open lots of corporate doors and treasuries. Radio and television stations are required to run public service spots, so advertising is free. The big drawback to being nonprofit is that you can get voted out if you don't structure your organization properly. You don't actually "own" the company. So don't set your business up as a nonprofit entity unless you're prepared to do it right. Otherwise, the IRS will come down on you like a ton of bricks.

---

7. The extra fees result from the delays in learning when some of your Internet sales have been questioned or deemed fraudulent. Due to the mail delay, you might not get the notice in time to respond and save your sale—or your standing with the bank.

TABLE 3.1 Summary of Tax Considerations for C- and S-Corporations, Partnerships, and Family Trusts

Tax Considerations	C-Corporation	S-Corporation	General Partnership	Limited Partnership	LLC	LLP	Family Trusts
Taxation	Corporation is taxed on profits. Shareholders are taxed on dividends.	Corporation is generally not taxed. Shareholders are taxed on profits passed on as dividends.	Partners pay taxes on their pro-rata share of income/ losses.	Partnership is not taxed. Partners pay taxes on their pro-rata share of profits. Partners have passive loss restrictions.	Taxation method is dependent on whether a corporation or a partnership is elected.	Partnership is not taxed. Partners pay taxes on their share of profits.	Generally, income is allocated to beneficiaries at year-end.
Pass-Through of Income/Loss	No	Yes	Yes	Yes	It depends.	Yes	Yes
Property Exchanged for Ownership Interest	Nonrecognition treatment if control requirements are satisfied under IRC §351. Liabilities transferred in excess of basis may result in gain.		More flexibility than corporations. Generally no gain or loss is recognized at either entity or partner level. Guidance under IRC §721.	More flexibility than corporations. Generally no gain or loss is recognized at either entity or partner level. Guidance under IRC §721.	More flexibility than corporations. Generally no gain or loss is recognized at either entity or partner level. Guidance under IRC §721.		Property or money is transferred into or sold to trust.
Initial Basis	Basis in stock = stock purchase price + cash + adjusted basis of property transferred to the corporation. Liabilities do not increase basis.		Same as corporations except that a partner's share of liabilities increases basis.	Determined in same manner as general partnerships	Determined in same manner as general partnerships	Determined in same manner as general partnerships	Fair market value of assets at time of transfer to the trust
Income Allocation to Family Members	Not applicable	Family members providing services must first be compensated prior to allocating income and loss to other family members.	Same as S-corps. Capital must be an income-producing asset in order for income to be allocated to a partner who is a family member and has received interest by direct or indirect gift.		Same as partnerships		Specified in terms of trust agreement

Alternative Minimum Tax	Subject to AMT.	Not subject to AMT at entity level.	Not subject to AMT at entity level.	Not subject to AMT at entity level.	Not subject to AMT at entity level.	Not subject to AMT at entity level.	Yes, either to the trust or beneficiary(ies)
Passive Loss Rules	Can generally offset passive losses against nonpassive income. C-corps are not subject to PAL rules except personal service corporations and closely held C-corps.	Shareholders may be subject to passive loss rules.	General partners are considered to participate materially if they meet any of seven tests in Reg. 1.469-5T, but LPs are more restrictive. Limited partners have only three tests by which they can be considered to "materially participate."		LLC members are treated as a general partner who has to satisfy one of the seven tests.	LLP members are treated as a general partner who has to satisfy one of the seven tests.	Subject to passive activity loss rules
Fringe Benefits	Few restrictions	Restrictions on 2% or more S-corp shareholders (may pay tax on fringe benefits)	Insurance, health, and welfare programs paid by partnership on behalf of partners are taxable to individual partners, deductible by entity, and reported as guaranteed payments to partners subject to SE tax.		Same rules as a partnership	Same rules as a partnership	Generally same rules as corporations
Double Taxation	Yes	No	No	No	No	No	No
Highest Marginal Tax Rate	Top rate: 35%	Flow-through depends on individual's tax rate bracket. Top rate: 35%	Flow-through depends on individual's tax rate bracket. Top rate: 35%	Flow-through depends on individual's tax rate bracket. Top rate: 35%	Flow-through depends on individual's tax rate bracket. Top rate: 35%	Flow-through depends on individual's tax rate bracket. Top rate: 35%	May flow through to individual or may be taxed as an entity. Top rate: 35%
Filing Costs at Creation	Filing fee with the state	Filing fee with the state	None	Filing fee with the state	Filing fee with the state	Filing fee with the state	None
Tax Forms and Applicable Publications	Form 1120/IRS Pub. 542	Form 1120-S/IRS Pub. 589	Form 1065/IRS Pub. 541	Form 1065/IRS Pub. 541	Form 1065/IRS Pub. 541	Form 1065/IRS Pub. 541	Form 1041/IRS Pub. 559
Tax Return Due Date	15th day of third month following entity's year-end.	15th day of third month following entity's year-end.	15th day of fourth month following entity's year-end.	15th day of fourth month following entity's year-end.	15th day of fourth month following entity's year-end.	15th day of fourth month following entity's year-end.	April 15; Generally trusts must use a calendar year.

TABLE 3.2 Summary of Nontax Considerations for C- and S-Corporations, Partnerships, and Family Trusts

Nontax Considerations	C-Corporation	S-Corporation	General Partnership	Limited Partnership	LLC	LLP	Family Trusts
Ease of Formation	File and incorporate in any state for permission to conduct business.	File and incorporate in any state for permission to conduct business.	General partners must agree to form partnership. No state permission is required.	Certificate of Limited Partnership must be filed with the state.	File with state for permission to conduct business. Must follow specific procedures for formation and operations.	Register election of LLP with the secretary of state.	Set up trust, appoint trustee, and identify beneficiaries.
Legal Status	Corporate legal identity independent of shareholders	Corporate legal identity independent of shareholders	Legal business entity independent from partners	Legal business entity independent from partners	Legal business entity independent from members	Legal business entity independent from partners	Independent taxable entity
Eligible Entity	No restrictions	Citizens, resident aliens, estates, certain trusts	No restrictions. Any person or entity qualifies as an eligible partner.	No restrictions. Any person or entity qualifies as an eligible partner.	No restrictions. Any person or entity qualifies as an eligible partner.	No restrictions. Any person or entity qualifies as an eligible partner.	No restrictions
Management	Board of directors and officers are elected or selected by shareholders.	Board of directors and officers are selected by shareholders.	Partners generally have equal voice in decision-making.	General partners manage according to partnership agreement.	Operating agreement outlines management.	Partners generally have equal voice in decision-making.	Trustee decides on most issues.

	C Corporation	S Corporation	General Partnership	Limited Partnership	LLC	LLP	Trust
Choice of Tax Year	No restrictions	There are certain restrictions in choosing a fiscal tax year. (Section 444 election)	Must adopt year-end as partner(s) with 50 percent interest. When no partner with 50 percent interest have same year-end, must adopt same year-end of principal partners with 5 percent interest in profits and capital. Otherwise, calendar year is adopted or show a business purpose.	Must adopt year-end as partner(s) with 50 percent interest. When no partner with 50 percent interest have same year-end, must adopt same year-end of principal partners with 5 percent interest in profits and capital. Otherwise, calendar year is adopted or show a business purpose.	Must adopt year-end as partner(s) with 50 percent interest. When no partner with 50 percent interest have same year-end, must adopt same year-end of principal partners with 5 percent interest in profits and capital. Otherwise, calendar year is adopted or show a business purpose.	Must adopt year-end as partner(s) with 50 percent interest. When no partner with 50 percent interest have same year-end, must adopt same year-end of principal partners with 5 percent interest in profits and capital. Otherwise, calendar year is adopted or show a business purpose.	IRC §645 provides tax year as the calendar year. Exempted are tax-exempt trusts under 501(a) and charitable trusts under 4947(a)(1).
Dissolution or Liquidation	Perpetual life. Shareholder approval normally is required. State law dictates approval procedure and necessary percentage of shareholders that can effect a liquidation.	Shareholder approval normally is required. State law dictates approval procedure and necessary percentage of shareholders that can effect a liquidation.	Death of partner may cause dissolution.	Generally limited to a fixed amount of time	Generally limited to a fixed amount of time	Generally limited to a fixed amount of time	Generally limited to a fixed amount of time
Owners' Liability	Shareholders are typically not personally liable for the debts of the corporation.	Shareholders are typically not personally liable for the debts of the corporation.	Partners may have unlimited liability.	General partners have unlimited liability and limited partners have limited liability.	Members not typically liable for the debts of the LLC.	Partners not typically liable for the debts of the LLP.	Owner is not generally liable for debts of trust.
Ability to Raise Capital	Sell shares of stock or bonds to raise capital	Sell shares of stock or bonds to raise capital	Obtain additional partners or investments from existing partners	Obtain additional partners or investments from existing partners; bank loans	Possible to sell interests, subject to operating agreement restrictions	Obtain additional partners or investments from existing partners	Owner can sell assets in trust. Income from assets is held in trust.
Transferability of Interest	Shares of stock in a corporation are easily transferable.	Yes, subject to shareholder consent	Depends on partnership agreement	Depends on partnership agreement	Possibly but usually restrictive	Limited partners may transfer their interests subject to partnership agreement.	No

You can start out with a nonprofit entity to establish yourself, your image, and your credibility. Use that as a jumping-off point to create a parallel business, funneling part of your profits to your nonprofit. You'll be helping yourself and doing good at the same time. Simply take a decent compensation as director of your nonprofit and make a remarkable improvement in the world around you. That's what Fred Jordan did. His Fred Jordan Mission started by feeding and sheltering Los Angeles's skid-row homeless. Today it helps people as far away as Africa and Hong Kong. Or take actress Carmen Zapata of the Bilingual Foundation of the Arts, which promotes cross-cultural understanding by bringing the Latino experience and culture, through the medium of bilingual theater, to English-speaking and Spanish-speaking audiences. And there's Rose Martin, whose Peace Neighborhood Center in Ann Arbor, Michigan, raises millions each year to help local people in need—and shares the wealth with other organizations in need.

Don't you admire people who can bring their passion to their work and create a win-win situation for all concerned? That could be you—and your family.

Entities We're Not Discussing

This book didn't cover the use of trusts or cooperatives as a business format. There are advantages to all of those forms, too, along with pitfalls. If you're feeling really aggressive, consider chatting with your advisory team about those alternatives.

All the Highlights in One Place

Let's summarize what you need to know about entities. First of all, avoid Nevada and Delaware corporations, unless you're located in Nevada or Delaware. Don't hide income offshore.[8] Cut taxes, but don't make that your only consideration. Factor in long-term issues, such as health, retirement, and your family and staff's needs.

The following overview lays out reporting requirements for each type of entity discussed in this chapter.

---

8. To the IRS, "offshore" means "outside the United States." That includes Canada, Mexico, and all those tempting tax-free islands and havens, like the Caymans and the Bahamas. See Chapter 5 for a discussion of offshore income and abusive schemes.

Sole Proprietorships

Report income and expenses on the following forms:

- Use Schedule C for most businesses.
- Use Schedule F for farms, florists, and ranches.
- Use Form 4835 if your farmland was leased to a tenant farmer. Income from this form is not subject to self-employment tax.
- Use Schedule E, page 1 for rentals of real estate or equipment.
- Use Schedule E, page 1 to report your royalties from books, films, and other intangibles.
- Use Form 8829 to deduct your home office.
- Use Form 4562 to deduct depreciation.

All Partnerships and LLCs Reported as Partnerships

Report income and expenses on the following forms:

- The overall tax return is Form 1065. Use page 1 to report your general business income and expenses.
- Use Form 1040, Schedule F to report farm and ranching income. Include it with Form 1065.
- Use Form 8825 to report your real estate rental activities. Include the form with your Form 1065 package.
- Schedule K-1 is issued to each partner or member, reporting their share of income, expenses, and credits.
- Use Form 4562 to deduct depreciation.

S-Corporations

Report income and expenses on the following forms:

- The overall return is Form 1120-S.
- Use Form 8825 to report your real estate rental activities. Include the form with your Form 1120-S package.
- Schedule K-1 is issued to each partner or member, reporting their share of income, expenses, and credits.
- Use Form 4562 to deduct depreciation.

Corporations

Report income and expenses on the following forms:

- The overall return is Form 1120.
- Use Form 8825 to report your real estate rental activities. Include the form with your Form 1120 package.
- You will generally need Form 4562 to report your depreciation, amortization, and business miles driven.
- Use Form 4562 to deduct depreciation.

Your Big Decision

You have the tools to decide. Before you go to the next chapter, how will you set up your business, your legacy? What will the body of your vision be? Will it be you alone or one of those alluring corporate or partnership entities? You'll need to know how your business will operate before you can set up the structure of your accounting system. Don't agonize over the decision. Please, don't let it paralyze you. Pick an entity. If you're wrong, it's all right. You can always change it later. Sure, it will cost a bit of money to convert to another entity. Don't worry about it. By then, you'll have the money. So, before turning to Chapter 4, decide!

Entity Resources

- **Online etymology dictionary.** www.etymonline.com
- **Form 1040, U.S. Individual Income Tax Return.** www.irs.gov/pub/irs-fill/f1040.pdf
- **IRS Publication 334, Tax Guide for Small Businesses.** www.irs.gov/publications/p334/index.html
- **Form 1040, Schedule C, Profit or Loss from Business.** www.irs.gov/pub/irs-pdf/f1040sc.pdf
- **IRS Publication 541, Partnerships.** www.irs.gov/publications/p541/index.html
- **Form 1065, U.S. Return of Partnership Income.** www.irs.gov/pub/irs-pdf/f1065.pdf
- **IRS Publication 542, Corporations.** www.irs.gov/publications/p542/index.html

- **Form 1120, U.S. Corporation Income Tax Return.** www.irs.gov/pub /irs-pdf/f1120.pdf
- **Form 1120S, U.S. Income Tax Return for an S-corporation.** www.irs .gov/pub/irs-pdf/f1120s.pdf
- **Form 4835, Farm Income and Expenses, Not Subject to Self-Employment Tax.** www.irs.gov/pub/irs-pdf/f4835.pdf
- **Form 8825, Rental Real Estate Income of a Partnership or S-corporation.** www.irs.gov/pub/irs-pdf/f8825.pdf
- **States' business start-up information.** www.bankrate.com/brm/news /biz/Green/states/states_text.asp: Bankrate.com provides fundamental information on licensing and start-up tips and links to various state agencies.
- **State tax forms.** www.taxadmin.org/fta/link/forms.html
- **LLCs and LLPs.** www.barw.com/pdf/Sept%20LLC%20Charts%201%20 &%202.pdf: A state-by-state tax treatment and overview by attorney Bruce P. Ely, Partner at Bradley Arant Rose & White LLP.
- **The Company Corporation.** www.accountstreet.com, (800) 315-9420: Register your corporation, LLC, or other formal structure at this site, which has much lower prices than attorneys.
- **Hubco.** www.inc-it-now.com, (800) 443-8177: Register your corporation, LLC, or other formal structure and handle most of it yourself—the cheapest option. Also, a great source of corporate supplies, such as the corporate seal, binders, and so on.
- **TaxSites.com.** www.taxsites.com: A great starting point for any tax or accounting search.
- **Legalbitstream.** www.legalbitstream.com: This site is a free tax law research website offering comprehensive and timely updated searchable databases of federal tax law, consisting of tax cases from the federal courts and IRS materials that were issued from the present ranging back to 1990 in most cases (contains fifty thousand documents).
- **Bottom Line Personal and Tax Hotline.** www.bottomlinepersonal.com: This site has a searchable database with at least the last three to five years of issues online. This is an excellent place to start a search. Subscribe to the Tax Hotline for $39 per year for a quick summary of important tax issues and excellent articles. They're written in plain English, so you'll have no trouble understanding them.

RECORD KEEPING

Always do right; this will gratify some people and astonish the rest.

—Mark Twain

You've probably never thought about it this way, but record keeping is a language. In fact, it's a series of different languages, depending on who will be using or reading your records. In Chapter 3, you made the big decision. You picked out the body your business will be wearing—even if it's just for the short term. Now, it's time for you to learn to communicate properly for the body you've chosen.

While the roots of the languages are all the same, the dialects are different—just as French, Spanish, Portuguese, and Italian all come from Latin. English also has a strong Latin influence. If you listen closely to those other languages, you'll find you can understand them a little, because you speak English.

It's the same thing with your records. The basics are the same across the board. The words used to describe concepts and transactions are the same, but the nuances and details are different the higher up the food chain your business gets. Refer to the glossary later in this chapter to demystify the terminology tax professionals and accountants use.

Types of Accounting Systems

It's very important for you to track your incoming funds and your expenditures if you want to have success as a small business. The simplest of accounting systems is just a summary of your various sources of income and a list of your expenses. Since that's essentially a list of numbers, there's no real way to tell if anything's missing. That's called a single-entry system. Whether you maintain these records manually or on a computer—using something like Quicken or Nitro Tax Helper— you have no cross-reference to ensure your books are in balance.

Here's an example of a single-entry system's transactions. In August, John fixed his car for $250. He paid his printer $150. John picked up office supplies for $75. His rent was $550. He bought a copy machine for $775 using his credit card. John's expense records might look like this:

Description	Amount
Auto Expenses	$250
Printing	$150
Office Supplies	$75
Rent	$550
Copy Machine	$775
Total August	$1,800

As you can see, there's nothing to show you how much money came from his bank account or from increasing the balance due on his credit card.

There's no balancing factor in single-entry systems. Being in balance is an obsession for accountants and bookkeepers. It tells us all the pieces of the puzzle are there. That's why businesses generally use a double-entry accounting system. Both sides of each transaction are recorded, and when the numbers don't balance—we know something's missing or something's entered incorrectly. In a double-entry system, John's transactions for August would look like this:

Description	Amount
Asset—Bank Account	($1,025)
Asset—Copy Machine	$775
Liability—Credit Card	($775)
Auto Expenses	$250
Printing	$150
Office Supplies	$75
Rent	$550
Total for August	-0-

Using a double-entry system, you always come out to zero, because assets = liabilities + capital.

Not everyone will need a double-entry bookkeeping system. Corporations will. Very small businesses can get by with the most casual of records. Although, if you start out with a balanced bookkeeping system, even for a tiny business, you'll already have it when growth is better than you expect. You can save the cost of converting, or entering a year's worth of data.

While paper-based bookkeeping systems are perfectly adequate, I recommend that you don't use them. If you're starting a business in this millennium, do your accounting on a computer. It's much easier and faster to correct posting errors. Reports are at your fingertips whenever a banker, your tax professional, or anyone asks. The software will give you enough information to prepare budgets or to catch fluctuations in costs or income.

One of the things I love about today's computerized accounting systems is that you no longer have to sort checks into numerical order or invoices into date order before you enter them. You just enter everything in any order you find them—and the computer puts each transaction into the right order. Working with people who haven't done bookkeeping for years, this is especially helpful. As I come across checks or invoices from other years, I can enter them into QuickBooks as I go along. I just need to remember to set the paper aside and file it in the box or drawer for the right year. You'll find that feature very helpful if you have receipts in your car or your kitchen or with your children, your boss, or your staff. As you get things in piecemeal, you don't need to stress about re-doing the entries to get them into the right month.

Another advantage to the computerized system is that it will give you reports for any time period. If you need to get a profit and loss statement for January through May, in order to compute your estimated tax payment, it takes seconds with a good software program.

One feature some of the accounting software companies are offering these days is online accounting. You pay a monthly fee, and they keep the software updated. You can access your accounts from practically anywhere on this planet. You and your tax professionals don't need to exchange files. You can go online together and discuss the accounting and make revisions or corrections any time you like. The only drawback is that when you use an online accounting system you can only use it for one company. If you buy bookkeeping software, on the other hand, you can generally use it for as many companies as you like.

Do yourself a favor, get the computer and the accounting software—or use an online system—whatever works for you. Just be sure to automate your accounting.

Doing It by Hand

If, on the other hand, you really prefer to do your bookkeeping by hand, take a look at Tables 4.1 and 4.2, which show how to set up a thirteen-column spread-sheet. As you can see in both tables, all the numbers to the right of the totals must be added together to equal the total in Column D, the "Total Check" column.

If you're going to do your bookkeeping by hand, be sure to total each page separately. Then have a total page for the month for both cash receipts and cash disbursements reports. Once the month is balanced, total all twelve months to get the whole year.

Use the "Other" column for expenses that are not necessarily recurring. At the end of the month, subtotal each item in the "Other." Add those sums together for the year.

Hand all these pages over to your tax professionals, who can review them and use the information to complete your business taxes.

The IRS Says It All

If you prefer not to take a full-blown bookkeeping course, start out by reading (or skimming) two IRS publications. The first one is IRS Publication 583, Starting a Business and Keeping Records (available at www.irs.gov/publications/p583/index .html) and the second is IRS Publication 334, Tax Guide for Small Business (available at www.irs.gov/publications/p334). Keep a highlighter pen and a pad of small Post-its handy to mark the passages that apply to you.

Fiscal Year

In general, you will set up your bookkeeping system using a calendar year for most entities. Sole proprietors may only use calendar year bookkeeping systems. Partnerships and pass-through entities may use the year of the majority owner. If that owner is a person, it will be a calendar year. When corporations or other partnerships own the majority interest, the partnership may use the fiscal year of the owners.

Corporations may select any year that suits them. Once the year is established, however, you may only change it with written approval from the IRS.

TABLE 4.1 Company Do-Re-Mi Cash Receipts Journal, November 2004

A	B	C	D	E	F	G	H	I
Date	Item #	Received From	Total Check	Net Sales	Sales Tax	Shipping Income	Reimb. Exp.	Rental Income
11/1/04	2245	Newman Sound Systems	650.00	577.37	47.63	25.00		
11/5/04	813	Ansty Tennant	825.00					825.00
11/17/04	11612	Speakers City	923.18				923.18	
		Total November	2,398.18	577.37	47.63	25.00	923.18	825.00

Totals in Columns E through I must equal the total in Column D.

TABLE 4.2 Company Do-Re-Mi Cash Disbursements Journal, November 2004

A	B	C	D	E	F	G	H	I	J	K	L
Date	Check #	Paid to	Total Check	Product Purchases	Office Supplies	Travel	Meals & Ent.	Rent & Utilities	Phone, Fax, Internet	Auto	Other (Describe)
11/1/04	811	Janice Janeway	321.83			200.00	75.83			46.00	
11/5/04	812	Landlord	1,165.00					1,165.00			
11/17/04	813	Electric Company	224.16					224.16			
11/21/04	814	Sally Staff	115.94		32.00		61.99		21.95		
11/26/04	815	City of LA	109.00								109.00 (Bus. license)
		Total November	1,935.93	0.00	32.00	200.00	137.82	1,389.16	21.95	46.00	109.00

Totals in Columns E through L must equal the total in Column D.

Accounting Styles

Either you use cash or accrual accounting—right? Nope, there's also the hybrid method and percentage of completion.

The cash method of accounting is the simplest and the most confusing. As with all things tax, there's always a dichotomy. It's the easiest method for people to use because you only report income from money you've actually received. You only report expenses for bills you've paid.

If it's that simple, why is it confusing? Perhaps it has something to do with the definitions of what is considered "received" and what is considered "paid," and the exceptions to the rule. Chapter 5 will explain "constructive receipt"—or define when money is considered received. Chapter 6 will explain when it's considered spent—and the few exceptions that crop up.

A key area of confusion for people who have not studied accounting (in other words, most of the business population) is why they can't write off bad debts—bills clients or customers never pay.

That's because you must be on an accrual basis to use bad debt write-offs. Even then, it's not as useful as you might think. You see, when using an accrual basis, you're reporting income when you send out the invoice to the client. So, you're paying tax on income you haven't received—or may never receive. That's why you may write off bad debts, when you can't collect the money. You've already included that debt in income.

Why would anyone in their right minds want to use accrual accounting (aside from the times it's required by law)? Because you also get to deduct your bills before you pay them. Some companies have customers who pay them quickly, so their accounts receivable (money from clients) is low. But they have sixty-day or ninety-day due terms on their accounts payable (bills they pay), so they have large unpaid balances—that they get to deduct at the end of the year.

Typically, businesses, such as doctors, who have large unpaid accounts receivable balances should always be on a cash basis. There are always more and more invoices that patients are refusing to pay. By using the cash basis of accounting, the doctor never has to report all the income he or she never received.

Larger corporations tend to use the accrual method. This lets them enter all their purchase orders, purchases, and shipping manifests or bills of lading into accounts payable in their accounting system. Doing this makes it easier to match up purchase orders with what was actually delivered. The company then has the invoice in its cash management system and can do a better job of tracking when to pay the bill. Companies on the accrual system also enter all the invoices for their sales into the system. That way, if customers pay off only part of an invoice, the computer can keep track of the amount of money the customer still owes.

If you use the accrual method and know how much cash you have, how much you expect to come in, and how much you have to spend, it becomes much easier to take advantage of vendors' discounts.

The hybrid method allows a business to use the accrual method for their stock and inventory, but the cash method for everything else.

Percentage of completion is generally used for large projects, like construction and engineering. You report your income and expenses based on the percentage of the project that has been completed. So if 15 percent of the bridge has been built, you'll report only 15 percent of the contractual income—even if you've received 30 percent of the payment. And since you often must buy half the materials in advance, you'll still only deduct 15 percent. The rest will be inventory.

Records You Must Keep

In our office, we keep everything. Our office and storage area is overflowing with paper. Why? I don't trust magnetic media to be readable when I need it. It's happened in the past, when something we meticulously backed up was corrupted by time or heat or . . . never got backed up properly to begin with. Besides, how many times have you changed your backup devices? You've used discs, then ZIP drives, then tapes, then CDs, and now DVDs. Do you still have a 5¼" "floppy" drive to read those old discs? Of course, if you're brave, you're welcome to scan all the documents and store the images electronically. Just make sure you get the front and the back, as needed.

What Kind of Paper Should You Keep?
- **Most important, make copies of all checks.** When customers pay you, copy their check. Then copy their check again, this time with your deposit slip. Put the check copy in your customer file, with their invoice. Put the deposit slip into your banking file. Later, when you reconcile your bank account, if you've overlooked an entry, you can find the details quickly.

  Consider making two copies of the invoices you send to clients, one to go in the client's file and the other to go into a master invoice file. All the invoices in the master file should be in numerical or date order. If you use numbers on your invoices, make sure you have each one, even if it's voided. The IRS looks for gaps in numbering sequence. To them, that means you invoiced someone and pocketed the cash off the books. To you, it probably meant your printer ate it or you messed up and prepared a new one. Just reprint it, mark it "void," and add it to the stack.

Making copies will also help you during an audit if the check you're depositing happens to be a loan from you or a cash advance. It will be easy to prove to an auditor that this was not income.

- **Next, save the cancelled checks as a record of your spending.** You don't need to copy them, just be sure to keep them safe and dry. You need them to prove you paid a bill when a vendor says they never received your check. You'll also need cancelled checks for tax agencies. And you'll need the information for audits.
- **It's very important to save paid bills.** Some people chill my soul: When they pay a bill, they throw it out. *Nooooooo!* The IRS wants to see what you're paying, not just how much. Do you like doing this with credit card bills? Please stop. Save all your paid invoices and your credit card statements.
- **Save bank statements.** Keep them all—from all accounts.
- **Save receipts.** Save receipts when you've been out of the office doing shopping. Bring back all the receipts for the money you took from petty cash and for the things you charged on your credit cards. You'll be able to match the invoices up with the statements. If there are errors, you'll catch them and get your refunds. Sometimes, the computer system produces posting errors, or they get hacked. With the receipt in hand, you have proof of the correct charge.
- **Keep copies of purchase contracts on all assets.** When you buy a car, a copy machine, a computer, or whatever, keep copies of all purchase contracts in a master file. You'll need copies of those invoices to support your depreciation expenses. Even though the IRS can, technically, only go back and audit you for three years, if there is something on a tax return that was bought six years ago, the IRS has a right to request the original documentation. For instance, you bought an editing machine for $30,000 in 1998. You didn't need the deduction the first year, so you depreciated it over seven years. Your last year will be in 2005. An auditor comes along to audit in 2004. He or she may audit 2001, but the year 2000 is not permitted. However, you bought this editing machine in 1998, and it's still generating a deduction. So the auditor may ask to see the purchase document. Save time—just have it handy.
- **Keep information about loans.** Keep a copy of the full loan contract, with all the details on the payoff terms. To verify the interest deduction, the IRS will want to see the contract so they can do their own calculations. It will also be a big help to you in case the interest charges are in error. I have seen

banks and finance companies make errors all too often. You can prove the correct interest using your paperwork and your own loan amortization schedule. Use Bankrate.com's loan calculators and print out the report (it's available online at www.bankrate.com/brm/popcalc2.asp).

- **Retailers, keep cash register receipts.** Always make sure that you match the information on your cash register receipts with the entries in your accounting system. If your cash register software is properly programmed, it should give you separate totals for cash and for credit card payments by customers. Match that up with your accounting entries. If the cash is short because you kept some of it to use for purchases and errands, record the total income received. Then, deduct the amount you kept as a charge to petty cash on hand. Be sure to bring back the receipts. For some reason, I find that with retail establishments, somehow the income on the books rarely seems to match the tape. We spend a great deal of time tracking down inconsistencies. Please make sure your tax professional helps you reconcile any differences.

- **Save tax returns of all kinds.** You file paperwork with your city, county, state, and federal governments. Keep copies of each one, in their own file in date order, with the most recent on top. Add up all your sales tax returns to make sure you've reported the same income on your income tax return as you did on your sales tax return.

How Long Should You Keep Records?

Keep all tax returns forever. Ignore what anyone else tells you. There have been too many times that the IRS or the state have made demands on tax returns filed eight or ten years ago, saying they were never filed. If you have a copy, you can insist it was filed.

If you send money in with those tax returns, keep a copy of the cancelled check in the file with the returns. If you got a refund—make a copy of that, too. If they grabbed your refund, you won't have any check copies, but you'll have a letter saying they grabbed the refund from a given year. One of these three items will prove that your return was filed.

Keep copies of all asset purchases for the life of the asset plus ten years, or for the life of the loan on the asset, plus ten years. If it's real estate, keep the paperwork until you sell it, plus ten years.

Basically, keep everything for at least ten years after its useful life or tax return filing date is past.

You realize, of course, there is this rule in the universe: As long as you keep it, you won't need it. The minute you throw it out, everyone will need it.

Until two years ago, I kept all my client records, from way back in the 1970s. Finally, I got bold and decided to give the records to the clients whose addresses I still had—and shred the files of people I couldn't reach. I only shredded files that were at least five years old—plus my own personal records.

One hour after I finished shredding, a client who'd filed bankruptcy a couple of years earlier, owing me money, called. He wanted the paperwork on the money he owed me so he could pay it off. (He had never listed my debt in the bankruptcy.) Well, I didn't have the papers, so I couldn't prove what he owed me. If it had been anyone else, I could have waved good-bye to that money. Luckily with Adam, he just shrugged and sent me what he thought he owed me.

Glossary of Bookkeeping Terms

Above the line. Accounting industry jargon for expenses that are deducted on the first page of Form 1040. These expenses are generally deductible as adjustments to income. They reduce your adjusted gross income, which allows you to increase medical expenses and miscellaneous itemized deductions. (*Also see* Below the line.)

Accounts payable (or A/P). Invoices you've received, or are expecting, for things you have purchased or things you have had delivered to your place of business or to your clients. For record-keeping purposes, only accrual basis companies report A/P on their financial statements.

Accounts receivable (or A/R). Money owed to you by your customers or clients after you have sent them an invoice. A/R does not include loans that are being repaid to your business, or anything else. It is just income due to you, in whatever form, as a result of a business transaction.

Accrual. An accounting method that includes all your company's sales and purchases, even if you haven't collected the money from clients or paid your vendors. Most people in business alone are wise to avoid this method. It involves an assortment of complexities and rules. (*See* Cash basis.) Accrual accounting is good when your outstanding business debt is high, but your accounts receivable are low.

Adjusted basis. The tax cost of your asset, with improvements added in, and things such as depreciation and casualty losses deducted. This is the tax cost after all adjustments mandated by the tax code have been applied to the cost. (*See* Basis.)

Adjusted gross income (AGI). The last number on the first page of your Form 1040. The lower this number is, the more apt you are to be able to deduct IRAs, take advantage of various credits and losses, and use medical expenses and miscellaneous itemized deductions. Several other numbers use this as a starting point. Please get familiar with AGI.

Advances. Loans, often to employees or owners, that will be repaid from their next payroll check or from their draws. They could also be funds given to workers before they go on a trip or to a business event. In that case, the worker must submit an expense report with receipts or mileage data adding up to the amount of money advanced. If they have money left over, they must either return it or have it deducted from their compensation. They may opt to have it added to their compensation and taxed, instead.

AGI. *See* Adjusted gross income.

Amortization. Derived from the Latin word for "death," the value of certain designated assets prorated over a period of time. You deduct a portion of it each year, much like depreciation.

Assets. Things the business owns that aren't part of the product being sold. Assets include bank accounts, investment accounts, inventory, vehicles, loans to people, equipment. They also include intangibles such as patents, copyrights, client lists, and goodwill. Businesses on accrual will also report their accounts receivable under assets. Assets are the first section of the balance sheet.

Audit trail. The detail of all the transactions behind a number on the financial statements, including all adjustments. Most consumer accounting or bookkeeping software has good audit-trail features. It lets you run reports and then click on the number to get the detail within that account. However, it also lets you correct the entry directly. Once you do that, there is no evidence of the error. Professional accounting software requires you to make a journal entry to correct each error, leaving a history of entries.

Balance sheet (BS). A report that shows the following relationship of your finances: Assets = Liabilities + Capital (or Equity). The balance sheet does not include your expenses or income—just the profit resulting from them. The "income" line on the balance sheet must equal the net income line on the profit and loss statement. All prior year's profits are rolled over into retained earnings.

Basis. Tax cost of an asset. It generally consists of the purchase price. For some assets, the basis is the fair market value (FMV). To keep things interesting, when it comes to depreciating business assets, the basis is the *lower* of cost or FMV. But for estates, it's often the *higher* of cost or FMV. (*See* Adjusted basis, Fair Market Value.)

Below the line. Accounting industry jargon for *itemized deductions*. These are expenses deducted on Schedule A. They don't reduce your adjusted gross income.

Capital (also called owner's equity). Capital represents investments in the company. Depending on the type of company, it might include stocks (corporations), shares (LLCs, LLPs, partnerships), or simply owner's equity. The capital section of the balance sheet includes the money invested in the business, the draws taken from the business, and the profits or losses of the business. It will also include any money spent to buy back company shares or stock from owners or partners.

Cash basis. The most common method of accounting. As income, you only include the money for which you have constructive receipt. (*See* constructive receipt.) Under expenses, you include only the bills you've paid. Certain things that look like accruals also get picked up—payroll and sales taxes to be paid in January (or at the end of your quarter). Credit card purchases are included in cash basis reporting, even though you have not paid for the purchases. They are treated like loans you've taken out at the time you made the purchase.

Check register. That little booklet the bank sent you with your checks. You're supposed to list all the checks you write and the deposits you make. Add your deposits and deduct your checks and bank fees. *Et voila!* You know how much money is in your bank account, at a glance.

Closing the books. When a company finishes the accounting for a month, quarter, or year, and reconciles all the accounts, they close the books for that period of time. No more entries are made into those ledger or journal pages. If errors are found later, they must be corrected using a journal entry. You can't just go back and erase the wrong entry. You must either debit or credit the error to get it right. That's in formal accounting systems. Today's software doesn't require that you close the books. It lets you make corrections later, if that's when you reconcile your bank statements or decide to enter your transactions.

Constructive receipt. Money you've received at a specific time, with the right to use it. (*See* Cash basis.) Usually this is important at year-end. A check was mailed to you by your customer in December, but you received it on January 2. Did you have constructive receipt of that check in December or January? Here are some common examples.

- If someone gives you a post-dated check, you don't have the right to deposit that check until the date.
- On the other hand, let's say you own a controlling interest in another business. That business owes your company $5,000, but you tell them to hold on to your money until next year. The IRS considers this as if you have constructive receipt of that money. You're the one who is in control of when that check is issued.
- A third case is where someone owes you money. You tell them to pay that money to a third party, to whom you owe money. Even though that check never hit your books, the IRS treats that as if you had constructive receipt of the money. You controlled how that money was spent.

Credit. In accounting, a credit is the negative half of an accounting entry (debits and credits). It reduces the balance of the account it's posted to. On the asset section of a balance sheet, it reduces the asset. A credit to the bottom of the balance sheet increases liabilities or equity. On the profit and loss statement (P&L), a credit increases income and decreases expenses. A credit balance on the P&L means you have a profit. (*See* Debit.)

Debit. The reverse of a credit. (*See* Credit.) A debit balance on the P&L means you have a loss—you're in the red. When you debit your bank account on your books, it means you've made a deposit. When the bank debits your bank account on *their* books, it means you have drawn money from it. Debits and credits are a confusing concept if you can't visualize both sides of the transaction.

Depreciation. The act of writing off the cost of an asset over a specific period of time, as designated by the tax code. Chapter 6 expands on this issue.

Double-entry bookkeeping. A balanced system in which each transaction has two sides, i.e., when you write a check for office supplies, you reduce the balance in your checking account and increase the balance in an account called office expenses.

Draws. In partnerships, or pass-through entities, these are funds paid to partners or members. They are considered advances against income. This is not income. Draws are reported on the books as a negative amount under capital. At the end of the business year, they are netted against retained earnings—or the owner's capital account. (*See* Owner's equity.)

Expense report. A worksheet submitted by employees wanting reimbursements for out-of-pocket expenses. It may also be an accounting for monies advanced before a business trip or shopping trip was made. Generally, receipts are attached to substantiate the expenses.

Fair market value (FMV). The price a stranger would pay for your asset in an arm's-length transaction. If you put it up for sale, what would someone pay for it? Try to avoid using sample prices you find on eBay as your source for FMV because you'll end up with a lower value.

General journal. Within the bookkeeping system, this is where adjustments are entered.

Journal entry. An accounting entry posted to the general journal. Most entries come into the books via money transactions—deposits or purchases. They are entered in the cash receipts journal or cash disbursements journal. However, corrections, depreciation, amortization, splitting payments between loans, and interest—all those noncash or correcting transactions are entered in the general journal. Year-end adjustments are entered on the books using journal entries.

Liabilities. These represent money the business owes, including unpaid payroll and sales taxes, accrued at the end of the year; credit card debt; loans; and monies owed to employees or officers. Accrual basis companies will include their accounts payable here.

Nexus. This is a business presence in a state or tax area. See Chapter 12 for a detailed explanation.

Offshore income. Income held in accounts outside the United States. *Offshore* doesn't necessarily mean "on an island." It could just as easily be in an account right across the border in Mexico or Canada.

Owner's capital account. An account in the equity or capital section of the balance sheet that tracks the partner's, shareholder's, or member's ownership interest in the business. When the investor contributed very little money but has received a lot of draws or losses, his or her capital account may be negative. When capital is negative, an investor is usually not permitted to deduct any more losses.

Owner's equity. *See* Capital.

Pass-through entities. Business entities that do not pay federal taxes. They pass their profits and losses through to owners, who report it on their personal tax returns. Chapter 3 explains this concept.

Payroll. Wages and salaries. Payroll is not just any money you hand to the workers. Payroll has a specific meaning. If you use *payroll* to refer to the compensation you're paying your freelancers within earshot of an auditor, you've just turned them into employees. Chapters 9 and 10 cover this topic.

Percentage of completion. Another accounting method. It is a way of reporting income when you're on a long-term project and receive progress payments. This is used in construction and engineering projects, among others.

Profit and loss statement (P&L). A financial report summarizing a business's income and expenses, resulting in either a profit or loss at the bottom line. (*See* Balance sheet.)

Purchase order (PO). A written document letting a company know that someone in authority approved a particular order. It also defines what was ordered and usually includes a promise to pay for a specific number of units at a specific price.

Quarter. When used in financial reporting, this is generally a three-month period. There are four each year. You'll often see quarters noted as Q1, Q2, and so on. They usually run as follows—Q1 = January–March; Q2 = April–June; Q3 = July–September; Q4 = October–December. The IRS, of course, has a whole different schedule for quarters (see Chapter 11). Quarters are particularly important for payroll, sales taxes, and estimated taxes. In the financial world, publicly traded corporations release their profit and loss statements each quarter—to the acclaim or jeers of analysts.

Retained earnings. Profits the business has earned that have not been distributed to owners or shareholders. (*See* Draws, Balance Sheet.)

Tax year (also fiscal year). The accounting year established by your business. In general, it should start on January 1 and end on December 31. However, corporations have the option of selecting their own year-end, to simplify accounting. If taxes will be deferred (delayed) more than three months, the IRS may require the company to pay the difference earlier, as estimated tax payments.

Terms. This includes the period of time by which an invoice must be paid and it may also include a discount code. For instance 2/10 means if you pay the invoice within ten days, you're welcome to deduct 2 percent of the invoice.

Trades. An advertising industry term, this term describes formalized barter transactions.

Transposition of numbers (also called "transpo"). When writing numbers or keying them into your accounting program, sometimes, your fingers get dyslexic and two numbers switch places. Instead of typing "976," you type "796." The difference is 180. You can always recognize a transpo because your out-of-balance number will add up to a multiple of three.

Trial balance. A list of all the accounts your company uses in its accounting system, with a balance in each account. When you total up the balances in all the accounts, you should get zero.

Wages. *See* Payroll.

Record-Keeping Resources

Online Glossaries
- **The AICPA (American Institute of Certified Public Accountants).** www .aicpa.org/members/glossary/a.htm: Has a glossary of terms, acronyms, and abbreviations.

- **VentureLine.** www.ventureline.com/glossary.asp: Offers an extensive tax and accounting glossary.

IRS Forms and Publications
- **Publication 583, Starting a Business and Keeping Records.** www.irs.gov /publications/p583/index.html

Bookkeeping Resources
- **One-Write.** www.one-write.com (double-entry cash journals): This is one of the older manual systems for small businesses. Basically, it's designed so when you write your checks, the information is duplicated directly into the cash disbursements journal. At the end of each day, week, or month— depending on how many transactions you have—you just total up each page. Just follow the formula at the bottom of the page to see if you're in balance. It's a little old-fashioned, but I remember having more free time when we used this system. You will still need to enter the data into a general ledger. Or have your tax pro do that for you. They also offer a software system.
- **Dome.** They produce a variety of record books and bookkeeping systems that are inexpensive. You can find their products at all office supply stores and at online bookstores, including a thirteen-column columnar pad in a three-ring binder, with tabs for cash receipts pages, cash disbursements pages, payroll journal, and general journal. Your tax professional can show you how to set it up.
- **Nitro TaxHelper.** www.nitrotaxhelper.com: This is the simplest software system—a single-entry bookkeeping system with easy-to-customize accounts. It lets you track mileage right up front. Reports include P&L and expense or income detail. They have a version for multi-level marketers, too, available at www.mlmtaxhelper.com.
- **Microsoft Money.** www.microsoft.com/money/buy/default.asp: The business version is substantially cheaper than QuickBooks and is very popular. I haven't used it in years because when I tested it in 1999, the software permitted you to make entries that didn't balance. By now, they've undoubtedly fixed that glitch. For the price, it's well worth considering, and you can bet there's some excellent support behind it.
- **Quicken.** www.quicken.com: This is a single-entry system with lots of bells and whistles. With its banking and investment tools, it has terrific value for personal use. But don't use it for business. Buy its big sister, QuickBooks, instead.

- **Peachtree.** www.peachtree.com: This is very popular with larger businesses and accountants but is more complex than QuickBooks. It's easier to use if you have some accounting or bookkeeping background. Generally, users set it up to work with account numbers, which are harder to use when trying to make entries quickly. The software is slow. I have tried it with various systems and it is always slow.

- **QuickBooks.** www.quickbooks.com: A full double-entry system for small businesses, QuickBooks is available in many versions, including customized versions for various industries and point-of-sale systems for retail shops. This program can work with online banking systems. Add-on payroll systems are available. When buying the box, instead of using the online version, you may track many companies. It's one of the most popular systems. Intuit is buying up smaller companies, so a few years from now, it may be the only one left standing. But, as they improve it, it gets more and more confusing to users. Newer versions are not backward compatible. So to enable your tax pro to review your work, or for you to see your tax pro's changes, you both have to constantly buy updates, which can be very frustrating. Mac and PC versions are available.

- **MYOB.** www.myob.com/us: This system offers software for both Windows and Mac systems, with accounting software for several countries and currencies. It's a more sophisticated system, allowing you to add more modules as your business expands to include manufacturing, payroll, and other accounting functions. They offer free conversions from QuickBooks.

- **ACCPAC.** www.accpac.com/products/finance: Another step up, this system works best for larger organizations needing a more formal accounting environment. They offer free conversions from QuickBooks and MYOB.

- **CFS Tax Software.** www.taxtools.com: This site has an excellent, inexpensive array of tax tools and special calculation tools, including payroll tools, you won't find anywhere else.

- *TMI Quickfinders Handbook.* www.quickfinders.com/book2.asp: Good for daily look-ups on how to handle issues, this book contains worksheets and basic explanations, with index versions for individuals and businesses. Great for at-a-glance information.

The following publishers provide tax updates and resources to accounting firms and colleges. You can get a copy of the tax code, regulations, or analyses on any tax issue. They have books for specific industries and entities. Teaching tools and study guides are available, too.

- **Bureau of National Affairs (BNA).** www.bna.com, (800) 372-1033: They provide folios and in-depth analyses of tax issues.
- **Commerce Clearing House.** http://cch.com, (800) 248-3248
- **Kleinrock.** http://kleinrock.com/taxsuite/Index.aspx, (877) 728-9776: They offer a full, searchable tax library on CD.
- **Prentice Hall.** http://vig.prenhall.com/catalog/academic/discipline /0,1142,6,00.html, (800) 227-1816
- **Lexis Nexis Matthew Bender.** The original in-depth legal database, teamed up with a major analytical publisher. http://bender.lexisnexis.com, (800) 227-4908.
- **Thompson-Ria.** Publishes in-depth analyses of tax and accounting issues. (800) 950-1216.

5

INCOME

You don't seem to realize that a poor person who is unhappy is in a better position than a rich person who is unhappy. Because the poor person has hope. He thinks money would help.

—Jean Kerr

Money In, Money Out, Wave Your Hands All About

You'd think income would be the easiest concept for a business owner to grasp. It seems completely obvious to you, right? Income is the money that came into the business. Clearly, it's all the money that was deposited into your account.

But what if you don't have a business account? Or you use your personal account most of the time instead? Then, how much is income?

The following question is typical of a new business owner:

I am self-employed as a carpenter. When someone pays me for a job I've done, and they pay me by check, how can I keep "supply" costs separate from "labor" costs? For example: If I charge $500 to do a job and spend $800 in supplies, I'll get a check for $1,300 in payment. I don't want the IRS to think I've earned $1,300 when in fact I've only earned $500. Help!

Other troubling concepts involve understanding the difference between income and deposits to the business account. They're not necessarily the same thing. Let's take a little test. All of the following are examples of items deposited in your business account. Can you tell which ones are income?

- Client reimbursement of your out-of-pocket expenses
- Customer's payment for completed work
- Your money, deposited to prevent an overdraft
- Cash advance from a credit card or your home equity
- Royalty for the oil under your home
- Money from investors or partners
- Money you borrow from Mom (Shhh. Don't tell Dad.)
- Insurance settlement for your pain and suffering arising from a work-related auto accident
- Money you took from your IRA to cover payroll
- Repayments of advances you took earlier

Which ones are income? Only the first two. All the rest are often deposited into business bank accounts, but they have nothing to do with income.

It's really important to get this right because most small business owners don't bring their bookkeeping with them to their tax appointments. Instead, many only bring their profit and loss statements, some neat printouts on a spreadsheet, or a couple of scribbled pages of data. Your tax professional generally never gets to see your income records. So, when you overstate your income, they have no way of knowing. The good news is that if you've reported these deposits as income, your audits will result in refunds.

A Capital Idea

If eight of these sample transactions aren't income, then what are they? Most of them are capital transactions. The rest were strictly personal and never belong in a business account at all. Money you receive for personal reasons, such as the royalties related to your residence and personal injury settlements, should be deposited into your personal bank accounts. If your business really needs that money, fine—write a check and lend it to the business. Then, you'll have an audit trail of a loan transaction.

Capital transactions are things that belong on the balance sheet side of your financial statements. They include loans, credit card debt, and investment assets bought or sold for business use.

Investor's Money

How do you report the money you receive from an investor? It depends on the nature of the investment. If an investor lent you money, which your business must repay, it's a loan. Sometimes the money they lend you is a hybrid of a loan and profit sharing: You're going to pay the investors their money back, plus 6 percent interest, plus 10 percent of profits. It's still a loan. Report the funds as a debit to the bank account and a credit to a loan account. Be smart. Use the name of the person as the name on the account, i.e., Loan from Rich Guy Malone.

To make it an investment, as opposed to a loan, the investor must have bought a percentage of your business—not just a percentage of your profits. We discussed the nuances of this in Chapter 3. Record this as a debit to the bank account where the money was deposited. The credit will go to stock, if it's a corporation. It will go to owner's equity—George Generous, if it's a partnership.

What if you're a sole proprietor? Well, if you sold part of your business, you're no longer alone. If you file no formal paperwork, you're automatically a partnership. Remember to get your federal identification number for the new entity.

Did I tell you the best thing about investor's money? If everything falls apart, you don't have to repay it. That's the big difference between a loan and an investment. Lenders avoid risks. Investors share the risk with you. You succeed—the investors get a windfall. You fail, and so do they.

So, if these eight transactions weren't income, what is?

What *Is* Income?

Income is all the compensation you receive for your goods or services. Note the word *compensation*, as opposed to *money*. Sometimes you don't get money—you get stock or a share in a partnership or LLC. Perhaps you trade your expertise for services or two chickens, or you get a painting or your lawn mowed.

To determine whether an unfamiliar transaction is income, ask yourself this—"Would they have given this to me if I didn't provide them with a product or service?"[1] If the answer is no, you have income.

If the answer is yes, you probably have a gift. Of course, what if your family and friends are using your services just to help you out? Well, even if it's a pity sale, it's still a sale.

---

1. Read the income chapter of IRS Publication 334, www.irs.gov/publications/p334/ch05.html#d0 e3424.

Look back to Chapter 3 to review which IRS forms to use to report your income.

Timing of Income

Chapter 4 explained the difference between accounting on a cash or an accrual basis. Most small businesses are on a cash basis. Essentially, you report your income when you get the money. But even for cash basis businesses, there are times when money received is not income, such as the following:

- **As a landlord you receive a security deposit, that's not income.** It's not your money. You must return that money to the tenant if they leave the premises in good condition when they move out.
- **You're an attorney and receive a settlement from an insurance company for your client.** That's not your money. It belongs in your trust account, until you pay all the costs and all the parties. Once the case is settled, the fee is income. When you draw money from the trust account specifically as fees, it's income.
- **You're a contractor and receive a third of the project cost from your client for the building you're erecting.** That money might be required to last several months, as the construction progresses. You're only entitled to draw money for yourself at certain stages of completion. You'll be reporting that income on a "percentage of completion" basis.
- **You're a retailer and someone buys something on layaway.** The money isn't yours until they finish paying for it and pick up the merchandise. If they never do, how much of that money are you entitled to keep before you refund the difference? There may be a processing fee at the time the transaction is cancelled. The fees will depend on your layaway contract. Until then, the money is a deposit.
- **You put on seminars or workshops.** People pay an attendance fee weeks or months in advance. They are entitled to a refund, less a cancellation charge, at any time before the event. Before the event, the only part of the money you've received that is considered income is the cancellation charge. Once the event takes place, naturally, the rest of it is realized as income.[2]

You're getting the idea. Money isn't treated as income until you earn it.

---

2. "Realized" in tax lingo means the event has now taken place, or the income is now earned.

Tip

The abbreviated explanation of income: when there are strings attached to money, it becomes income when the strings are gone.

A Brief Note About Accrual Basis

Small businesses that work on the accrual basis report the income as it is invoiced.[3] You only send invoices when you've earned the money. So when people pay you a retainer or advance for services to be rendered, you record the money received as a debit to cash and a credit to accounts receivable, instead of as a credit to income. It gets treated as income when you work off your obligation. When you issue your invoices for this work, you'll be crediting income and debiting accounts receivable.

Sales Taxes Received—Are They Your Money?

Bookkeeping can frequently be a messed-up area, but it's actually much simpler than it looks. You want your books and your deposits to balance to the income reported on your tax return. To do that, you must include the sales tax you collect as part of your income. Simple. Yes, include it.

Then, see the line of your tax return that asks about tax expenses? Deduct the sales taxes you paid to your state on that line. In fact, this is one of those expenses you get to deduct even before you pay it. Since you received all the sales taxes with your sales by December 31 (or your fiscal year-end), you deduct it in the year the taxes were collected. You'll be paying it by January 31, or the alternate due date, if it falls on a weekend.

Income Rarely Reported

There are three kinds of transactions most people either forget to report or don't bother—illegal income, offshore income, and barter. I'll cover each of these briefly, just so you know the issues associated with these types of income.

---

3. *Accrual basis* means that you report income when you send out the invoice. You report expenses when you receive the invoice, or when the merchandise you bought is received into your office or warehouse. See the glossary in Chapter 4.

Illegal Income—Can't Report It?

If you're engaged in criminal activities, the last thing you want to do is report your income to the IRS and turn yourself in. You're not an idiot. Well . . . you are a criminal, so there's room for doubt.

Remember, the arm of the IRS is all-powerful. Before Homeland Security was created, the IRS was the only agency of the U.S. government that operated on the Napoleonic Code—guilty until proven innocent. The IRS has the distinction of catching Al Capone, where the relentless pursuit of the FBI brought no results.

So, yes, if you're a drug lord, thief, illegal prostitute (it's legal in some states), embezzler, whatever—report the income. You're welcome to call it "other" income. But report it. Since being a criminal is a business, report it on Schedule C and pay the self-employment taxes on it. Enter 999999 as the activity code on Schedule C— it stands for unclassified establishments, or unable to classify. If you consider yourself a professional, use 541990—all other professional, scientific, and technical services.

Oh, go ahead, pay the tax. Just because you're a criminal doesn't mean you can't be a good citizen, too.

Offshore Income and Abusive Tax Schemes

Offshore income[4] means income generated outside the United States. Sometimes you have transactions with businesses outside the United States. As a U.S. citizen or resident, your business is taxed on its worldwide income, not just the domestic revenues. With the Internet, it's easy to open a bank account in another country without ever setting foot there. You can deposit your offshore sales into that account and keep it as a secret nest egg until you're ready to retire. Or just have the bank issue you a debit card and you can spend the money here at home. Most people think that the IRS will never see a record of that money, but those people aren't thinking straight.

The world is getting smaller and smaller. The IRS already has arrangements with Visa and MasterCard (your debit cards) to audit their offshore accounts. Small countries often rely on U.S. financial assistance or tourism. When the U.S. government starts threatening to withhold those benefits, countries often elect to enter into treaties that effectively rat you out.

---

4. The IRS's Abusive Tax Schemes warning is available at www.ustreas.gov/irs/ci/tax_fraud/abusive taxtschemes.htm.

There are some very heavy fines, penalties, and even jail time if you're caught. The IRS is making a powerful effort to make the public aware of this—and paying rewards for information. So, beware. Your friends who don't have money offshore might just get irked enough that you're flaunting your wealth. That reward is really nice.

Seriously, don't go there. It's not worth the price.

There are legitimate ways to legally set up businesses and partnerships with people or businesses in other countries. If your business is heading that way, go for it. Be sure to report all your earnings when you do. It's done all the time. You've seen Coca-Cola, Motorola, McDonald's, Federal Express, and many other very successful international businesses do it. When you reach this point in your business, add an expert in international taxation to your advisory team. Otherwise, you're bound to step on the toes of other countries' tax systems, too.

Bartering—You May Not Even Know You're Doing It

Barter happens more often than you realize. It's not just a function of formal barter clubs or exchanges.

You do it without even thinking. Barter is older than speech. It's the foundation of civilization. Barter made it possible for people to specialize. I cook. You weave. I farm—and give you food. You shoe my plow horse and make my tools.

How does this translate into today's world? You have skills and trade your services for someone else's products. When each side of the transaction has equal value, and both sides are providing something related to business, it's not nearly such a problem when you don't report it. There would be no tax effect.

The advertising industry commonly gets columns, space, or air-time in "trade." Instead of paying for the ads, their client provides goods or services. When I was working for a radio station, we had flowers delivered to each office every Monday by FTD. On Fridays, we'd all get Winchell's donuts. Licorice Pizza provided records (what, you were expecting pizza pie?). When the Shubert Theatre opened in Century City, we were all invited to a private, press-only performance of *Grease*. For the most part, both sides of the transactions were business-oriented. Even though it may look personal, the station received certain merchandise and used it in the course of business. Staff benefited from all the goodies so we could use it and spread word-of-mouth recommendations.

However, barter isn't usually done by contract. It's usually a casual exchange of a business product or service for a personal one. For instance, you're a plumber with a shop on Main Street. You provide $1,200 of plumbing services to your gardener at his home. In exchange, your gardener mows your lawn and maintains your landscaping for a year. You must record the value of your plumbing services as a sale. You have $1,200 in income.

Since the gardener is providing you with a personal service, you don't get to deduct the cost of the gardening. The gardener must report the $1,200 he would have been paid for his services as income. May the gardener deduct your plumbing bill? Perhaps a part of it. The gardener has an office using 33.3 percent of his home. He'll be able to deduct one-third of the expense. As a result, the gardener has net income of $800 from this transaction.

When you add them together, that's $2,000 worth of income never reported to the IRS. The IRS understands this. Wherever they stumble across barter during an audit, they're assessing taxes. Your innocent remarks may incriminate you, even when you didn't realize you've done anything wrong.

So, please be careful. When trading with people, be sure to think through the details of the tax implications of your transaction.

1099s Your Business Receives

1099 Forms are only sent to sole proprietors and partnerships. Corporations don't get them at all, except for doctors and lawyers. While a business might get an assortment of 1099s, here are the principal kinds to expect, in order of frequency:

- **1099-MISC.** Your company provides services to another company or person.
- **1099-INT.** Your company lent money to another company or person.
- **1099-DIV.** Your company used some excess cash to invest in stocks. This might also come when you receive income from a corporation your company owns.
- **1099-B.** Your company sold stock or engaged in barter transactions.

The IRS's computer receives millions of 1099s from all over the country and matches up the amounts with everyone's tax returns. If a 1099 was issued to you, the IRS is going to be looking for that number on your tax return. You'd be wise to include the full amount shown on that 1099—even if it's wrong. Chapter 13 explains what happens when the numbers don't match. Here are some tips to ensure you don't get those nasty notices.

What if They Sent You a 1099 with the Wrong Amount?

Of course, a person would be daft to pay tax on money he or she has never received. How can you fix the problem without getting yourself into trouble? You have two choices—contact or correction.

Contact whoever issued the 1099 and ask them to issue a correction. Or, as I always like to do, ask them to pay you the difference. Pity, they rarely do.

If they are smart enough to hold off filing the 1099s with the IRS until they've received feedback from recipients, the company will be most agreeable. Simply provide some proof or documentation explaining why the 1099 is too high. The company will be happy to help—or they will show you why you're wrong. See how easy that is?

I wish it were so. Unfortunately, this avenue usually results in an argument with some closed-minded bureaucrats who stubbornly refuse to help. They get defensive because they didn't have the foresight to wait for feedback from the recipients. They've already submitted the 1099s and don't want to file amended forms. Amending them attracts attention. They also are used in audits or court cases when examiners are looking for evidence of fraud. One of my longest, nastiest audits started when a corporation was audited and the examiner happened across an amended 1099 with my client's name on it. He jumped on that amended 1099, deciding he'd found fraud. In fact, the auditor was so aggressive, he was shooting for a RICO audit.[5] But . . . that's a story for another day . . . and another book.

What if the Money Is from Last Year?

Be aware that sometimes the 1099 will be right. But it's a timing difference. Take the example of my client, Eddie the Entertainer. Eddie is on the road most of the year. He does his darnedest to keep up with his bookkeeping, but it's tough when you're rarely home. As a result, my office always calls Eddie's agent to verify his earnings for the year. In 2002, the agent reported $20,000+ more than Eddie had on his books. That's a large sum. Eddie couldn't really account for the difference. Tracking down the payments, we learned the agency issued some checks at the end of 2002 that Eddie didn't receive until 2003. That accounted for the difference. As far as the agency was concerned, they paid the bill in 2002—they wanted the deduction. There was no error.

---

5. *RICO* is the acronym for the Racketeer Influenced and Corrupt Organizations Act—we're talking about organized crime here!

How can you fix this when it happens to you? When the money was sent out in one year, but you received it the next, report the full income, but adjust your expenses to account for the difference in income. The tax code, when it comes to cash basis taxpayers, operates on the doctrine of "constructive receipt." You don't report the income until you receive the money in such a way that you can actually use it. (For example, a post-dated check received on December 20 that is dated January 15 is considered received in January.)

As far as I am concerned, this is the easiest and fastest course of action. If the amount in dispute is really large or if it's a substantial part of your overall income for the year, it would be wise to attach proof with your deduction.

To prove you received the money in the following year, here are some things you can use:

- **A copy of the postmarked envelope the check arrived in will help.** If the envelope was postmarked on December 31, no matter where you are, you didn't get it until the following year. If it was postmarked earlier, maybe the 28th or 29th, it will depend on how far you are from the sender. So be prepared to describe the normal travel time for letters between your locations. If the envelope has stamps or notations about being misdelivered, that will also help demonstrate you got it later.
- **A copy of the check and the deposit slip can also prove your case.** In Chapter 4 you were advised to make copies of all deposits, with the deposit slips. Here's a perfect example of an instance when you'll need it.
- **A signed statement from your bookkeeper or accountant that states you didn't receive the check until the following year can help.** If they don't really have firsthand knowledge, don't put them on the spot. Be kind to your staff.
- **When all else fails, you can use your bank statement.** Circle or highlight the deposit in the following year. I don't like providing bank statements if I don't have to. It gives the IRS too much information about your bank account. And there might be some innocent deposit of a loan or something that the IRS will jump on as unreported income. So use this as a last resort.

There's one timing issue that may be a gray area with respect to constructive receipt. Suppose the check was sent so that it arrived at your business before December 31, but you were out of town or the office was closed. There was no one to receive or deposit the check until January. When do you report it?

Use your best judgment. The answer to this question will depend on how well you can support your position that you didn't have constructive receipt.

When the Issue Is Not a Timing Difference

Suppose you flat out disagree with the amount on the 1099. You know you keep good records, and you know you never got that money. What do you do?

First, let's examine why the 1099 is wrong. Did the company you worked with report that they paid your whole invoice, but didn't really pay you? Check with the company's accounting department. They may have a check that never cleared, got lost in the mail, or is sitting in someone's drawer, forgotten. All of these scenarios are common. Who knows, perhaps you just found some money. Collect the money—and include the adjustment to your tax return. Regardless, ask them to give you a printout of checks they paid to you. Sometimes, you'll catch a posting error. Perhaps they posted someone else's payment to your name.

If the company you are working with refuses to cooperate and the difference is substantial, you may want to pursue the issue. After all, they might owe you money. Most likely, you're no longer working with them.

At the very least, you should look into why they are so insistent on reporting a larger amount. Who else have they done this to? What other fraud is going on? Send a letter via certified mail, return receipt requested, asking for the detail on all their payments to you. Give them ten business days to respond. If they don't, be prepared to go to small claims court, or superior court depending on the amount, to collect the difference. Clearly, if they say they paid you that much money, but you didn't get it—they owe it to you. You'd be surprised how quickly a company will cooperate with you once they've been served with a lawsuit. You'll either get your information—or your money.

If it's not a lost check and not unpaid bills but simply a completely wrong number, it will be up to you to convince the IRS you're telling the truth. In this case, be very sure all your bookkeeping is up to date and that you've identified all your mystery deposits. (Yes, even I have those—when my filing hasn't been done for a while and I can't find my copies of the deposits where they should be.) Attach a statement to your tax return, containing a listing of the checks you did receive from that company, with the dates and check numbers. Include some words about the steps you took to straighten it out and the company's lack of cooperation.

To What Do You Attach All These Statements?

The tax return you use will depend on the business format you've chosen. Chapter 3 will give you the details and the forms. For our purpose, you need to know where on those forms to put your adjustments.

- **Sole proprietorships.** Look at page 2 of your Schedule C, as shown in Figure 5.1. There are empty lines in "Part V Other Expenses." On one of those lines, enter "1099 income in error. See Statement XXX attached." Replace the XXX with the heading you put on the statement. Incidentally, if you run out of lines on Part V, you're welcome to attach a list of expenses. Simply save one line for this purpose and on it write "See additional expenses on Schedule XXX attached." After you've listed the overflow of expenses, put the total on the line you saved for this schedule.
- **Partnerships or LLCs filing as partnerships.** Line 20 on Form 1065 (see Figure 5.2) is for "Other deductions (attach schedule)." Most business expenses end up on that attached schedule. On one line of that listing of other deductions, simply enter "1099 income in error. See Statement XXX attached."

You can add the statements even when you file electronically. Simply be sure to check the box on your software that says the note or statement is to be printed or included with the tax return. All the major software providers give you this option.

If you're worried about this getting you audited, don't be. I'm going to give you some really great news. The IRS hardly ever reads these statements—especially not when you file electronically. Your electronically filed return is rarely touched by human hands.

What about that difference you just adjusted? The IRS's computers only match up to the income reported on line 1 of your Schedule C and line 1a of your Form 1065. So be sure to include the full amount of the 1099 on those lines. The computers doing the matching have no way of cross-referencing your miscellaneous expenses.

What Should You Do if the 1099 Never Showed Up?

The purpose of the 1099 system is for the IRS to catch cheaters. It's not designed for you to have someone else do your bookkeeping, though many small business owners rely on 1099s for just that purpose. If you're already doing everything right by keeping proper books, the way you were taught in Chapter 4, you already know your income. Don't wait for the 1099s to come in. If you haven't received one by March 15, use your own records.

Generally, when companies send out 1099s, they tend to be correct. If you get one later and it's wrong, be prepared to amend your tax return solely to report the additional income and deduct it back out at the bottom. Usually, that's not a

FIGURE 5.1 Schedule C, Form 1040, Profit or Loss From Business

SCHEDULE C **(Form 1040)** Department of the Treasury Internal Revenue Service (99)	**Profit or Loss From Business** (Sole Proprietorship) ▶ **Partnerships, joint ventures, etc., must file Form 1065 or 1065-B.** ▶ **Attach to Form 1040 or 1041.** ▶ **See Instructions for Schedule C (Form 1040).**

OMB No. 1545-0074

20**03**

Attachment Sequence No. **09**

Name of proprietor

Social security number (SSN)

A Principal business or profession, including product or service (see page C-2 of the instructions)

B Enter code from pages C-7, 8, & 9 ▶

C Business name. If no separate business name, leave blank.

D Employer ID number (EIN), if any

E Business address (including suite or room no.) ▶ ....
City, town or post office, state, and ZIP code

F Accounting method: **(1)** ☐ Cash **(2)** ☐ Accrual **(3)** ☐ Other (specify) ▶ ....

G Did you "materially participate" in the operation of this business during 2003? If "No," see page C-3 for limit on losses . ☐ Yes ☐ No

H If you started or acquired this business during 2003, check here . . . . ▶ ☐

Part I Income

1	Gross receipts or sales. **Caution.** If this income was reported to you on Form W-2 and the "Statutory employee" box on that form was checked, see page C-3 and check here . . . . . . ▶ ☐	**1**	
2	Returns and allowances	**2**	
3	Subtract line 2 from line 1	**3**	
4	Cost of goods sold (from line 42 on page 2)	**4**	
5	**Gross profit.** Subtract line 4 from line 3	**5**	
6	Other income, including Federal and state gasoline or fuel tax credit or refund (see page C-3) . . .	**6**	
7	**Gross income.** Add lines 5 and 6 . . . . ▶	**7**	

Part II **Expenses.** Enter expenses for business use of your home **only** on line 30.

8	Advertising	**8**		**19**	Pension and profit-sharing plans	**19**	
9	Car and truck expenses (see page C-3)	**9**		**20**	Rent or lease (see page C-5):		
					a Vehicles, machinery, and equipment .	**20a**	
10	Commissions and fees . .	**10**			**b** Other business property . .	**20b**	
11	Contract labor (see page C-4)	**11**		**21**	Repairs and maintenance . .	**21**	
12	Depletion	**12**		**22**	Supplies (not included in Part III) .	**22**	
13	Depreciation and section 179 expense deduction (not included in Part III) (see page C-4) . .	**13**		**23**	Taxes and licenses	**23**	
				24	Travel, meals, and entertainment:		
14	Employee benefit programs (other than on line 19) . . .	**14**			**a** Travel	**24a**	
15	Insurance (other than health) .	**15**			**b** Meals and entertainment		
16	Interest:				**c** Enter nondeductible amount included on line 24b (see page C-5) .		
	a Mortgage (paid to banks, etc.) .	**16a**					
	b Other	**16b**			**d** Subtract line 24c from line 24b .	**24d**	
17	Legal and professional services	**17**		**25**	Utilities	**25**	
				26	Wages (less employment credits) .	**26**	
18	Office expense	**18**		**27**	Other expenses (from line 48 on page 2)	**27**	
28	**Total expenses** before expenses for business use of home. Add lines 8 through 27 in columns . . ▶					**28**	

29	Tentative profit (loss). Subtract line 28 from line 7	**29**	
30	Expenses for business use of your home. Attach **Form 8829**	**30**	
31	Net profit or (loss). Subtract line 30 from line 29.		
	• If a profit, enter on **Form 1040, line 12**, and also on **Schedule SE, line 2** (statutory employees, see page C-6). Estates and trusts, enter on Form 1041, line 3.	**31**	
	• If a loss, you **must** go to line 32.		
32	If you have a loss, check the box that describes your investment in this activity (see page C-6).		
	• If you checked 32a, enter the loss on **Form 1040, line 12**, and also on **Schedule SE, line 2** (statutory employees, see page C-6). Estates and trusts, enter on Form 1041, line 3.	**32a** ☐ All investment is at risk.	
	• If you checked 32b, you **must** attach **Form 6198.**	**32b** ☐ Some investment is not at risk.	

For Paperwork Reduction Act Notice, see Form 1040 instructions. Cat. No. 11334P Schedule C (Form 1040) 2003

continued

FIGURE 5.1 *continued*

Schedule C (Form 1040) 2003   Page **2**

Part III	**Cost of Goods Sold** (see page C-6)

33 Method(s) used to value closing inventory: **a** ☐ Cost   **b** ☐ Lower of cost or market   **c** ☐ Other (attach explanation)

34 Was there any change in determining quantities, costs, or valuations between opening and closing inventory? If "Yes," attach explanation . . . . ☐ **Yes**   ☐ **No**

35	Inventory at beginning of year. If different from last year's closing inventory, attach explanation . .	**35**
36	Purchases less cost of items withdrawn for personal use	**36**
37	Cost of labor. Do not include any amounts paid to yourself	**37**
38	Materials and supplies	**38**
39	Other costs	**39**
40	Add lines 35 through 39	**40**
41	Inventory at end of year	**41**
42	**Cost of goods sold.** Subtract line 41 from line 40. Enter the result here and on page 1, line 4 . .	**42**

Part IV	**Information on Your Vehicle.** Complete this part **only** if you are claiming car or truck expenses on line 9 and are not required to file Form 4562 for this business. See the instructions for line 13 on page C-4 to find out if you must file Form 4562.

43 When did you place your vehicle in service for business purposes? (month, day, year) ▶ ..../........../...... .

44 Of the total number of miles you drove your vehicle during 2003, enter the number of miles you used your vehicle for:

a Business .... **b** Commuting .... **c** Other ....

45 Do you (or your spouse) have another vehicle available for personal use? . . . . ☐ **Yes**   ☐ **No**

46 Was your vehicle available for personal use during off-duty hours? . . . . ☐ **Yes**   ☐ **No**

47a Do you have evidence to support your deduction? . . . . ☐ **Yes**   ☐ **No**

   b If "Yes," is the evidence written? . . . . ☐ **Yes**   ☐ **No**

Part V	**Other Expenses.** List below business expenses not included on lines 8–26 or line 30.

---	

48 Total other expenses. Enter here and on page 1, line 27	**48**

Schedule C (Form 1040) 2003

FIGURE 5.2 Form 1065, U.S. Return of Partnership Income

Form **1065**	**U.S. Return of Partnership Income**	OMB No. 1545-0099
Department of the Treasury Internal Revenue Service	For calendar year 2003, or tax year beginning .... , 2003, and ending .... , 20.... . ▶ **See separate instructions.**	**2003**

A Principal business activity	Use the IRS label. Other-wise, print or type.	Name of partnership	D Employer identification number
B Principal product or service		Number, street, and room or suite no. If a P.O. box, see page 14 of the instructions.	E Date business started
C Business code number		City or town, state, and ZIP code	F Total assets (see page 14 of the instructions) $

G Check applicable boxes: **(1)** ☐ Initial return **(2)** ☐ Final return **(3)** ☐ Name change **(4)** ☐ Address change **(5)** ☐ Amended return
H Check accounting method: **(1)** ☐ Cash   **(2)** ☐ Accrual   **(3)** ☐ Other (specify) ▶ ....
I Number of Schedules K-1. Attach one for each person who was a partner at any time during the tax year ▶ ....

Caution: *Include only trade or business income and expenses on lines 1a through 22 below. See the instructions for more information.*

Income	**1a** Gross receipts or sales	**1a**	
	b Less returns and allowances	**1b**	**1c**
	2 Cost of goods sold (Schedule A, line 8)		**2**
	3 Gross profit. Subtract line 2 from line 1c		**3**
	4 Ordinary income (loss) from other partnerships, estates, and trusts *(attach schedule)* . . .		**4**
	5 Net farm profit (loss) *(attach Schedule F (Form 1040))*		**5**
	6 Net gain (loss) from Form 4797, Part II, line 18		**6**
	7 Other income (loss) *(attach schedule)*		**7**
	8 **Total income (loss).** Combine lines 3 through 7		**8**
Deductions (see page 15 of the instructions for limitations)	**9** Salaries and wages (other than to partners) (less employment credits)		**9**
	10 Guaranteed payments to partners		**10**
	11 Repairs and maintenance		**11**
	12 Bad debts		**12**
	13 Rent		**13**
	14 Taxes and licenses		**14**
	15 Interest		**15**
	16a Depreciation (if required, attach Form 4562)	**16a**	
	b Less depreciation reported on Schedule A and elsewhere on return	**16b**	**16c**
	17 Depletion **(Do not deduct oil and gas depletion.)**		**17**
	18 Retirement plans, etc.		**18**
	19 Employee benefit programs		**19**
	20 Other deductions *(attach schedule)*		**20**
	21 **Total deductions.** Add the amounts shown in the far right column for lines 9 through 20 .		**21**
	22 **Ordinary income (loss)** from trade or business activities. Subtract line 21 from line 8 . .		**22**

Sign Here	Under penalties of perjury, I declare that I have examined this return, including accompanying schedules and statements, and to the best of my knowledge and belief, it is true, correct, and complete. Declaration of preparer (other than general partner or limited liability company member) is based on all information of which preparer has any knowledge.		May the IRS discuss this return with the preparer shown below (see instructions)? ☐ Yes ☐ No
	▶ _____ Signature of general partner or limited liability company member	▶ _____ Date	

Paid Preparer's Use Only	Preparer's signature		Date		Check if self-employed ▶ ☐	Preparer's SSN or PTIN
	Firm's name (or yours if self-employed), address, and ZIP code	▶			EIN ▶	
					Phone no.	( )

For Paperwork Reduction Act Notice, see separate instructions.   Cat. No. 11390Z   Form **1065** (2003) problem. Then again, if you're working with a spouse, partner, or boss who doesn't remember to tell you everything, here's what might happen to you.

One of my clients, the Big Macher, is the embodiment of the entrepreneurial spirit. He's the golden boy that everyone trusts and loves. You probably know someone like him—or are like him. Family and friends gave him lots of money to invest in real estate. In the 1980s, Mr. Macher was the limited partnership king. He was the general partner in dozens of partnerships, owning millions of dollars of property across the U.S.A. His management company wasn't incorporated—he filed on a Schedule C. He operated his business on a handshake. While emotionally satisfying for him, it was a nightmare to his accountant. Trying to get the details of agreements and contracts was harder than holding on to a snowflake. Not surprisingly, Macher received an audit notice. The IRS was concerned about him because he never reported $33,000 of interest income from a company in Long Beach, California. That made no sense. I logged in each 1099 meticulously. If it wasn't reported, we never received it. Besides, if we'd received $33,000, I'd know about it. It never happened.

The auditor faxed me a copy of the incriminating document. I asked Macher if he knew anything about this. He just shrugged it off, saying, "I don't think so." Furious, I called the company who issued it. Bob explained what it was. Macher was a partner in one of Bob's partnerships. The venture came up short and they had to borrow money. Macher was responsible for his share of the interest payments. However, Bob happened to owe Macher a chunk of money. So, Bob wrote a check to Macher for the $33,000 interest. Macher endorsed the check back to Bob to pay his own obligation. That's why I had never seen the income. Bob sent me a copy of the front and back of the check Macher had received and endorsed. He also sent me paperwork on the interest Macher was paying. (He never explained why he didn't send us a copy of the 1099 in the first place.)

Net tax effect? $33,000 interest income was received. $33,000 interest expense was paid. Taxable total = 0.

Cost to Macher? Plenty! Lots of fees. Despite the fact that there was clearly no taxable error, the auditor insisted on auditing three years' worth of tax returns. He felt this was a big enough omission that he wanted to see what else was missing. After months of work, he found—ta daaaa! A couple of thousand dollars of expenses he disallowed. There was no tax due—just a minor reduction of the net operating loss carryforward.

The key points of this story are:

1. No matter how careful you are, there's always something outside your control.
2. For heaven's sake, if you're the Big Macher, have pity on your support staff and debrief them at the end of each day. If you're not a report and staff meet-

ings kind of person, set up a voice mailbox you can call, using your voice-activated, hands-free cell phone (no accidents or distractions, please). You can tell the story of your last meeting. Be sure to brag and include all the details and nuances you're so proud of. Your assistant will be able to check the messages throughout the day. One of those offhand remarks will alert your assistant to ask you about a contract, order, or whatever.

So, What the Heck *Is* Income?

And you thought this was easy. Income is more complex than you think it is. Some funds you intuitively consider income aren't. Other things you'd never dream are income really are. If you're not sure, call your tax advisor.

The best thing to do, to keep yourself on track, is to have your accountant or tax professional review your books each quarter. Errors will be caught before they cost you money.

Income Resources

- **IRS Publication 334, Tax Guide for Small Business.** www.irs.gov /publications/p334, (800) 829-3676: Order this book; it is a must-have reference source, covering all the tax-related aspects of your business.
- **IRS on Barter.** www.irs.gov/taxtopics/tc420.html
- **IRS on Barter Clubs and Exchanges.** www.irs.gov/businesses/small /article/0,,id=113437,00.html
- **TaxMama on Barter.** www.taxmama.com/Articles-cur/Barter.htm: Shows a real case.

COMMON DEDUCTIONS

*I only speak one language really, mathematics, but I dabble in
others like English just enough to answer questions and buy
groceries.*

—RENE DESCARTES

The best part about being in business for yourself is all those luscious deductions.
You can't go to a cocktail party, networking meeting, or any place people gather
without hearing how someone deducted a cruise, a party, their luxurious car—
frankly most of their living expenses. Owning your own business is great, they say,
because most of your living expenses are deductible.

So if you listen to what other people say, you might as well get the best of
everything—the most expensive briefcase, watch, PDA, computer, and cell phones
for everyone! After all, it's practically free. It's all tax deductible.

Could you please curb your euphoria for just a moment? Even if all of those
things are acceptable as deductible business expenses in your particular business,
your tax savings is only a percentage of the amount you spend. It's not more than
50 percent of the price. So you're still spending $100 for every $50 you save. And
no, you can't make it up in volume.

So how do you know what you can deduct and what you can't? This chapter
explains it all for you.

Rule of Thumb

Actually, you're really rather right to rejoice in your expenses. Let's face it, if you
must spend the money, you might as well enjoy what you've bought. In most cases,

the IRS doesn't really have the right to dictate how much you spend on any given item. So, if you'd like to have your business carry you around first class—go for it.

In looking at the cost of something I want to use for business, this is my rule of thumb: How many hours will it take me to pay for this thing or this experience? Do I want to devote that many hours, after I've consumed this trip or bought this device?

Think about it. Money, once you develop a business, will come. But time, on the other hand, is not a renewable resource. Think about that when you pull out that credit card.

Universally Deductible

As long as we're in a spending frame of mind, what shall we spend money on that we know the IRS is used to seeing on business tax returns? The following are some of the items you can deduct.

Mixed-Use Assets

Car, computers, cameras, cell phones, and even other things that don't start with a *c* are mixed-use assets—things you need both personally and for business. We'll talk more about them later in this chapter.

Office Expenses

Especially when working at home—out of your back pocket, so to speak—you overlook a substantial part of your office costs. You may pick up supplies while you're out running around, shopping for the family, but you often forget to split the receipts you've collected. Some of those family supplies were used in the business office. This category is often used as a catchall for all general business expenses. Don't dump everything in here—or in office supplies. Look at each purchase and put it in the category where it belongs. Stamps and postal supplies belong in postage, or postage and shipping. Software, if it's renewed annually, should be considered computer supplies. Software that has a long-term life is capitalized. It's an asset that gets depreciated. Auto expenses, including gasoline and parking, don't belong in office expenses. They belong in auto expenses and parking, respectively. The $1,000 down payment on the copy machine doesn't belong here either. That's an asset. Here's how you enter the copier purchase on your books.

When you take out a loan to buy an asset, such as a copier, you must put the full cost of the copier on the books, as well as the loan. Here are the entries you'll be making when you purchase the copier (1), and when you make payments (2):

Account Name (Description)	Debit	Credit
Copy Machine (cost of asset)	$5,000	
Bank Account (wrote check)		$1,000
Loan Payable (borrowed money)		$4,000
(1) Record the purchase of the copier		
Interest Expense (make loan payment)	$25	
Loan Payable (principal part of payment)	$75	
Bank Account (wrote check for payment)		$100
(2) Record monthly loan payment		

Cost of Goods Sold

This deduction is generally for merchandise or inventory. When you're selling a product, wholesale or retail, your merchandise is considered your cost of goods sold.[1] That cost gets reported on the second page of the Schedule C, for proprietorships, and on the second page of the 1065 or 1120 for other entities. Other costs of goods sold include the labor to make it, to get it ready for sale, or to install it. Freight to ship it to your facility is also a cost of goods sold. The freight to ship it to customers, however, is part of the sales costs.

For attorneys, your cost of goods sold would be the clients' costs on a specific case, e.g., the filing fees for the case, the doctor's bills, investigators' costs, and things like that. For someone putting on seminars, the cost of goods sold would include the fees to instructors or speakers, the cost of the facility and the refreshments you provide, and the costs of the handouts or books. When you're involved in manufacturing, there is a raft of direct and indirect costs that may end up in this part of the tax return. Be sure to have your tax professional set up your accounting system, so you get it right.

---

1. Cost of goods sold is the hard costs involved with producing your product or delivering your service.

Advertising, Marketing, and Publicity

The IRS clearly has no trouble with these obvious expenses. For some reason, though, people don't deduct these correctly. When I see a business growing that doesn't show anything on the advertising line, I wonder where they mis-posted those costs. You may include trade shows where you exhibit your company; print, radio, television, or Internet advertisements; open houses, if you're a realtor; and mailers, brochures, and flyers.

Commissions and Fees

Be sure to issue 1099s to anyone you pay $600 or more to in a year. Chapter 9 tells you how to make the experience painless. Be careful in this category. If your professional code of ethics doesn't permit commissions to be paid to anyone who isn't licensed in your field, you may not want to report illegal commissions. (Those are also known as bribes.) On the other hand, even during an audit, I haven't seen examiners question the legality of commission paid by realtors to unlicensed individuals.

Interest Expense

Most businesses borrow money. In fact, it's a good idea to establish a business line of credit now, when you don't need it. Your bank will give you a better rate of interest now—when you're flush with cash—than when you're broke and begging.

Do you understand how lines of credit work? The money is available for your use whenever you need it. You pay no interest unless you use the money. And if you're really sweet, your banker will waive the annual fees. So, what interest expenses are deductible?

- If it's a business loan, deduct the interest.
- If it's a personal loan, the interest deduction does not belong on your business books.
- If it was a personal loan and you used all the money for the business, put the proof into a file with each year's tax return. You may deduct the interest.
- Credit card interest is easy to deduct if you use a separate card for all your business purchases. Personal interest expenses are not deductible. So, if your funds are limited and you have to choose between paying off the balance on a personal credit card or the business one—pay off the personal card first. Let the business card earn the interest fees. Those are deductible. When using

the same card for both personal and business use, you'll have to do some computations to see what percentage of the interest on that card can be treated as a business deduction. For the future, set aside one card just for business use. It will make your life much easier, and your record keeping, too.

- For vehicle loans, if you use the car for personal purposes, be sure to deduct only the business percentage of the auto interest. For example, if you use the car personally 15 percent of the time, deduct only 85 percent of the vehicle loan interest.
- Be careful with loans from owners. Write up a loan contract for each loan, with an interest rate. Even if you don't pay the interest, compute it for the year and accrue it. (Journal entry: debit to interest expense. Credit to interest payable [or to loan from officer])

Rent and Utilities

The IRS expects going concerns to rent office or manufacturing or storage space. That won't attract any attention. But if you're trying to deduct your home office expenses, please read Chapter 7 for instructions.

Insurance

Business insurance premiums, including workers' compensation, business liability, malpractice, and facility and equipment coverage, are all deductible. When it comes to health insurance or life insurance, Chapters 9 and 10 explain what you may and may not deduct.

Taxes and Licenses

One of the things I always find in this account is estimated payments on the owner's personal income tax. Sorry, my friend, those are not an expense of your business.

Education

It doesn't matter what industry you're in, whether you're a professional or a tradesperson, you must keep up with the latest news, information, and technology relating to your business. Classes, seminars, workshops, books, and magazines—all of these are acceptable—and expected. You're entitled to deduct travel costs. So, why not look for courses in places you'd like to visit? Combine your personal and business interests. Who knows, if you're having fun, you may even attract other people who are apt to become future clients or customers.

You may not deduct courses taken toward your degree if having that degree is a minimum requirement of the job. Nor may you deduct the cost of education to learn a new career. These sound like foolish rules, but that's the law. You would think our legislators would do everything in their power to encourage Americans to have the best education and skills in the world. Besides, I have seen major shifts in the workforce several times over the years. You've seen times when entire professions or trades were put out of work. (Engineers in the 1970s, teachers in the 1980s, engineers in the 1990s, data entry folks in the 1990s . . . just to name a few.) It's important that people and businesses look toward the future and learn skills to fall back on if things go poorly in your present industry. That can cut social welfare costs way down.

Travel and Transportation

General business travel and travel to attend trade shows or courses is deductible. However, if your spouse or family members come along just for fun, you don't get to deduct their expenses. You may only deduct their travel expenses if they are an integral part of the business.

You have a choice of keeping careful receipts and deducting the actual cost of your lodging. However, if you're frugal, the IRS's standards, called per diem rates, may be higher. Look up current, or prior, per diem rates at the General Services Administration website, available at http://policyworks.gov/org/main/mt/homepage/mtt/perdiem/travel.htm.

Meals and Entertainment

Except for places in the business of serving food (like restaurants and day-care centers), you only get to deduct 50 percent of this expense. That's why it's so important that you post your travel expenses properly. You don't want to find yourself in shock right before an audit, when you pull out those credit card receipts and see that a hefty part of your travel deduction was really meals.

Uniforms

Aside from the tax deduction, there are other advantages to having uniforms. You know exactly what you're going to wear each day, and your wardrobe costs drop. Uniforms create brand awareness, spreading your company name wherever you go. They also can give you and your staff a sense of pride. *And* they're deductible. You can turn anything into a uniform. Simply sew your logo onto your jackets, shirts, or other garments. Establish a particular look to enhance your image and to be remembered. (OK, don't look, there's a guy wearing a brown shirt and shorts, with heavy shoes. Who is he? We all know it's the UPS guy.) Create your own look so that people seeing you will instantly associate you with your business.

Now that you know different specific items you can deduct, let's look at expenses specific to some industries.

It's All About You

Each industry has certain characteristic deductions to consider. These deductions won't apply to all members of the industry, but they apply to enough to make them worth knowing. To find out the deductions unique to your industry, the best place to start is with your industry association. Often, national trade and professional associations hear from their members when they face audits relating to the industry. The better associations track the information about what was handled incorrectly by members. Either they will educate members to avoid that accounting practice or they will lobby to change the law, so it coincides with industry practices.

While there's no room to cover all industries, here are some tips on a few industries. Use a search engine on the Internet, such as www.google.com, and look for your own trade or profession to find tax issues relative to your business. That's how I find my best resources.

Beauty Salons and Barbershops

If you own a beauty salon or barbershop, your biggest issue is determining if the people working at your shop are employees or independent contractors. Chapter 9 describes the results of a barber's audit. To avoid paying employment taxes on your tenants (or people renting out chairs in your shop), get rental contracts signed with your operators, holding them responsible for rents, even on weeks they are not using their station. When renting out space in your salon, don't deduct the money from customers' payments. Have the operator write you a monthly or weekly check. If you are processing customers' credit card payments, the contract should include a provision allowing you to do that, spelling out the fees or percentage you will charge the operator for this service.

Remember to include laundry costs for the towels and robes you clean at home each day.

The following are some sites you will find useful:

- **The Salon Association.** www.salons.org: This national association of salon owners and beauticians provides information, resources, trade shows, and more. In fact, they get involved in lobbying.
- **The Tax Fairness and Compliance Act of 2001.** www.salons.org/news /tax_fairness.html: This is the salon industry's reply to provisions affecting them in the 2001 Tax Act.
- **IRS's Salon Industry Audit Procedures, Including Allowable Expenses.** www.irs.gov/pub/irs-mssp/beauty.pdf: This is the IRS's guide for their auditors to use when they audit salons and shops.

Child-Care Providers

If you run a child-care business from your home, IRS Form 8829 has a special computation for your office in home. Rather than basing your business use on square footage, yours is based on the percentage of hours your facility is in operation. It's very important that you keep daily logs. Often, you have parents coming very late to pick up their children—that's still business time. The IRS has new standard per diem/per student rates for the food you provide. The amounts appear to be low, to my eyes, so track your actual food costs. At the end of the year, see whether your actual costs or the IRS's rates are better. When buying groceries and class supplies, get separate receipts for your school purchases and household purchases.

For more information on how the IRS looks at child-care businesses, go to the IRS's Child-Care Providers Industry Audit Procedures and Allowable Expenses, available at www.irs.gov/pub/irs-mssp/childcar.pdf.

Construction Industry

Most states have rules requiring construction businesses to pay their workers as employees if they are not licensed contractors. While you may not have specific uniforms, for many trades, you can only wear your jeans or shirts once. After that, they are too caked with cement or other dirt to be washed. Since those items of clothing are disposable, pick up the costs. Keep receipts for all your tools, gloves, boots, safety equipment, and the tool box on the back of your truck. Your office in home (see Chapter 7) probably includes the whole garage and additional storage units you've built. Taking that into consideration, your ratios of business use may change. On some projects, using percentage of completion costing will let you delay paying taxes on some of the money you've received. Sometimes, the completed contract method will work better for you. Check with your tax professional for some tricks of the trade.

Some online resources for the construction industry are McGraw-Hill's Construction Industry Resources at www.construction.com and the IRS's Construction Industry Audit Procedures, Including Allowable Expenses, available at www.irs.gov/pub/irs-mssp/build.pdf.

Multi-Level Marketing Industry (MLM)

Surprisingly, the IRS does not list an audit guide for MLM companies, yet they have instituted an aggressive push to shut down abusive MLM schemes, such as the 2001 Tax People prosecution in Kansas.[2] Think carefully before treating this as a business. If you're only buying the products or services for personal use, then all your expenses are personal. If you get a 1099 for your sales, to yourself, report the income and on page 2 of the Schedule C, on the "Other Expenses" line, enter "Not income—personal use discount only" and deduct the same amount. If you're getting a discount on merchandise you purchase for use in your business, your commissions are income. Add the commissions to your business income. However, if you are actively and aggressively building your down lines,[3] selling products, and generating revenues, then you should take all the deductions you're entitled to. In case your income never builds up enough to show a profit, keep a log of all your marketing activities and marketing expenses. You'll need them to fight the IRS in the event of a hobby-loss or fraud audit.

Truckers

If you're a trucker, you're subject to a variety of gasoline, road, and vehicle taxes; tolls; and weight charges. Keep all the receipts for those fees in a safe place for each year. Even though you're probably an owner-operator, you've contracted with one or two companies that give you the majority of your runs. Have you ever

---

2. Analysis by attorney Jeffrey A. Babener of the 2001 prosecution of Kansas–based company Renaissance, The Tax People, available at www.mlmlegal.com/taxpeople.html.

3. In multi-level marketing terminology, "down lines" are the members that you have recruited to the company. These are the people whose sales earn you a commission.

looked at the pay stubs they give you? They have deducted for at least two kinds of insurance and several fees they share with you. Usually, the 1099 they issue to you is for the *gross* amount of your income, or the contracted fee. Yet the check you actually get might be at least 10 percent less. Ask the accounting department if this is the case. Or, hold on to every single check from that company and add them all up. Odds are, you haven't been taking a deduction for this 10 percent or so worth of fees. There's also an annual heavy vehicle use tax, $550, due every August (Form 2290).

The IRS's per diem rates allow truckers to get a standard daily meal allowance of $41 for every night they're on the road ($46 outside the continental United States). Please note, if you are subject to "hours of service limits" by the Department of Transportation, you may still use 70 percent of the per diem amount in 2004 (75 percent in 2005 and 80 percent in 2006).

Here are some resources to cut your time and costs of tax administration.

- **Flatbed Owner Operator Tutorial.** http://flatbedowneroperatorjobs.com /TruckTutorial6.html: A tutorial about the kinds of deductions you can expect your carrier to take from your check when you drive for a truck line.
- **Drivers' Daily Logs.** www.driversdailylog.com: A software tool to help you maintain daily logs and hours of service.
- **Trucking Success's Tax Organizer for the Road.** www.truckingsuccess .com/record_detail.php3?recordid=130: This tool will help make it easy for you to keep your tax data and records in one place.
- **IRS's Trucking Industry Audit Procedures, Including Allowable Expenses.** www.irs.gov/pub/irs-mssp/truck.pdf: It would be wise to get familiar with the IRS's perspective on what is and isn't deductible by truckers.
- **Form 2290, Heavy Highway Vehicle Use Tax Return.** www.irs.gov/pub /irs-pdf/f2290_03.pdf: You must file Form 2290 within the first month that you put any heavy highway vehicle, with a taxable gross weight of 55,000 pounds or more, into use.
- **Form 2290-EZ, Heavy Highway Vehicle Use Tax for Single Vehicle Owners.** www.irs.gov/pub/irs-pdf/f2290e03.pdf: If you only have one truck, you're entitled to use Form 2290-EZ.

Mixed-Use Assets

Mixed-use assets were introduced earlier. Now is the time to look at them in depth. Cars, computers, cell phones, cameras, and other property used for entertainment, recreation, or amusement are called "Listed Property"[4] and have the honor of occupying their own special place, taking up most of the second page of Form 4562. (See Figure 6.1.)

Computers, video equipment, cameras, monitors, and beepers—you can't run a business today without them. They're no longer a luxury. In fact, they're so reasonably priced that many children have their own electronics. Parents and their businesses no longer share the home computer. Since the initial public offerings (IPOs) of the 1990s, everyone is trying so hard to re-create the phenomenon, who has time for a personal life anymore? Besides, with digital cameras and reality television, everyone's family and home is going online.

Let's talk about how you can make the most of your deductions with each of these mixed-use assets.

Cars, aside from real estate or a complete manufacturing plant, are likely to be the biggest one-shot expense to a small business. In the American economy, your car is the key to your image. Chapter 8 tells you all of the most effective ways to squeeze deductions out of it—whether you lease or buy.

Would you like to get even more money out of your car dollars and be able to get something better than you thought you could afford? Go to the dealer selling the model of your dreams—and buy a used model. New luxury cars lose value instantly when taken off the lot. That's not just an old wives' tale. So, let someone else pay for that quick devaluation. You buy the completely refurbished one- or two-year-old dream machine with most of the warranty left, and have the dealer detail it for you before you pick it up. If you don't squeal, people will think you bought the car new.

The listed property rules with respect to just about everything except cars, televisions, and stereos are obsolete. They should be removed from the tax code. Even the IRS isn't paying attention. The IRS used to target the split usages of listed property. Aside from personal use of cars, I haven't seen an auditor ask about personal use of property (except for television or cable) since the early 1990s.

What Do the Listed Property Rules Mean to You?

For all listed property you want to deduct, you must track the business and personal usage so you know what percentage of that usage is for business. If you want to treat your camera, stereo, DVD player, and television as business property, you have to keep logs of all the usage with a separate column for business. That's right.

---

4. Internal Revenue Code §280F(b) applies to less than 50 percent business use of listed assets.

FIGURE 6.1 Form 4562, Depreciation and Amortization

Form 4562 (2003)   Page **2**

Part V   **Listed Property** (Include automobiles, certain other vehicles, cellular telephones, certain computers, and property used for entertainment, recreation, or amusement.)

Note: *For any vehicle for which you are using the standard mileage rate or deducting lease expense, complete **only** 24a, 24b, columns (a) through (c) of Section A, all of Section B, and Section C if applicable.*

Section A—Depreciation and Other Information (Caution: *See page 7 of the instructions for limits for passenger automobiles.***)**

24a   Do you have evidence to support the business/investment use claimed? ☐ **Yes** ☐ **No**   24b If "Yes," is the evidence written? ☐ **Yes** ☐ **No**

(a) Type of property (list vehicles first)	(b) Date placed in service	(c) Business/investment use percentage	(d) Cost or other basis	(e) Basis for depreciation (business/investment use only)	(f) Recovery period	(g) Method/ Convention	(h) Depreciation deduction	(i) Elected section 179 cost
25 Special depreciation allowance for qualified listed property placed in service during the tax year and used more than 50% in a qualified business use (see page 6 of the instructions) **25**								
26 Property used more than 50% in a qualified business use (see page 6 of the instructions):								
		%						
		%						
		%						
27 Property used 50% or less in a qualified business use (see page 6 of the instructions):								
		%				S/L –		
		%				S/L –		
		%				S/L –		

28   Add amounts in column (h), lines 25 through 27. Enter here and on line 21, page 1 . .   **28**

29   Add amounts in column (i), line 26. Enter here and on line 7, page 1 . . . .   **29**

Section B—Information on Use of Vehicles

Complete this section for vehicles used by a sole proprietor, partner, or other "more than 5% owner," or related person.

If you provided vehicles to your employees, first answer the questions in Section C to see if you meet an exception to completing this section for those vehicles.

	(a) Vehicle 1		(b) Vehicle 2		(c) Vehicle 3		(d) Vehicle 4		(e) Vehicle 5		(f) Vehicle 6	
30 Total business/investment miles driven during the year (**do not** include commuting miles—see page 2 of the instructions)												
31 Total commuting miles driven during the year												
32 Total other personal (noncommuting) miles driven												
33 Total miles driven during the year. Add lines 30 through 32.												
34 Was the vehicle available for personal use during off-duty hours?	Yes	No	Yes	No	Yes	No	Yes	No	Yes	No	Yes	No
35 Was the vehicle used primarily by a more than 5% owner or related person?												
36 Is another vehicle available for personal use?												

Section C—Questions for Employers Who Provide Vehicles for Use by Their Employees

Answer these questions to determine if you meet an exception to completing Section B for vehicles used by employees who **are not** more than 5% owners or related persons (see page 8 of the instructions).

	Yes	No
37 Do you maintain a written policy statement that prohibits all personal use of vehicles, including commuting, by your employees?		
38 Do you maintain a written policy statement that prohibits personal use of vehicles, except commuting, by your employees? See page 8 of the instructions for vehicles used by corporate officers, directors, or 1% or more owners		
39 Do you treat all use of vehicles by employees as personal use?		
40 Do you provide more than five vehicles to your employees, obtain information from your employees about the use of the vehicles, and retain the information received?		
41 Do you meet the requirements concerning qualified automobile demonstration use? (See page 9 of the instructions.) . .		

Note: *If your answer to 37, 38, 39, 40, or 41 is "Yes," do not complete Section B for the covered vehicles.*

Part VI   **Amortization**

(a) Description of costs	(b) Date amortization begins	(c) Amortizable amount	(d) Code section	(e) Amortization period or percentage	(f) Amortization for this year
42 Amortization of costs that begins during your 2003 tax year (see page 9 of the instructions):					
43 Amortization of costs that began before your 2003 tax year **43**					
44 **Total.** Add amounts in column (f). See page 9 of the instructions for where to report . . . **44**					

⊕   Form **4562** (2003)

Can you just see yourself sitting down to watch television and making a notation in your log with the date, starting time, and listing of the programs you're watching? Be sure to include a few lines about how you're using the time or the programming for business purposes. If other family members use the TV, they have to make log entries, too. After all, your family's time counts toward total use of the asset. At the end of the year, you'll be able to deduct about 20 percent of the expenses, based on the few business hours you actually logged. Yes, it's a pain. That's the point. Congress wants to discourage you from deducting personal assets.

Many entertainment industry folks set up their equipment in a separate screening room, even if it's just a separate bedroom, to use for business viewing.

The main thing you need to know is when business use of the asset falls to less than 50 percent, you can't take a depreciation deduction for the asset. If you've been depreciating over several years and business use falls below 50 percent, you may have to recapture, or pay back, some of the depreciation. This is what you have a tax professional for—to help you in times like that.

As to the special rules for cars—and there are many—we've devoted Chapter 8 to this subject. But we didn't explain what depreciation is all about—that comes next.

Depreciation

Back in the good old days, a depreciation deduction was provided so companies could write off a portion of the cost of their large capital expenses (buildings, equipment, fixtures, and so on) over the item's useful life. This was to provide them with the incentive to put that money aside so they could replace items as they wore out. Back then, depreciation life was related to how long a piece of equipment or building would last without substantial repairs or improvements.

Depreciation was also easy to figure out back then. Using a simple mathematical formula or two, you could determine depreciation without a scientific calculator or slide rule—just a pencil and paper . . . and perhaps an extra finger or toe. Really, depreciation was logical—you could use straight line, declining balance (DB), or sum-of-the-years digits.

Straight line was the easiest type of depreciation. For this, you just had to divide the cost of the asset by the number of months in its useful life. Then multiply that result by the number of months the asset is in use this year:

cost ÷ useful life months × months used this year

Straight Line

Trixie bought a computer for $1,200 on September 5. It had a five-year useful life. 5 years = 60 months. Dividing $1,200 by 60 = $20 per month. She used the computer for four months this year. The deduction is 4 × $20 = $80.

Next year, Trixie will depreciate it for a whole year: $20 × 12 = $240, or 20 percent per year.

In double-declining balance (DDB) or a 1.5 declining balance (1.5DB), you simply took the first formula and multiplied it by 2 or 1.5:

$$(\text{cost} \div \text{useful life} \times \text{months used this year}) \times 2$$

or

$$(\text{cost} \div \text{useful life} \times \text{months used this year}) \times 1.5$$

The only difference in the declining balance method is that you multiply your resulting percentage against the undepreciated balance of the asset. Let's go back to Trixie, shall we?

Double-Declining Balance (DDB)

Divide the number of months the asset was in business use this year by the total life. Trixie had four months of use, divided by sixty months' life. Her straight line depreciation rate would be 6.67 percent. Using DDB, she would multiply that rate by 2 = 13.33 percent. Trixie's first year depreciation would be $160 (13.33 percent × $1,200).

The following year, Trixie deducts the $160 already written off from the full purchase price of $1,200 to equal $1,040. She would multiply this reduced asset cost by the second year's depreciation. In Trixie's second year, she used it twelve months out of a total of sixty. That's 20 percent. Remember, we multiply by that number by two to equal 40 percent. So the second year, Trixie's depreciation is $416 ($1,040 × 40 percent). From then on, Trixie's rate would be 40 percent, but the balance will keep decreasing. In the third year, the asset cost is $624 ($1,040 − $416). Multiplying $624 by 40 percent gives Trixie a smaller deduction than last year, equal to $250. And so forth.

The formula is:

(cost ÷ useful life × months used this year) × 2 × (cost − previous depreciation)

or

(cost ÷ useful life × months used this year) × 1.5 × (cost − previous depreciation)

Halfway through the useful life, you'd switch back over to straight line.

Depreciation in Today's World

Aside from mere historical value, there's a reason for explaining the old way of determining depreciation to you. The present depreciation system still has a little resemblance to these two computation methods.

The IRS changed their depreciation rules in 1986. They introduced concepts such as Accelerated Cost Recovery System (ACRS) and Modified Accelerated Cost Recovery System (MACRS). For the present, you'll be using MACRS, which is based on the two systems described above.

Depreciable assets are categorized in groups called classes. You can look them up in IRS Publication 946—How to Depreciate (available at www.irs.gov/publica tions/p946/index.html) or read IRC §168. Most businesses only need to know about these four classes. The life is called a recovery period.

- **Three-year property.** This property includes manufacturing equipment, certain racehorses, tractor units, and rent-to-own property.
- **Five-year property.** This category includes autos, taxis, small aircraft, trailers, computers and peripherals, office equipment, apparel manufacturing equipment, certain construction equipment, and fixtures and appliances used in rental properties.
- **Seven-year property.** Office furniture, manufacturing equipment (not already included in the first two classes), oil, gas and mining equipment, agricultural buildings or structures, and anything that isn't classified anywhere else fits here.
- **Real estate (buildings only, not land).** Commercial real estate is depreciated over 39 years using a straight-line method. Residential real estate is depreciated over 27.5 years, straight line.

Don't worry, you won't have to do the calculations. You'll be able to look up depreciation in the tables. Table 6.1 gives you the most commonly used depreciation table for small businesses. Table 6.2 covers residential real estate (apartments and homes rented out) and commercial and business property. This also includes your home office. Although you're living in the house, the office part makes it subject to the 39-year rules.

TABLE 6.1 MACRS Depreciation: 3-, 5-, 7-, 10-, 15-, and 20-Year Property; Half-Year Convention

| | Depreciation Rate for Recovery Period | | | | | |
Year	3-Year	5-Year	7-Year	10-Year	15-Year	20-Year
1	33.33%	20.00%	14.29%	10.00%	5.00%	3.750%
2	44.45	32.00	24.49	18.00	9.50	7.219
3	14.81	19.20	17.49	14.40	8.55	6.677
4	7.41	11.52	12.49	11.52	7.70	6.177
5		11.52	8.93	9.22	6.93	5.713
6		5.76	8.92	7.37	6.23	5.285
7			8.93	6.55	5.90	4.888
8			4.46	6.55	5.90	4.522
9				6.56	5.91	4.462
10				6.55	5.90	4.461
11				3.28	5.91	4.462
12					5.90	4.461
13					5.91	4.462
14					5.90	4.461
15					5.91	4.462
16					2.95	4.461
17						4.462
18						4.461
19						4.462
20						4.461
21						2.231

TABLE 6.2 Residential Rental Property Mid-Month Convention Straight Line—27.5 Years

Year	Month property placed in service											
	1	2	3	4	5	6	7	8	9	10	11	12
1	3.485%	3.182%	2.879%	2.576%	2.273%	1.970%	1.667%	1.364%	1.061%	0.758%	0.455%	0.152%
2-9	3.636	3.636	3.636	3.636	3.636	3.636	3.636	3.636	3.636	3.636	3.636	3.636
10	3.637	3.637	3.637	3.637	3.637	3.637	3.636	3.636	3.636	3.636	3.636	3.636
11	3.636	3.636	3.636	3.636	3.636	3.636	3.637	3.637	3.637	3.637	3.637	3.637
12	3.637	3.637	3.637	3.637	3.637	3.637	3.636	3.636	3.636	3.636	3.636	3.636
13	3.636	3.636	3.636	3.636	3.636	3.636	3.637	3.637	3.637	3.637	3.637	3.637
14	3.637	3.637	3.637	3.637	3.637	3.637	3.636	3.636	3.636	3.636	3.636	3.636
15	3.636	3.636	3.636	3.636	3.636	3.636	3.637	3.637	3.637	3.637	3.637	3.637
16	3.637	3.637	3.637	3.637	3.637	3.637	3.636	3.636	3.636	3.636	3.636	3.636
17	3.636	3.636	3.636	3.636	3.636	3.636	3.637	3.637	3.637	3.637	3.637	3.637
18	3.637	3.637	3.637	3.637	3.637	3.637	3.636	3.636	3.636	3.636	3.636	3.636
19	3.636	3.636	3.636	3.636	3.636	3.636	3.637	3.637	3.637	3.637	3.637	3.637
20	3.637	3.637	3.637	3.637	3.637	3.637	3.636	3.636	3.636	3.636	3.636	3.636
21	3.636	3.636	3.636	3.636	3.636	3.636	3.637	3.637	3.637	3.637	3.637	3.637
22	3.637	3.637	3.637	3.637	3.637	3.637	3.636	3.636	3.636	3.636	3.636	3.636
23	3.636	3.636	3.636	3.636	3.636	3.636	3.637	3.637	3.637	3.637	3.637	3.637
24	3.637	3.637	3.637	3.637	3.637	3.637	3.636	3.636	3.636	3.636	3.636	3.636
25	3.636	3.636	3.636	3.636	3.636	3.636	3.637	3.637	3.637	3.637	3.637	3.637
26	3.637	3.637	3.637	3.637	3.637	3.637	3.636	3.636	3.636	3.636	3.636	3.636
27	3.636	3.636	3.636	3.636	3.636	3.636	3.637	3.637	3.637	3.637	3.637	3.637
28	1.97	2.273	2.576	2.879	3.182	3.485	3.636	3.636	3.636	3.636	3.636	3.636
29							0.152	0.455	0.758	1.061	1.364	1.667

Nonresidential Real Property Mid-Month Convention Straight Line—39 Years

Year	Month property placed in service											
	1	2	3	4	5	6	7	8	9	10	11	12
1	2.461%	2.247%	2.033%	1.819%	1.605%	1.391%	1.117%	0.963%	0.749%	0.535%	0.321%	0.107%
2-39	2.564	2.564	2.564	2.564	2.564	2.564	2.564	2.564	2.564	2.564	2.564	2.564
40	0.107	0.321	0.535	0.749	0.963	1.177	1.391	1.605	1.819	2.033	2.247	2.461

In addition to recovery periods, you have "conventions" that dictate adjustments in the MACRS tables. Did you notice that "half-year" designation in the title of Table 6.1? It refers to the date you bought your assets.

- The half-year convention treats all of your property as if you bought it in the middle of the year.
- The mid-month convention applies to real estate. It treats all buildings as if they had been bought in the middle of the month.
- The mid-quarter convention comes into play if more than 40 percent of your assets (based on cost) were bought in the last three months of your tax year.

I'm sorry, despite the title of this book, there is no way to make depreciation easy. All this and we haven't even talked about the part you're most excited about—bonus depreciation.

Bonus Depreciation

We have not one, but two bonuses, and a Section 179 deduction. What largesse! Let's go over your options.

Bonus Number One

To help the economy recover after September 11, the legislature provided for a special 30 percent bonus depreciation deduction, included in the Job Creation and Worker Assistance Act of 2002. It remains in effect for property bought through December 31, 2004 (extended from September 11, 2004). The bonus depreciation deduction can be used for qualified property[5] placed in service after September 10, 2001. You may use this additional first-year depreciation deduction for both regular tax and alternative minimum tax purposes. It may only be used on new property—not used. However, many states have not agreed to go along with the federal law on this deduction.[6] As a result, you may have to use a "state if different" computation on your state tax returns to make the required adjustment. If you don't need the higher deduction, you don't have to use it.

---

5. Qualified property is defined in IRC §168(k)(2) and Revenue Procedure 2002-33.

6. *Taxing Subjects* provides a list of states that have and have not conformed as of September 2002 at www.taxingsubjects.com/ARCHIVES/ISSUE9%20ARTICLES/artcl2.html.

Bonus Number Two

The Jobs & Growth Tax Relief Reconciliation Act of 2003 created an extra bonus depreciation of 50 percent for property if:

- You bought after May 5, 2003, and before January 1, 2005, and didn't have a written binding contract in effect before May 6, 2003.
- You bought new.
- You used it for business before January 1, 2005.
- You made an election to use this 50 percent instead of the 30 percent.

In other words, the 50 percent bonus doesn't apply to used property. You must attach a statement to your tax return stating that you choose to use this bonus depreciation—and you must buy the assets before the end of 2004 [except §168(k)(2)(B) property].

The 30 percent bonus depreciation still exists for those taxpayers that prefer to use it instead of the 50 percent. Or you may use no bonus amounts at all.

Section 179 Depreciation

The name 179 comes from the Internal Revenue Code section that covers this, the original bonus depreciation. Section 179 depreciation may be used for new or used property. This tax code provision lets you write off up to $100,000 of equipment or vehicles that are placed into business use from January 1, 2003. This is a deduction, not a credit.

There are strings attached to the Section 179 deduction.

- If more than $400,000 of property is placed in service during the year, the allowable Section 179 expense must be reduced by the amount in excess of $400,000.
- The Section 179 election can't cause income from all trades or businesses to be reduced below zero.
- Any amounts expensed under this provision reduce the depreciable basis of the assets placed in service during the year. In other words, you can't expense part or all of the cost of an asset and also depreciate the same costs.
- If the property is disposed of prior to the end of its useful life, you will be required to recapture some of the Section 179 deduction previously taken. *Recapture* means that a portion of your Section 179 deduction must be included as taxable income on your tax return.

Large corporations have entire departments devoted to tracking assets and recording their disposal. Take the cost of administration into account when you discuss the value of depreciation deductions.

If the Section 179 deduction will take your business income to zero, cut back on how much you use. A good tax professional will play with the numbers to give you the highest deduction you can get without throwing you into alternative minimum taxes, or having you waste the deduction. When the Section 179 depreciation you take is too high, the rest of it gets carried forward to next year.

Affecting Pass-Through Entities

When using bonus depreciation and Section 179 depreciation for partnerships, LLCs, S-corps, or other pass-through entities, talk to the partners, members, or shareholders first. If you take the deduction on the business return, but they can't use it, they'll be forced to carry it forward. It might be wasted.

Depreciation is one of the most complex tax computations. So many other forms, schedules, and limits are affected that it's like playing multidimensional chess. Even the best tax software doesn't always get this right. If you talk to your tax advisors, they'll admit they check their software's depreciation calculations to make sure all affected forms and limits are taken into account on your tax returns.

More Deductions Than You Can Imagine

We've just scratched the surface of how to use expenses, and we haven't delved deeply into the expenses you can't use. Some businesses are subject to passive loss limitations or alternative minimum taxes and the intricacies of net operating losses. These are things you'll need to have your tax professional explain, if they pertain to you. After all, you need to have something to call them about, now that you've learned all you need to know to run your business.

Incidentally, a word to the wise—don't spend *all* your time learning to run the business. At some point, you have to take action—and start working.

Deduction Resources

- **Form 4562, Depreciation.** www.irs.gov/pub/irs-pdf/f4562.pdf
- **IRS Publication 946, How to Depreciate.** www.irs.gov/publications/p 946/index.html

- **Per Diem Rates from the U.S. General Services Administration.** http://policyworks.gov/org/main/mt/homepage/mtt/perdiem/travel.htm
- **IRS Audit Guides for Specific Industries from the Market Segment Specialization Program (MSSP).** www.irs.gov/businesses/small/article /0,,id=108149,00.html
- **McGraw-Hill's Construction Industry Resources.** www.construction.com
- **Small Business Taxes and Management.** www.smbiz.com. Tax updates, summaries, and news for small businesses.
- **TaxMama.com's Resource Pages.** www.taxmama.com/resources
- **Open, by American Express.** http://open.americanexpress.com. For discounts on business supplies and services.

7

OFFICE IN HOME

No matter under what circumstances you leave it, home does not cease to be home. No matter how you lived there—well or poorly.

—Joseph Brodsky

Brodsky Is Right: Let's Stay Home

In 2001, the latest year for which IRS statistics are published,[1] more than 1,853,000 business returns were filed, reporting nearly $69 billion in sales. In total, those small businesses also reported a little more than $54 billion in expenses. Less than 1 percent of those deductions were for an in-home office. Does it appear that people are afraid to use the office-in-home deduction? Apparently.

For a new business, having your office at home is an excellent idea because it keeps your overhead low. You can get away with earning less, so you can concentrate on building the business instead of paying the bills. Not only do you save money on renting an office space, but you also save precious time by not having the distractions and office politics of a shared suite.

For me, moving out of the penthouse suite on Ventura Boulevard meant a savings in tangible dollars of more than $1,000 per month. I no longer paid rent, additional annual common area costs, parking for staff and myself, parking validations for clients, tips to the valets, or utilities. I saved at least another $1,000 per

---

1. IRS report on Non-Farm Sole Proprietorships of businesses with and without net income (2001) page 57, Table 2, available at www.irs.gov/pub/irs-soi/01solep.pdf.

month in my staff's increased productivity because they didn't have all the distractions that came with managing a suite with several tenants. Many tenants had too much free time and liked to hang around chatting with my charming staff.

Another advantage to working from home is that when your family needs you, you're there. Once all the interruptions end, or the family time is over, you can slip back into your office, perhaps late at night, without having to dress up and drive across town. You can step in for just a minute, even on days off, to take care of something quickly and conveniently.

Besides, you can take expenditures you're already making and have them help reduce your business profit and the related self-employment taxes. Which expenses do double duty like this? Your rent. Or if you own a home, your mortgage and property taxes. You're already paying those bills, right? With an office in the home, a percentage of those costs will move to your Schedule C.

It's a Red Flag; It's Just Asking for an Audit

Sure it's a red flag! So what? If you are operating a real business out of your house, shouldn't you be entitled to take legitimate deductions for it? True, having an office-in-home deduction and using Form 8829 (see Figure 7.1) will definitely increase your chances of an audit. But if you keep good records, you have nothing to worry about. You'll need to be able to prove exactly what part of your home you used for business. It's also important to define what the business use was for each area you're claiming as business space. But with the instructions that follow, you'll be able to prove to the IRS that you're entitled to the deduction. And, if you're ever audited again, you'll have proof that the IRS accepted your evidence in the past.

Why does having a home office seem risky to many small businesses? Here's the background on the issue. It relates to the Pomarantz case.[2]

---

2. The Ninth Circuit Court recently concluded that an *emergency* care physician's home office was not his "principal place of business" under §280A. See *Pomarantz v. Commissioner*, 867 F.2d 495 (9th Cir. 1988). The Ninth Circuit ruled that Pomarantz could not deduct home office expenses because he consistently spent more time on duty at the hospital than he did at home. The essence of his profession was the hands-on treatment of patients, which he did only at the hospital and never at home. Finally, he generated income only by seeing patients at the hospital, not by studying or writing at home.

FIGURE 7.1 Form 8829, Expenses for Business Use of Your Home

Form **8829**	**Expenses for Business Use of Your Home**	OMB No. 1545-1266
Department of the Treasury Internal Revenue Service (99)	▶ File only with Schedule C (Form 1040). Use a separate Form 8829 for each home you used for business during the year. ▶ See separate instructions.	**2003** Attachment Sequence No. **66**
Name(s) of proprietor(s)		Your social security number

Part I Part of Your Home Used for Business

1 Area used regularly and exclusively for business, regularly for day care, or for storage of inventory or product samples (see instructions) . . . . | **1** |
2 Total area of home . . . . | **2** |
3 Divide line 1 by line 2. Enter the result as a percentage . . . . | **3** | %

• For day-care facilities not used exclusively for business, also complete lines 4–6.
• All others, skip lines 4–6 and enter the amount from line 3 on line 7.

4 Multiply days used for day care during year by hours used per day . | **4** | hr.
5 Total hours available for use during the year (365 days × 24 hours) (see instructions) | **5** | 8,760 hr.
6 Divide line 4 by line 5. Enter the result as a decimal amount . . . | **6** | .
7 Business percentage. For day-care facilities not used exclusively for business, multiply line 6 by line 3 (enter the result as a percentage). All others, enter the amount from line 3 . . . . ▶ | **7** | %

Part II Figure Your Allowable Deduction

8 Enter the amount from Schedule C, line 29, **plus** any net gain or (loss) derived from the business use of your home and shown on Schedule D or Form 4797. If more than one place of business, see instructions | **8** |

See instructions for columns (a) and (b) before completing lines 9–20.

		(a) Direct expenses	(b) Indirect expenses	
9	Casualty losses (see instructions)	**9**		
10	Deductible mortgage interest (see instructions) .	**10**		
11	Real estate taxes (see instructions)	**11**		
12	Add lines 9, 10, and 11	**12**		
13	Multiply line 12, column (b) by line 7		**13**	
14	Add line 12, column (a) and line 13			**14**
15	Subtract line 14 from line 8. If zero or less, enter -0- .			**15**
16	Excess mortgage interest (see instructions) . .	**16**		
17	Insurance	**17**		
18	Repairs and maintenance	**18**		
19	Utilities	**19**		
20	Other expenses (see instructions)	**20**		
21	Add lines 16 through 20	**21**		
22	Multiply line 21, column (b) by line 7		**22**	
23	Carryover of operating expenses from 2002 Form 8829, line 41 . .		**23**	

24 Add line 21 in column (a), line 22, and line 23 . . . . | **24** |
25 Allowable operating expenses. Enter the **smaller** of line 15 or line 24 . . . . . . | **25** |
26 Limit on excess casualty losses and depreciation. Subtract line 25 from line 15 . . . . . | **26** |
27 Excess casualty losses (see instructions) . . . . | **27** |
28 Depreciation of your home from Part III below . . . . . . | **28** |
29 Carryover of excess casualty losses and depreciation from 2002 Form 8829, line 42 | **29** |
30 Add lines 27 through 29 . . . . | **30** |
31 Allowable excess casualty losses and depreciation. Enter the **smaller** of line 26 or line 30 . . | **31** |
32 Add lines 14, 25, and 31 . . . . | **32** |
33 Casualty loss portion, if any, from lines 14 and 31. Carry amount to **Form 4684**, Section B . . | **33** |
34 Allowable expenses for business use of your home. Subtract line 33 from line 32. Enter here and on Schedule C, line 30. If your home was used for more than one business, see instructions ▶ | **34** |

Part III Depreciation of Your Home

35 Enter the **smaller** of your home's adjusted basis or its fair market value (see instructions) . . | **35** |
36 Value of land included on line 35 . . . . | **36** |
37 Basis of building. Subtract line 36 from line 35 . . . . | **37** |
38 Business basis of building. Multiply line 37 by line 7 . . . . | **38** |
39 Depreciation percentage (see instructions) . . . . | **39** | %
40 Depreciation allowable (see instructions). Multiply line 38 by line 39. Enter here and on line 28 above | **40** |

Part IV Carryover of Unallowed Expenses to 2004

41 Operating expenses. Subtract line 25 from line 24. If less than zero, enter -0- . . . . . . | **41** |
42 Excess casualty losses and depreciation. Subtract line 31 from line 30. If less than zero, enter -0- . | **42** |

For Paperwork Reduction Act Notice, see page 4 of separate instructions. | Cat. No. 13232M | Form **8829** (2003)

Until 1998, the IRS knew an office-in-home audit was one easy way to generate money for Uncle Sam's coffers.

Why? Until the end of 1998, the rules for in-home offices were dictated by the results of a court ruling against Dr. Pomarantz. He was a physician whose work took place in a hospital. But he did have a legitimate office at home where he took care of all of his business transactions, planning, and calling and where he maintained his records. Since he didn't meet with patients at home, under a strict definition of the tax code, he was not permitted a deduction for an office at home.

Pathetic, isn't it?

The same treatment applied to such people as plumbers (they didn't fix their customers' pipes by bringing them to their own home and working on them there), laundromat owners, traveling salespeople (a whole other problem), actors, and . . . you're getting the idea.

Looking at these businesses' returns, odds were in the IRS's favor to score some good money by auditing office-in-home returns. But no more.

Under the rules that took effect as of January 1, 1999 (based on a law that passed two years earlier . . . why it took so long, I have no idea!), you no longer have to meet customers in your home to qualify for the office-in-home deduction.

IRS Publication 587 outlines the present requirements:

1. Your use of the business part of your home must be:

   a. Exclusive
   b. Regular
   c. For your trade or business

and

2. The business part of your home must be one of the following:

   a. Your principal place of business
   b. A place where you meet or deal with patients, clients, or customers in the normal course of your trade or business

or

   c. A separate structure (not attached to your home) you use in connection with your trade or business

That little item you see in 2a opened up the door to you if your office in home is only used for administrative purposes, even if you generally work at customers' locations. But this must be the *only* business office you have. The office in home doesn't have to be a whole room; it may be part of a room. It doesn't have to be just a room; it may also include closet space, garage space, carport, or parking pad for your primary business vehicle or tools (tractors, cement mixers, clown cars, drill presses, whatever you use or store).

Under the present rules, pretty much everyone who operates a business from home will have a legitimate claim to an office in the home. Since 1999, the odds of the IRS finding fault with the office-in-home deduction on a tax return have decreased dramatically.

Oh, there's no doubt that many people who are taking the deduction are not really entitled to it. But, it's no longer a sure thing that you'll get audited. These days, to get the IRS's attention, you need to have both an office in home and a loss on Schedule C. (See Chapters 5 and 6.)

Another Attractive Change to the Law Affecting Homeowners Only

Before May 6, 1990, there was a consideration even more daunting than IRS audits for people who planned to sell their homes within a few years. You would lose the $250,000 ($500,000 for couples) personal residence exclusion on the business portion of your home. As a result, when you had a large gain on the sale, you would have to pay tax on the business percentage of that gain. For instance, let's say you used 15 percent of your home as your office. Your home was worth $200,000, but you bought it for $100,000 several years ago. In the past, when you sold the house, $170,000 would have been treated as sale of your personal residence. The gain would not have been taxable, since it's less than the $250,000 exclusion per person. But $30,000 ($200,000 × 15 percent) would have been treated as the sale of business property. Without going through all the numbers, essentially, you would have had to pay $3,000–$5,000 in IRS and state taxes on the sale, depending on how much depreciation you had taken.

That additional tax is no longer an issue. Under the present law, you get to treat the whole house as your personal residence when you sell it. You only have to pay tax on the depreciation you've deducted. Since most people don't get to deduct more than $500 per year of depreciation, the tax doesn't usually amount to much. So relax. It's all right to use office-in-home deductions if they apply to your business.

Inner Space

Now that you're comfortable taking the deduction, just how much of the home's area can you deduct?

Carefully measure out the square footage of the space(s) you use. You'll find you use substantially more of your home for business than you realize. After all, most businesspeople use their car for business more than 40 percent of the time. Have you ever noticed how much space your garage takes up? While you may have a 1,400-square-foot home, your two-car garage may add 800 square feet (about $20' \times 40'$). If half that garage is used for your 75 percent business-use car—that amounts to 300 square feet (800 $\times$ 50 percent $\times$ 75 percent). Add in the storage for your files, inventory, tools, and records (about 10×20 square feet)—that's another 200 square feet. You've just found 500 square feet in the garage alone!

Look at the space you're using in the house. You have that area at the back half of the living room. You have a desk (or two to make an L-shape), a bookcase or three, a cabinet for your printer, several upright or lateral files. You're talking about $12' \times 15' = 180$ square feet. Don't forget the closet filled with office supplies—another $6' \times 4' = 24$ square feet. So far, we have 704 square feet! (24 + 180 + 500) divided by the total square footage of the house and the garage (1,400 + 800) of 2,200 square feet results in a business use of 32 percent of your home. You can use the worksheet in Figure 7.2 to help you.

Just using your unimaginative desk area, you'd have had 180 ÷ 1400 = 12.9 percent.

As long as the areas you're taking for the deduction are really used for business, you will have no problem in an audit.

Just remember one thing—you can't add in space that is not exclusively used for business. If you do your work on the kitchen counter and then clear it all away to make and serve family meals, that's *not* office space. On the other hand, if you use the dining room as your office and never use it for family meals—that is office space.

Isn't this exciting?

Two Critical Reminders

Let's pause for just a second here. Please do be careful about two things when claiming this deduction.

1. You really do have a business with a profit motive.
2. You really are using your home as your principal place of business.

FIGURE 7.2 The Home Office Spaces

Total Business Square Footage

Area of your desk and main files   _____

Primary supply closet   _____

Additional in-house storage   _____

Office lavatory   _____

Vehicle parking area   _____

Garage or carport storage area   _____

Additional structures   _____

Total Business Square Footage   **(A)** _____

Total Home Square Footage

Area of primary residence   _____

Area of garage or carport   _____

Area of additional structures, if used in the business   _____

Total Home Square Footage   **(B)** _____

Percentage of Business Use

(A) ÷ (B) = (C)   **(C)** _____%

While the IRS isn't chasing after office-in-home deductions per se, they are looking for fraud. So, please don't be frivolous about this because the IRS really doesn't have a sense of humor in this area.

Incidentally, having gone through this exercise to see how much of your home you're using for business may get you to do some thinking about your business space.

Is there really enough space to run your business the way you'd like? Would you be better off in a traditional business facility? Or would you be better off in a bigger house? Perhaps, looking all this over will help you realize that you not only need more space, but that your business can afford to pay for it.

Prove It, Baby!

Okay, you're comfortable using the home office. You've learned how to determine how much of the home is a business. Now, how do we prove it to the IRS in the event of an audit?

After all, if they do audit you, it will be about two or three years after the year you used the area. You might have remodeled that area by now—or moved away. How do you protect your deduction? Simple: take photographs. Take lots of pictures of the office spaces in the house, and remember to include the closets and storage areas. Take photos of the garage area and any business space out there.

I know you love your digital camera. It makes life so easy. But print those snapshots. Keep a hard copy in your permanent file for the house and another copy in your tax file. Who knows if you'll still be able to read the same digital medium in 2006?

Make a schematic drawing of the home. It doesn't need to be fancy. Just make an outline of the house, garage, and storage areas, putting lines in to separate each room. (Remember those old-fashioned things called rulers? They come in really handy for making neat, straight lines. If you don't have a ruler handy, use the edge of a book or your *TV Guide*.) Write in the lengths and widths of each room. Then add up the total square footage and list it neatly in a corner of the page. Next, identify all the areas you use for business and add up their measurements. Enter the total business square footage on the page. Finally, show the computation of the business percentage (business square feet divided by total square feet).

Do not use the number of rooms used for business divided by the total rooms in the house. It doesn't work that way. You must use square footage.

Set up a permanent office-in-home file. Put a copy of this schematic into that file and another copy in your tax file for each year that you operate from this home. That way, in case of an audit, you won't have to scramble to find a copy.

Now that you have the measurements, what can you deduct?

What Are Office-in-Home Expenses?

Don't get too carried away here. I've seen people drag in everything they spend money on and try to turn it into a business expense. Don't get greedy. If you don't have clients coming to your home, don't deduct things like your gardener, pool guy, or other outside maintenance expense. When it comes to your housekeeper, if you don't even let her set foot in your office, don't take that deduction. I'm not trying to spoil your fun—just trying to keep you looking good.

Rent Is Easy

If you don't own your home, multiply the business percentage (you've already computed it) times your total rent. For example, let's say you pay $12,000 per year for rent plus $500 for renter's insurance. Earlier, you computed your business use as 32 percent. Your deduction then is $4,000 (12,500 × 32 percent). That's it. Drop that number onto line 20—"Other expenses" on Form 8829 (see Figure 7.1).

If You Own, You Depreciate

Since the home area is being used for business, you'll need to use the nonresidential real property tables to look up your depreciation. Business property is depreciated over 39 years. If you can't get your hands on a depreciation table, just do the computation yourself. There are 468 months in 39 years (12 × 39). Divide your depreciable cost by 468. That gives you the depreciation per month. Then, multiply the monthly amount by the number of months you used the space for business this year.

It's important to figure out the value or cost of your office in home. It's not quite as easy as it looks. The number might start with your purchase price of the home. Or, if the current market value of the home is lower than your purchase price plus improvements, that's your starting point. That will give you a basis (tax cost) for the home. You can't depreciate land. To determine the cost of the land, look at your appraisal, if you have a copy. Most professional appraisers include that information. If you're in the process of buying the home, or refinancing, ask for a copy of the appraisal. Be sure to ask the appraiser to define the land value. You can't get your hands on an appraisal? Use a copy of your property tax assessor's statement or annual invoice. It shows land and building value. Don't use the value shown. Use the percentage (divide the land value by the total value of the property). Apply that percentage to your basis to get the cost of the business portion of your home. Use the worksheet in Figure 7.3 for guidance.

Add in any major improvements that weren't previously depreciated. Have you ever taken a casualty loss deduction on your home? If you live in a flood, tornado, or earthquake zone you might have. Be sure to reduce your basis by the amount of the casualty losses you deducted. Line D in Figure 7.3 will give you the adjusted basis.

Figure 7.4 will guide you on the rest of the depreciation calculation.

There are still expenses you may take.

Utilities (gas, electric, sewage, trash, water). Rather than using the square foot method, what I like to do is this.

- Start with your utility bills from before the office was in your home. Add up a year's worth. Take the average (divide by 12). That number is your average

FIGURE 7.3 Depreciation of Home

Lower of cost of home or fair market value		_____
Improvements to home before becoming office		_____
Less:		
Cost of land		_____
Casualty loss used		_____
Total Adjusted Basis	(D)	_____
Divide (D) by 468 (months)	(E)	_____
Multiply (E) by months of business use in current year		
Total Depreciation	(F)	_____

monthly utility charge. Deduct this amount from your present monthly utility total. The difference is your business expense. For instance, before working from home your electricity bill was $50. Now that you're working from home, with all the computers and air conditioning, your bill is $150. The $100 increase is your business expense.

- If your office was always at home, you're stuck using the same percentage as your square footage of business use. If you have a way of proving that your home office uses more power or water than is needed for regular living, use it. One way would be to get copies of a neighbor's utility bills for a year. Even three months would be great. Find someone who works outside of the home, has a similar number of people living in the home, and won't mind letting you use their utility invoices for your audit. Follow the instructions above.
- Generally, doing the calculation this way will result in a higher and more reasonable deduction. (Put this worksheet into your permanent office-in-home file.)

Internet Access. If your family is using the same lines, you'll have a hard time justifying the deduction. You might get away with deducting the difference between dial-up and a high-speed line, using the logic that you wouldn't have gotten the high-speed line if not for the business.

Cable TV. To get this deduction, you'll need to keep a log of the shows watched and which were for business purposes. Keep a notebook outlining how that program related to your business. Deduct only the business use. (When I take this

FIGURE 7.4 Home Office Deduction Overview

Total Business Profit from Schedule C	**(G)**	_____
Indirect Expenses: Shared with Home		
Rent or mortgage interest	_____	
Property taxes	_____	
Home insurance	_____	
Utilities	_____	
Repair and maintenance	_____	
Other	_____	
Total indirect expenses	**(H)**	_____
Multiply this by the percentage in Figure 7.2 (C)	**(I)**	_____
Direct Expenses: Business Related Only		
Insurance	_____	
Repair and maintenance	_____	
Other	_____	
Other	_____	
Total Direct Expenses	**(J)**	_____
Depreciation from Figure 7.3	**(F)**	_____
Prior year carryforward from Form 8829		_____
Total Office-in-Home Expenses		
(I) + (J) + (F)		_____
Deduct profit from	**(K)**	(_____)
Deductible office-in-home expenses this year	**(L)**	_____
If the result is negative, you have a carryover to next year.		

deduction, even for my entertainment folks, I know it's usually a giveaway: one of those things you're prepared to give up during an audit.)

Repairs and Maintenance. If you repaint or repair any part of your business space, naturally, 100 percent of those costs are deductible. For instance, if you install an additional bathroom just for your office, you can deduct all of those expenses. However, if you make repairs or improvements to the whole house, such that it also benefits your business space, you'll only be able to deduct the business percentage we arrived at earlier. An example of such an improvement would be installing an air-conditioning system in the whole house.

Property Tax and Interest. Deduct the business percentage on Form 8829. Use the rest on Schedule A.

Insurance. Business liability insurance or business insurance just on your office space is fully deductible. You may use the business percentage of whatever you pay for homeowner's insurance or renter's insurance.

Household Supplies. You'll buy certain things at the supermarket or discount store for household cleaning or beverages or coffee. Some of those things may look like personal groceries. But if you are using them strictly for your clients or staff, they may be business expenses. Think about the expenses from this perspective— if you were in an outside office, you would have a "kitchen" area containing a coffeemaker, microwave, and refrigerator, and you would stock it with coffee, teas, cocoas, popcorn, and other supplies for visitors and staff. Are you doing the same thing at home? I like to separate out the groceries that are for the office from the ones for the house. The store doesn't mind ringing it up as two sales. If you keep separate receipts, it's easier to support your deduction. Be careful not to abuse this.

When You Can't Use Office-in-Home Deductions

If your business shows a loss, your office-in-home deductions are suspended. If your business shows a profit, but when you use the office-in-home expenses, your profit turns into a loss, you may only deduct enough expenses to zero out your profit. The unused expenses don't entirely go away. You carry them forward to next year's tax return. There's a line at the bottom of Form 8829 for carryovers.

Evaluate Your Options

You understand how to use the office in home. Now, the question arises, should you use it? There may be times when it's wise to just skip it.

These are some of the considerations I look at for my clients:

- Do you own or rent your home?
- If you own, will you still be living there two years from now?

- How soon *do* you plan to sell it?
- Will you have a gain or a loss if you sell it?
- Do you expect your business to show a profit after using these deductions?

If you are renting the residence, there are no long-term repercussions from using this deduction.

When you own your home, it has most likely appreciated since you bought it. You will have to pay taxes on the depreciation you've taken. Is it worth it, for the small amount of depreciation deduction you get anyway?

It may be worth it, if all the other office-in-home expenses really help reduce your taxable business profit. You don't get to use all the other office-in-home expenses without also using the depreciation. The tax code has a special rule about depreciation. It's called the "allowed or allowable" rule. That means if you should have taken depreciation, but didn't, the IRS will treat your tax return as if you had. It's complicated and nasty—and if you were in business for more than three years and didn't take the depreciation, but should have, it could cost you. This is definitely one of those areas that you want to discuss face-to-face with a good tax professional.

One of the questions above asks whether your business is profitable. I ask that for two reasons.

1. When your business shows a loss, your office-in-home deduction cannot be used. (Sure, it will carry over to the next year, but it's useless now.)
2. If you expect to be showing losses for several years, you may never get the advantage of the office-in-home deduction, but you will attract an audit for a hobby loss. (See Chapter 13.)

Generally, seeing a pattern like that, I avoid the deduction altogether. If you can stand the scrutiny and have a solid business plan that shows how and why your business will start being profitable five years from now, go ahead and use the office-in-home deductions.

Then there are times when you just want to throw out the whole deduction altogether. Which is what I did for one client, until I went all the way. Erica hadn't filed tax returns for a long time. I prepared seven years' returns for her, including her office-in-home deduction. It wasn't that hard because she was renting an apartment. As a self-employed publisher, she worked from home. You can just bet that a substantial portion of her home really was devoted to her business.

Erica had losses for the first six years. She could prove how deeply in the red she was by the very high balances on her credit card and bank loans. Seeing all those losses during the first years' returns and thinking of the added scrutiny the IRS gives to nonfilers, I went back and removed the office-in-home deduction. (I kept a printed copy of those pages in case I needed them again.).

Good thing, too. When I prepared the last year, she had $50,000 worth of profits. Suddenly, all those years with losses became very attractive. Putting the office-in-home deduction back in and carrying it forward each year wiped out most of Erica's $50,000 profit, including her self-employment taxes. In the end, Erica only owed a few hundred dollars for all seven years. (I love it when I can see the future like this, don't you?)

When I first removed the Form 8829, it was because she already had such high losses, that it was clear her net operating losses (NOLs) would wipe out income for years to come. The trouble with NOLs is that they don't wipe out self-employment taxes. The self-employment tax is 15.3 percent of your business's current year profit. Some people don't mind paying that money because it's for your own Social Security and Medicare coverage. Others are so broke or operating on such a tight budget that they can't look toward the future—only to keeping the lights on.

Working on this series of tax returns helped remind me that NOLs only had a limited use. It was also a defining moment for me. Preparing Erica's tax returns was how I came to understand that the office-in-home carryforwards are one of the few deductions that *will* reduce self-employment tax.

All the reading and education in the world doesn't help. You've got to go hands-on to understand the tax system.

A Final Note

Working at home can be really grand. You are free to indulge yourself when you simply need a break. You can spend time with friends, children, and lovers. Or, you can be interrupted constantly. How you structure the separation between working space/time and personal space/time is strictly up to you. But you will reduce your stress levels if you establish specific boundaries for your family and friends—and stick with them. When you work at home, people tend to treat you as if you're not really working. Or they will call you to service them at all hours of the day or night.

You can get some help and support with the issues you're facing from an assortment of online resources. All have articles and tools to help. Some also have forums where you'll find it a relief to talk to other people dealing with the same issues as you.

Office-in-Home Resources

IRS Forms
- **Form 8829, Expenses for Business Use of Your Home.** www.irs.gov
/pub/irs-pdf/f8829.pdf
- **IRS Publication 587, Business Use of Your Home.** www.irs.gov/publica
tions/p587/index.html

Books
- *The Home Daycare Complete Recordkeeping System* by Brigitte A.
Thompson. www.DaycareRecordkeeping.com
- *Minding Her Own Business: The Self-Employed Woman's Guide to
Taxes and Recordkeeping* by Jan Zobel. www.janztax.com/Minding_Her
_Own_Business/Minding_Her_Own_Business.htm: My readers and
clients have been using this book for years.

Online Support for Home-Based Businesses
- **Family Content** by Donna Schwartz Mills. www.family-content.com:
Articles, e-books, tools
- **Work at Home Moms** by Cheryl Demas. www.wahm.com: Resources,
tools, message boards, find local moms
- **Slowlane.com** by Chris Stafford and Jay Massey. www.slowlane.com: For
stay-at-home dads, this site has articles, tools, and forums.
- **WomanOwned.com** by Christiana Blenk. www.womanowned.com: Arti-
cles, resources, forum, networking

8

VEHICLES: EVERYONE'S FAVORITE DEDUCTION

I spent a lot of money on booze, birds, and fast cars. The rest I just squandered.

—GEORGE BEST

Autos, trucks, vans, minivans, trailers, SUVs, whatever you're using, it's probably one of your most costly assets. It's also your best source of business deductions, since you've got to have a set of wheels for personal use.

Vehicles are essential to your life and your business. Practically everyone has at least one car at home. You may have several, depending on your family size, hobbies, interests, and business requirements.

When it comes to using cars for business, select just one of those vehicles as the business vehicle. When more than one family member is involved in the business, assign one business vehicle to each person as a business vehicle, or have several family members or staff use one vehicle. Try not to keep switching around. Consistency of use makes it simpler to track business mileage. If you must use more than one vehicle, keep logs in each car to track total mileage and business mileage. Being able to track the actual miles may be more important for a "fleet" than for a single car.

When your business requires the use of a single-purpose truck or van, such as an outfitted plumbing truck or delivery van, you shouldn't have problems establishing that you used it 100 percent for business. That vehicle is not fit for personal use. Take a photo of the vehicle full of your usual equipment or inventory and put it in your tax file.

Clearly, certain vehicles really are used 100 percent for business by their very nature. But for regular vehicles, don't expect the IRS to allow you 100 percent business use. They realize that even if you have several cars, sometimes you're going to use your business car to shop for groceries, pick up your children, or run some personal errands. The IRS expects that you will record a reasonable amount of personal use.

Some of my clients have a separate business vehicle, or they work from home and practically all their driving is business. For them, it's easier to track the personal miles than the business miles. While they may not drive many miles during the year, the larger percentage of the miles they do drive will be business.

Deducting Auto Expenses

Figure 8.1 shows you two ways to report auto expenses—the mileage method and actual expenses. Yes, it looks like three ways. That's because actual expenses are different for owned and leased vehicles. Please note that the mileage method isn't nearly as easy as you may have thought. You have four different rates, depending on how you use your car. In addition, there's also a depreciation component built into each mile.

FIGURE 8.1 How to Deduct Auto Expenses and Mileage Rates

Mileage Method	Actual Expenses for Leased Vehicles	Actual Expenses for Purchased Vehicles
_____ cents per mile	Lease payments	Interest on auto loan
Parking/valet	Gasoline	Gasoline
Tolls	Repairs and maintenance	Repairs and maintenance
	Parts, washes	Parts, washes
	Insurance	Insurance
	License/registration	License/registration
	Parking/valet	Parking/valet
	Garage rent	Garage rent
	Tolls	Tolls
	Less the lease inclusion amount	Depreciation

Actual expenses used to be simpler before depreciation got so complicated. Now you have such a varied menu of depreciation options that it really does take a computer to find the best treatment.

Regardless which method you use to write off your auto expenses, you will need to know two mileage numbers for each car you use—total miles and business miles. The second page of Form 4562 still asks for the mileage breakdown. To make this as correct as possible, on January 1 of each year, note your vehicle's odometer reading on your calendar.

If you didn't make any notes during the year about your total miles, you can reconstruct the total miles. Find a repair invoice from early in the year and one from later in the year. Find the box showing the mileage when you brought it in for service. Deduct the miles shown on the earlier invoice from the miles on the later invoice (for example, the February 16 invoice shows 14,500 miles and the June 8 invoice shows 19,600 miles). Divide the difference by the number of days in between invoices (in our example, 5,100 miles ÷ 112 days = 45.54). Multiply the result by 30 to get the number of miles per month (returning to our example, 45.54 miles × 30 days = 1,366 miles per month). Then multiply by 12 to get the total miles for the year (1,366 miles × 12 months = 16,392 miles driven this year).

If you tracked the business miles, you'll be able to easily figure out your business use of your vehicle. If you only tracked your personal miles, deduct the personal miles from the total miles you drove to get your business miles (continuing our example, 16,392 total miles − 2,634 personal miles = 13,758 business miles). Divide your business use by the total miles to arrive at the percentage of actual expenses you're entitled to deduct (13,758 business miles ÷ 16,392 total miles = 83.9 percent business use of the vehicle).

Using the Standard Mileage Rate

Once you have the total miles and the business miles, enter them on the second page of Form 4562. If you're using the mileage rate, multiply the current year's rate by the total business miles (for 2004 using our example, 13,758 × 37.5 cents = $5,159) and pop it onto line 9 of your personal tax return's Schedule C, or onto a schedule on your business return. Steve Hopfenmuller at the Small Business Taxes and Management website maintains a list of mileage rates from 1997 to the present, available at www.smbiz.com/sbrl003.html. You can see a sample from previous years in Table 8.1.

Just a little note that no one seems to tell you—if you take advantage of any of the special depreciation methods, including the bonus depreciation or Section

TABLE 8.1 Standard Mileage Rates

Built into the standard mileage is a certain amount of depreciation per mile. Don't worry about the number until you sell the car. Then add up the miles you've deducted each year and multiply it by the depreciation rate for each year.

	Year and Rate per Mile				
Types of Miles	2004	2003	2002	2001	2000
Business	37.5	36.0	36.5	34.5	32.5
Charity	14.0	14.0	14.0	14.0	14.0
Medical	14.0	12.0	13.0	12.0	10.0
Moving	14.0	12.0	13.0	12.0	10.0
Depreciation	**16.0**	**16.0**	**15.0**	**15.0**	**14.0**

179, you may not use the mileage method to deduct your car expenses for the life of the vehicle.

When using actual expenses, follow the guide in Figure 8.1 to see what you can deduct for owned and leased vehicles. We'll examine the special vehicle depreciation rules later in this chapter.

Should I Lease or Buy?

Car ads make automobile leases sound awfully tempting. Before getting seduced by the temptation of driving a sleek Lexus for a low monthly payment, know that there are big-dollar tax ramifications lurking behind the small-dollar dealer hype.

The most frequent call I get is from business clients trying to decide whether to buy or lease a car. Being a number-cruncher, I computed several test scenarios, coming to the conclusion that there are too many variables to generate general answers. Instead, let's highlight the questions you need to ask yourself when facing this decision.

Thoughts to Ponder
- Do you plan to drive more than 12,000 miles per year?
- How many miles do you drive for business?
- How many commuting miles do you drive? (Commuting is not deductible.)

- What percentage of the total use of that vehicle will be for business?
- Do you have a second car for personal use?
- How long do you normally keep your vehicles?
- Do you mind having payments for the rest of your life?
- How frequently do you service your vehicles?
- How much money can you afford to put down on a vehicle?
- If you lease, how much of a "deposit" do they require?
- How good are you at keeping detailed records?

All these issues will affect your long- and short-term operating costs and tax benefits.

Aside from my being nosy, how do my clients' responses affect my recommendation? Let's examine each topic more carefully.

Driving Issues

Most leases penalize you for driving more than 12,000 miles per year. Take into account the additional costs for the excess mileage. This is usually prohibitive. Some people, though, don't mind.

If you live in your car, getting your wheels serviced can be a problem. Look for a lease or purchase that includes free loaner cars. I discovered that when buying or leasing an Infiniti from the dealer (even a used one), free loaner cars during scheduled service are included as a matter of company policy. For me, that's one of the most valuable accessories any car can offer. To be competitive, other car companies or dealers may offer the same deal if pressed—so ask.

Presently leases are advertised at very low, very tempting prices. But when you can buy a car with 0.0 percent interest and no down payment, buying may be better. Look closely at your options and compare them carefully.

The lease down payment is almost as much (or more) than the down payment to buy the car. That makes the total cost over the life of the lease less attractive—especially since you must turn your vehicles over every two years under most lease agreements. That's a lot of "down payment" money for something you'll never own!

Tax Issues

When deducting the lease expenses on your tax return, even if you use the car 100 percent for business, there is a mandatory "lease inclusion cost," described later in this chapter.

Whether you lease or buy, you still must maintain mileage logs to track what percent of the actual expenses to deduct. The best way to keep track of mileage is to keep a daily log in your car. Most people find that too onerous. I've found it's a good habit to record your mileage in your appointment book when you get into your car. Just put it at the top of the page, or in your PDA calendar for that date. Use the record-keeping tips you learned in Chapter 4 to track all your time and expenses.

You computed your business use percentage earlier in this chapter. In our example, it was 83.9 percent. Multiply your total expenses by that business percentage. Assuming you spent $5,400 on the lease; $250 for registration/license fees; $1,200 for insurance; $600 on gasoline; and $600 on car washes and routine service, total expenses equal $8,050. Your lease inclusion was $120, so net expenses are $7,930. Multiply that by 83.9 percent. Your total auto expenses are $6,653, plus parking.

The only expense that doesn't get hit by the percentage is parking. You're only including your business parking receipts in the first place.

My First Rule of Thumb

If you drive very few miles each year (10,000 or less) and more than 80 percent of that mileage is directly business-related, I recommend that you buy the vehicle, deducting the actual expenses.

Why? The numbers say it all.

The lease deduction based on a $450 per month lease would be nearly $6,600:

$450
× 12
− $71 lease inclusion on a $25,000 car
+ $1,200 insurance
+ $350 license
+ $800 fuel
+ $500 repairs and maintenance
+ $60 washes
× 80 percent business use

The purchase deduction based on the actual expense method would be $8,456:

$0 interest on a $25,000 loan
+ $1,200 insurance

+ $350 license
+ $800 fuel
+ $500 repair and maintenance
+ $60 washes
+ $7,660 first-year bonus depreciation
× 80 percent business use

My Second Rule of Thumb

If you drive 20,000 miles per year for business, I usually recommend that you buy.
Why?
The deduction based on buying the car and using the actual expense method would be nearly $9,900.

$0 interest on a $25,000 loan
+ $1,500 insurance
+ $350 license
+ $1,600 fuel
+ $1,200 repair and maintenance
+ $60 washes
+ $7,660 depreciation
× 80 percent business use

Your tax savings, if you're in a 28 percent tax bracket, is nearly $2,775. The deduction based on a $450 per month lease would be around $8,100—*and* you would have to pay back $1,200 per year to the leasing company for excess mileage![1]

$450
× 12
+ $71 lease inclusion on a $25,000 car
+ $1,500 insurance
+ $350 license
+ $1,600 fuel
+ $1,200 repair and maintenance
+ $60 washes
× 80 percent business use

---

1. The $8,100 deduction, in a 28 percent tax bracket, is worth $2,270.

Excess mileage is generally charged at $.15 × miles over 12,000 = 8,000 × $.15 = $1,200.

When you deduct the excess mileage penalty of $1,200, your net benefit from the lease alternative is barely $1,050! Owning your car would have saved you $1,725 over leasing.

Hmmm. I think you are coming to the conclusion that leasing is not the best tax alternative for moderately priced vehicles. You're right! Frankly, I just can't figure out why anyone would lease a car and saddle themselves with payments forever.

The only time you really get a tax advantage from leasing is when you lease a hyper-expensive motorcar. Paying monthly lease fees of $750 or more, plug your costs into the examples above.

When the depreciation deduction is limited, the tax benefits are far higher when you lease a BMW, Eldorado, Mercedes Benz, or other high-ticket car. On the other hand, wouldn't it be nice to have three to five years without a car payment? Buy it!

Lease Inclusion—Add It Back In

When you lease a vehicle, unless it is a commercial vehicle like a MACK truck, the IRS knows you will have some personal use. There is no 100 percent business use for leased personal vehicles. The IRS has established a formula to use, based on the value of the car. They publish new tables each year. In fact, they have now added tables for trucks, due to their new rates. You can look them up in IRS Publications 463 and 946, or at www.irs.gov. Or you can do it more quickly and easily by using the online tables provided by the folks at Small Business Taxes and Management. Their lease inclusion tables, at www.smbiz.com/sbrl003.html#alv, cover 1996 to the current year.

The Cons of Depreciation

Chapter 6 outlined how depreciation works. Now that you understand the principle, let me tell you how it's different for vehicles.

First of all, be aware that the rules for autos change slightly almost every year. Next, be aware that this aspect of taxes is a political football and also gets changed dramatically whenever Congress feels like it.

It's a really confusing area of tax law. It's not enough to know the numbers. You need to know when to use which numbers. Please have a tax professional set up depreciation for your vehicle(s)—at least for the year of purchase. You may also want to have your tax pro review the depreciation again in the fourth year when the limit drops to $1,775 to see if you can switch to mileage at that point.

You may only use bonus depreciation and Section 179 depreciation if your business use of the vehicle is more than 50 percent.

Once you've used up as much of the bonus depreciation as you can, it's time to take regular depreciation on your vehicle. When it comes to cars, you can forget everything you learned in Chapter 6 about depreciation methods. For vehicles, there are luxury auto limits, which brings in special limits on how much depreciation you may use each year.

Luxury Auto Limits

The IRS defines a *luxury vehicle* as anything costing more than $15,300, at the latest report. (This value has increased a whole $1,000 since 1993, when you could actually buy a car for under that price.) If you've looked at autos today, if you want luxuries, like carpets, radios, even air conditioning (which is not a luxury in the hot South), you're not apt to find anything but a Kia for under that price. Saturn has one model—the Ion—that would qualify.

Most cars you will use for business will fall under the luxury auto deduction limits. That means, regardless of what your total depreciation should be for the vehicle, you may deduct no more than the amounts shown at the top of Table 8.2 each year. Look at this table. Let's see how long it will take to depreciate a car if you buy a typical auto, priced at $23,000 including tax and license, in 2004 and use the maximum depreciation. Let's say you're only using the auto 86 percent of the time for business. Multiply the $23,000 by 86 percent to learn that $19,800 is the maximum depreciation available.

In the first four years, you could pick up $19,935 worth of maximum depreciation—if you used the car 100 percent for business. But you only used it 86 percent so, over the first four years, you'd write off $17,144 (19,935 × 86 percent). That would still leave $2,656 of the car to write off. It would take you six years to write off a Toyota Corolla. You might still have this car. The only reason you were able to write it off over six years is because of the bonus depreciation Congress added in 2002 and 2003.

Otherwise, you'd still be writing this off for nearly five more years ($7,650 ÷ $1,675).

Imagine if this were a Mercedes or a Lexus! At these rates, it could take you twenty years. (You have a $1,675 deduction limit per year after the first three years.)

TABLE 8.2 Depreciation Limits for Cars and Trucks

Depreciation on cars, light trucks, and vans is limited by the luxury vehicle rules. For 2003 and forward, the IRS has created two different limits—one for cars and one for trucks. In addition, all *new* assets qualify for either the 30 percent or 50 percent additional depreciation. The tables already include the extra $4,600 first-year allowance. Note: Bonus depreciation ends in 2005.

2003–2004 Depreciation Limits for Passenger Automobiles

Tax Year	Standard		30% Additional		50% Additional	
	2004	2003	2004	2003	2004	2003
First	$2,960	$3,060	$7,560	$7,660	$10,610	$10,710
Second	4,800	4,900	4,800	4,900	4,800	4,900
Third	2,850	2,950	2,850	2,950	2,850	2,950
Subsequent	1,675	1,775	1,675	1,775	1,675	1,775

1996–2002 Depreciation Limits for Passenger Automobiles

Tax Year	2002–2000	1999	1998	1997	1996
First	$3,060	$3,060	$3,160	$3,160	$3,060
Second	4,900	5,000	5,000	5,000	4,900
Third	2,950	2,950	2,950	3,050	2,950
Subsequent	1,775	1,775	1,775	1,775	1,775

Depreciation Limits for Trucks and Vans (must be built on truck chassis)

Tax Year	Standard	30% Additional	50% Additional
First	$3,360	$7,960	$11,010
Second	5,400	5,400	5,400
Third	3,250	3,250	3,250
Subsequent	1,975	1,975	1,975

TABLE 8.2 *continued*

Depreciation Limits on Electric Vehicles

The total depreciation deduction (including the Section 179 deduction and the special depreciation allowance) you can take for an electric vehicle that you use in your business and first placed in service in 2003 and forward is:

- $22,880 if you acquired it before May 6, 2003, and you claim the 30% special allowance
- $32,030 if you acquired it after May 5, 2003, and you claim the 50% or 30% special allowance
- $9,080 if you elect not to claim any special allowance for the vehicle, the vehicle is not qualified property, or the vehicle is qualified Liberty Zone property

---

OK, so, that's who this rule was written to penalize—people who could afford the Audis and the Rolls-Royces. Unfortunately, the average person is caught in this trap, too.

The SUV Craze

Despite the push to cut back on emissions and to discourage gas-guzzlers, there is a little loophole in the depreciation rules that rewards you for buying gas hogs. Intended to exempt trucks and commercial vehicles from the luxury auto rules, this loophole has been snapped up by clever planners to subsidize the cost of expensive cars.

Buying vehicles weighing more than 6,000 pounds provides dramatically better tax benefits. They are not subject to the luxury vehicle rules in Table 8.2. You might even be able to deduct the entire cost in one year, using the new $100,000 limits to the Section 179 depreciation that came into play with the new tax law and the special bonus depreciation. (See Chapter 6 for more information about depreciation.)

Driving Home Conclusions

Remember, if you sell the car or stop using it for business within five years, you will have to pay back some of that depreciation. So don't get too greedy.

If you're going for the moneybags image—such as a Mercedes or Rolls-Royce—lease that car.

If you want a good value, give yourself a break from payments and buy the vehicle! At least you'll be able to have something to sell when the payments stop.

Or better yet—breathe easy for a couple of years with no payments at all. What a concept!

Does all this confuse you? Me, too. Please, as I said earlier, don't try to figure this out alone. There are so many nuances to vehicles and depreciation. This is one of the easiest parts of your tax return to get wrong. To make the vehicle part of your business tax return work, here's what you need to do.

Give your tax professional a good summary of each of your auto expenses. Provide the total mileage and business mileage. Provide a copy of the purchase or lease contracts if you got a new car during the year. Be sure to provide copies of the sales documents if you sold the car.

With that information in hand, your tax pro can give you the best results.

Vehicle Resources

- **Bankrate.com Lease vs. Buy Calculator.** www.bankrate.com/brm/auto-advisers/br_buyvlease.asp
- **Mileage Rates for 1997–current year.** www.smbiz.com/sbrl003.html
- **Lease Inclusion Tables for 1996 to current year.** www.smbiz.com/sbr l003.html#alv
- **2004 Deduction Limits on Autos.** www.cshco.com/news/taxupdate _alertdetail.lasso?type=us&article=3: Excellent summary by Clark, Schaeffer, Hackett & Co. CPAs for owned and leased vehicles.
- **IRS Publication 463, Travel, Entertainment, Gift, and Car Expenses.** www.irs.gov/formspubs/page/0,,id%3D11531,00.html
- **IRS Publication 946, How to Depreciate.** www.irs.gov/publications/p 946/index.html
- **Form 1040, Schedule C.** www.irs.gov/pub/irs-pdf/f1040sc.pdf
- **Form 4562, Depreciation.** www.irs.gov/pub/irs-pdf/f4562.pdf

9

EMPLOYEES AND INDEPENDENT CONTRACTORS

Nearly all men can stand adversity, but if you want to test a man's character, give him power.

—Abraham Lincoln

On your last job, you came to realize you did all the work but got paid only a fraction of what you're worth. You quit and ranged out on your own. Now, with your own business, you get to keep all the money. You're better off, it's true, only now you have to do all the work yourself.

You may decide that you need help—if so, it's time to hire your own staff. Excellent idea—many companies can grow to great heights with the right employees and there are tax benefits to hiring employees. This chapter covers everything you need to know about categorizing employees, hiring family members, setting up payrolls, paying employee taxes, and much more.

Who Is an Employee?

Often, new small business owners are apt to think of people who work for them as temporaries or as freelancers. You may feel that since you haven't had employees until now, that you don't want to go through the hassles of setting up a formal payroll until you absolutely must.

You've got my sympathy. But not the IRS's.

Knowing the difference between an official employee by law and an independent contractor can be challenging. The following examples show just a small sampling of the wide range of possible employment situations.

- Nancy comes to Jackie's home to open mail, do filing, and pay bills. Nancy picks up a big stack of files and works on them at her own home. Is Nancy an employee?
- Joe hires Dan as his webmaster and site developer. Joe is gearing up for a big marketing push, making it clear that Dan must devote all of his time to the project. Dan agrees to work for Joe exclusively for 2004. Is Dan an employee?
- Perry is self-employed as a journalist. During the school yearbook season, Perry works for PhotoKiddie, snapping shots of schoolchildren for their yearbooks. Using their film, their contracts, and their forms, all the payments Perry collects are made out to PhotoKiddie. Is Perry an employee of PhotoKiddie?
- You do work for your corporation, but you have a full-time job. You're only working on corporate matters ten hours a week. Are you an employee?

All right, which one of these people are considered legal employees and how can you tell?

In actuality, the descriptions above don't provide enough information to make a decision. To determine if someone counts as an employee, you must ask more questions about each person you pay. As the positions are described above, it could go either way. With more information, however, there is an answer.

The IRS uses twenty common law factors that determine a person's employment status, and the factors don't all carry the same weight. Without experience facing employment audits, you won't know which factors matter. To make things more challenging, your state might have their own factors that don't match up to the IRS's. A tax professional whose practice specializes in small businesses and freelance work can evaluate the relative importance of each of the following factors for your business and industry.

The Twenty Common Law Factors the IRS Uses to Define Independent Contractors

1. Instructions are generally not given by the company that hires you.
2. Training is not essential and is not given by the company.
3. Your personal services are not required; you can assign the work to anyone.

4. The work you are performing is not essential to the company.
5. You set your own hours.
6. You have no continuing relationship with the company.
7. You control and hire your own assistants.
8. You are free to pursue other work.
9. Where you work is your choice.
10. You set your own work priorities.
11. No interim reports are required of you.
12. You work for more than one firm.
13. You pay your own business expenses.
14. You use your own tools and equipment.
15. You bear a risk of loss.
16. Your services are available to the general public (or industry).
17. You have a significant capital investment.
18. Right of discharge is limited by contract.
19. You are not compensated for incomplete work.
20. Timing of payment coincides with completion of job, rather than in regular intervals.

Consider those twenty factors whenever you need to decide if someone you hire should be on payroll or not.

Do They Act Like a Business?

If you're unsure how the IRS definition of *contractors* applies to your situation, consider this when looking at someone you want to treat as an independent contractor—people in business must look and act like a business. They must have all the licenses and certifications standard for their profession and their city, county, state, province, or other government division. They don't need to have a business name, but if your contractor uses Susan Johnson Consulting instead of plain old Susan Johnson, she'd have to get a fictitious name filing.

People you consider freelancers who are working for you, on your premises, using your equipment, and following your instructions are typically employees. Did you give them a key? Or access to one, to get in when you're away? That sounds like an employee relationship. If they feel like taking off, going down to the beach for the day and sending a colleague to do the work, may they? If not and you require that only the person you hired do the work, on your schedule—you have an employer-employee relationship. Essentially, it means that you control their work, their hours, and their staffing decisions. If they were in business for themselves, you couldn't do that, could you?

Now, if your new hire does fit the definition of an *independent contractor*, what should you do to prove it to the IRS, just in case they ever ask?

Protecting Yourself from Independent Contractor Claims

Whenever the IRS audits a business return that shows independent contractors, the first thing they check is whether the 1099s are filed. (You'll learn about them later in this chapter.) The second thing the examiner looks at is the worker's job duties. If the IRS decides you have an employee, not an independent contractor, they will create a payroll and assess you for payroll taxes you should have paid, plus penalties and interest.

To legitimize your claim of the independent relationship, use a checklist when hiring new vendors to provide rent or services of any kind. Simply hand the list to all new hires.

Alert: If needy friends beg you to hire them without putting them on the payroll, be wary. The biggest cause of employer audits is a nonemployee who is let go (even voluntarily) or gets sick. Suddenly, they realize they can't collect unemployment or disability insurance, but they file anyway—and turn you in. Yes, your best friend. Someone who was really in need and begged you to hire them under the table. Here is a horror story from one of my clients.

Bennie the Barber had a modest shop in Santa Monica that supported his family. Carlos came to him, begging for work. Bennie really couldn't afford it, but Carlos kept calling and coming by, telling Bennie how desperate he was for work. Relenting, Bennie gave him the second chair and turned customers over to Carlos. Bennie cut his own income because Carlos didn't bring in customers. Then Carlos started coming in late. Some days, he just didn't feel like coming in—no

---

Tip

Insist that all independent contractors provide all the information on the checklist in Figure 9.1 before issuing the first check. Make this a part of all contracts. It's easier to compel someone to provide an address and identification number when they want their check than it is in January when you want to file 1099s.

FIGURE 9.1 Independent Contractor Hiring Checklist

Obtain an Original from Independent Contractor

☐ Form W-9–Request for Taxpayer Identification Number (see Figure 9.1a)

☐ Business card

☐ Flyer, advertisement, brochure

☐ Contract or proposal

Obtain a Copy from Independent Contractor

☐ Current business licenses

☐ Professional license number, if applicable

☐ Sales tax certificate or license, if applicable

---

explanations. After two years of rudeness, Bennie finally got smart and let Carlos go.

What did Carlos do? You guessed it. He filed for disability. Carlos claimed he didn't know why he wasn't an employee. Carlos accused Bennie of cheating him. The state disability auditor was no dummy. But under the circumstances she had no choice. She audited Bennie. Digging deeply and looking at the whole situation, her audit assessment, with penalties and interest, was more than $5,000. IRS charges added another $10,000.

If you encounter a situation similar to Bennie the Barber's case, there's a way to reduce the IRS assessments when they decide your independent contractor is really an employee. You can use a safe harbor, which we'll discuss in the next section.

Before moving on, though, there's one very important thing you need to remember about independent contractors. Don't call them employees when talking about them, describing them, or speaking to them. Especially, do not use the word *employee* during an audit. You'd be surprised how many people trip themselves up that way. It's important that you change the word you use to think of these people. Get your mind around a new word, depending on what they do. Some options are *consultant, expert, contractor,* or *advisor.*

Also, they are not your associates or your partners—that's a different relationship. How you think of the person will determine what you instinctively say. At least, if the terminology is common in your industry, the safe harbors covered next may help reduce the damages.

FIGURE 9.1A Form W-9, Request for Taxpayer Identification Number and Certification

Form **W-9** (Rev. January 2003) Department of the Treasury Internal Revenue Service	**Request for Taxpayer Identification Number and Certification**	Give form to the requester. Do not send to the IRS.

Print or type
See Specific Instructions on page 2.

Name

Business name, if different from above

Check appropriate box: ☐ Individual/Sole proprietor ☐ Corporation ☐ Partnership ☐ Other ▶ .... ☐ Exempt from backup withholding

Address (number, street, and apt. or suite no.)

Requester's name and address (optional)

City, state, and ZIP code

List account number(s) here (optional)

Part I   **Taxpayer Identification Number (TIN)**

Enter your TIN in the appropriate box. For individuals, this is your social security number (SSN). **However, for a resident alien, sole proprietor, or disregarded entity, see the Part I instructions on page 3.** For other entities, it is your employer identification number (EIN). If you do not have a number, see **How to get a TIN** on page 3.

Note: *If the account is in more than one name, see the chart on page 4 for guidelines on whose number to enter.*

Social security number

or

Employer identification number

Part II   **Certification**

Under penalties of perjury, I certify that:

1. The number shown on this form is my correct taxpayer identification number (or I am waiting for a number to be issued to me), **and**

2. I am not subject to backup withholding because: **(a)** I am exempt from backup withholding, or **(b)** I have not been notified by the Internal Revenue Service (IRS) that I am subject to backup withholding as a result of a failure to report all interest or dividends, or **(c)** the IRS has notified me that I am no longer subject to backup withholding, **and**

3. I am a U.S. person (including a U.S. resident alien).

Certification instructions. You must cross out item **2** above if you have been notified by the IRS that you are currently subject to backup withholding because you have failed to report all interest and dividends on your tax return. For real estate transactions, item **2** does not apply. For mortgage interest paid, acquisition or abandonment of secured property, cancellation of debt, contributions to an individual retirement arrangement (IRA), and generally, payments other than interest and dividends, you are not required to sign the Certification, but you must provide your correct TIN. (See the instructions on page 4.)

Sign Here   Signature of U.S. person ▶   Date ▶

Purpose of Form

A person who is required to file an information return with the IRS, must obtain your correct taxpayer identification number (TIN) to report, for example, income paid to you, real estate transactions, mortgage interest you paid, acquisition or abandonment of secured property, cancellation of debt, or contributions you made to an IRA.

U.S. person. Use Form W-9 only if you are a U.S. person (including a resident alien), to provide your correct TIN to the person requesting it (the requester) and, when applicable, to:

  1. Certify that the TIN you are giving is correct (or you are waiting for a number to be issued),

  2. Certify that you are not subject to backup withholding, or

  3. Claim exemption from backup withholding if you are a U.S. exempt payee.

  Note: *If a requester gives you a form other than Form W-9 to request your TIN, you must use the requester's form if it is substantially similar to this Form W-9.*

Foreign person. If you are a foreign person, use the appropriate Form W-8 (see **Pub. 515,** Withholding of Tax on Nonresident Aliens and Foreign Entities).

Nonresident alien who becomes a resident alien. Generally, only a nonresident alien individual may use the terms of a tax treaty to reduce or eliminate U.S. tax on certain types of income. However, most tax treaties contain a provision known as a "saving clause." Exceptions specified in the saving clause may permit an exemption from tax to continue for certain types of income even after the recipient has otherwise become a U.S. resident alien for tax purposes.

  If you are a U.S. resident alien who is relying on an exception contained in the saving clause of a tax treaty to claim an exemption from U.S. tax on certain types of income, you must attach a statement that specifies the following five items:

  1. The treaty country. Generally, this must be the same treaty under which you claimed exemption from tax as a nonresident alien.

  2. The treaty article addressing the income.

  3. The article number (or location) in the tax treaty that contains the saving clause and its exceptions.

  4. The type and amount of income that qualifies for the exemption from tax.

  5. Sufficient facts to justify the exemption from tax under the terms of the treaty article.

Cat. No. 10231X   Form **W-9** (Rev. 1-2003)

Safe Harbor Rules

Section 530 of the Revenue Act of 1978 provides a safe harbor with special leniency toward certain employers.[1] Barbers and beauty salons are among those protected by Section 530.

Congress decreed that you had a reasonable basis for treating your staff as independent contractors if you can pass a test: You pass the test if you relied on:

- Judicial precedent, published rulings, technical advice, or letter ruling to the employer
- A past IRS audit in which no assessment was made on account of improper treatment of workers (even if the audit was not related to employee issues)
- A long-standing recognized practice of a significant segment of the industry in which the individual worked. (The IRS used to require the practice to span more than ten years, before 1979, or more than 50 percent of the industry. The new law requires no fixed amount of time and no more than 25 percent of the industry.)

Earlier, we posed some situations. The PhotoKiddie example would fit the safe harbor rules. Why? When an industry (photographers) treats its freelance workers as contractors, it can get the penalty reduction.

When the IRS decides you should have had an employee, they charge you for both halves of the Social Security/Medicare that should have been withheld from the worker's wages. They also charge you for a certain amount of the withholding. Then the IRS adds various penalties and finally tops off the whole thing with interest on the combined total. The final balance due may be hefty enough to shut down your business.

When facing an employment tax audit, be sure to ask your tax pro to invoke the Section 530 Safe Harbor rules. You'll be relieved of a substantial part of the Social Security taxes and IRS withholding you should have taken. Hopefully, you'll never need this rule.

---

1. Full text, plus amendments, of §530 of the Revenue Act of 1978 can be found at www.worker status.com/530text.html.

What Are 1099s?

You're familiar with W-2s. Think of 1099s as the same thing for people without full-time jobs. Form 1099 is also the IRS's way of catching tax cheaters. Before the program started in 1980, there was a huge under-the-table economy. It's still large, but getting smaller as enforcement improves. Using 1099s, the IRS can ensure freelancers report all their income. Knowing you'll be reporting their earnings to the IRS, they have two choices:

1. They can refuse to work for you, which has happened. If someone refuses to provide the requisite information, you're better off knowing this when the project starts. You don't want to find out that this person may not be ethical after giving them access to sensitive information or clients.
2. They can do like everyone else—earn the money and pay taxes on it.

There's always the other option—where they collect the fees and don't file. When they do that, the IRS sends out notices to companies who filed 1099s, insisting you withhold 28 percent of all checks to that person as backup withholding. You'll rarely face this issue. If it comes up for you, you'll find instructions and explanations in IRS Publication 1281—A Guide to Backup Withholding on Missing and Incorrect Names/TINs.

Some states realized that waiting until 1099s are filed and processed means the tax evader can stay on the job before being caught until July or August of the following year. To shorten the time, many states are coming up with solutions. California created Form 542, which companies must file with the state as soon as they pay anyone $600 or more. Since this is working for California, expect other states to request it, too.

Who Gets 1099s?

IRS instructions on the 1099 forms require you to send them out to people you've paid in the course of your trade or business. The forms are only issued to those who are not incorporated (individuals and partnerships), with two exceptions. 1099-MISC forms must be issued to all attorneys or medical professionals, even if incorporated.

Never issue 1099s for the purchase of products or supplies. Don't issue it for reimbursed expenses you pay to an independent contractor who gives you a copy of the receipt for something he or she purchased or for an expense report from a vendor or consultant.

When your business pays you, without a payroll, you'll need to issue 1099s to yourself. The only exception is if you're filing on a Schedule C. When you are an LLC filing on Schedule C, you may need to issue yourself a 1099 if your business is taking a deduction for payments to you.

Looking at the boxes on the form (Figure 9.2), even without reading the tax code or the instructions, you can readily get an idea of who gets 1099s. Let's review only the boxes that are apt to affect your business.

- **Box 1: Rents.** This is for payments to your landlord. Also, use it for equipment leases from private parties. If you pay for storage and the company is a partnership, they get one, too. If your business pays you rent, you get one.
- **Box 2: Royalties.** This applies if you have a graphic artist; you're licensing technology; you have a co-author or ghostwriter; or you're a publisher. If you are licensing something to your entity, issue this to yourself.
- **Box 3: Other income.** Be generous with this. If you're paying someone for something that clearly is not self-employment, use this box instead of Box 7.

FIGURE 9.2 Form 1099-MISC, Miscellaneous Income

Tip

Here's a 1099 secret. Hardly anyone knows this, but if you need extra time to file those 1099s, you can get another thirty days using Form 8809. I've included a copy here (see Figure 9.3), since you'll never see it anywhere else. If you're really in trouble and need still more time, send a note to the good folks at the Martinsburg Computing Center in West Virginia. (Remember to enter the year.) Their address is:

IRS–Martinsburg Computing Center
Information Reporting Program
ATT: Extension of Time Coordinator
240 Murall Drive
Kearneysville, WV 25430

They've been known to give small business owners one more break if they have a good reason. But don't abuse this.

Anytime you're not sure how to categorize payments to someone and have no one to ask, use box 3. Leave it up to them to decide how to report it on their own tax return.

- **Box 4: Federal income tax withheld.** Some of your vendors may want withholding (rarely). Usually you will withhold taxes when the IRS garnishes their income. This may also be a way for partners or LLC members to avoid making quarterly estimated tax payments (more on this in Chapter 11). When you do withhold, be sure to issue the 1099s early so recipients can file their tax returns on time.
- **Box 7: Nonemployee compensation.** All remuneration to anyone performing a service to your business gets reported here, including your tax pro, consultants, freelancers, web designers, outside services, virtual assistants, trainers, advertising agency, public relations firm, landlord, and equipment rentals. Attorney fees go into Box 14.

To the recipient, it's very important that you get the boxes right. Income reported in Box 1 and Box 2 is not subject to self-employment taxes. Taxpayers pay self-employment taxes on all income in Box 7. When they don't, the IRS sends them nasty letters (we'll discuss this in Chapter 13). Box 3 is a gray area. Generally the income in that box is not self-employment taxable—but it could be. The IRS's computers won't be looking for a match on Schedule SE for amounts in Box 3.

FIGURE 9.3 Form 8809, Application for Extension of Time to File Information Returns

Form **8809**

(Rev. July 2004)

Department of the Treasury
Internal Revenue Service

Application for Extension of Time To File Information Returns

(For Forms W-2 series, W-2G, 1042-S, 1098 series, 1099 series, 5498 series, and 8027)

▶ **Send to IRS–Martinsburg Computing Center.** See **Where to file** below.

OMB No. 1545-1081

Caution: *Do not use this form to request an extension of time to (1) provide statements to recipients, (2) file Form 1042 (instead use Form 2758), or (3) file Form 1040 (instead use Form 4868).*

Extension Requested for Tax Year 20_____
(Enter one year only.)

1 Filer or transmitter information. **Type or print clearly in black ink.**

Filer/Transmitter Name _____

Address _____

City _____ State _____ ZIP Code _____

Contact Name _____ Telephone number (____)_____

Email address _____

2 **Taxpayer identification number** (Enter your nine-digit number. Do not enter hyphens.)

3 Transmitter Control Code (TCC)

4 Check your method of filing information returns (check only one box). Use a separate Form 8809 for each method.

☐ electronic   ☐ magnetic media   ☐ paper

5 If you are requesting an extension for more than one filer, enter the total number of filers and attach a list of names and taxpayer identification numbers. Requests for more than 50 filers must be filed electronically or magnetically. See **How to file** below for details. ▶

6 For extension requests sent electronically/magnetically only, enter the total number of records in your extension file. **Do not** attach a list. ▶

7 Check this box only if you already received the automatic extension and you now need an additional extension. See instructions. ▶ ☐

8 Check the box(es) that apply. **Do not** enter the number of returns.

Form	✓ here	Form	✓ here	Form	✓ here
W-2 series		5498		8027	
1098 series, 1099 series, W-2G		5498-ESA		1099-INT/OID for REMIC	
1042-S		5498-SA			

9 If you checked the box on line 7, state in detail why you need an additional extension of time. You must give a reason or your request will be denied. If you need more space, attach additional sheets.

Under penalties of perjury, I declare that I have examined this form, including any accompanying statements, and, to the best of my knowledge and belief, it is true, correct, and complete.

Signature ▶   Title ▶   Date ▶

General Instructions

Purpose of form. Use this form to request an extension of time to file any forms shown in line 8.

Who may file. Filers of returns submitted on paper, on magnetic media, or electronically may request an extension of time to file on this form.

Where to file. Send Form 8809 to IRS-Martinsburg Computing Center, Information Reporting Program, Attn: Extension of Time Coordinator, 240 Murall Dr., Kearneysville, WV 25430. To avoid delays, be sure the attention line is included on all envelopes and packages containing Form 8809.

How to file. When you request extensions of time to file for more than 50 filers for the forms shown in line 8, except Form 8027, you must submit the extension requests magnetically or electronically. For 10–50 filers, you are encouraged to submit the extension request magnetically or electronically.

If filing on paper with 50 or less filers, you must attach a list of the filers' names and taxpayer identification numbers. If you are filing the extension request magnetically or electronically, you do not have to provide a list.

Also, see Pub. 1220, Specifications for Filing Forms 1098, 1099, 5498, and W-2G Electronically or Magnetically and Pub. 1187, Specifications for Filing Form 1042-S, Foreign Person's U.S. Source Income Subject to Withholding, Electronically or Magnetically.

Note. Specifications for filing Forms W-2, Wage and Tax Statements, magnetically or electronically, are only available from the Social Security Administration (SSA). Call 1-800-SSA-6270 for more information.

When to file. File Form 8809 as soon as you know an extension of time to file is necessary. However, Form 8809 must be filed

For Privacy Act and Paperwork Reduction Act Notice, see page 2.   Cat. No. 10322N   Form **8809** (Rev. 7-2004)

continued

FIGURE 9.3 *continued*

by the due date of the returns. See the chart below that shows the due dates for filing this form on paper, magnetically, or electronically. IRS will respond in writing beginning in January. Filers and transmitters of Form W-2, Wage and Tax Statement, whose business has terminated, should follow the procedures in the 2004 Instructions for Forms W-2 and W-3 to request an extension.

If you are requesting an extension of time to file several types of forms, you may use one Form 8809, but you must file Form 8809 by the earliest due date. For example, if you are requesting an extension of time to file both 1099 series and 5498 series forms, you must file Form 8809 by February 28 (March 31 if you file electronically). You may complete more than one Form 8809 to avoid this problem. An extension cannot be granted if a request is filed after the due date of the original returns.

The due dates for filing Form 8809 are shown below.

IF you file Form . . .	MAGNETICALLY or on PAPER, then the due date is . . .	ELECTRONICALLY, then the due date is . . .
W-2 Series	Last day of February	March 31
W-2G	February 28	March 31
1042-S	March 15	March 15
1098 Series	February 28	March 31
1099 Series	February 28	March 31
5498 Series	May 31	May 31
8027	Last day of February	March 31

If any due date falls on a Saturday, Sunday, or legal holiday, file by the next business day.

Caution: *You do not have to wait for a response before filing your returns. File your returns as soon as they are ready. For all forms shown in line 8, except Form 8027, if you have received a response, do not send a copy of the letter or Form 8809 with your returns. If you have not received a response by the end of the extension period, file your returns. When filing Form 8027 on paper only, attach a copy of your approval letter. If an approval letter has not been received, attach a copy of your timely filed Form 8809.*

Extension period. The automatic extension is 30 days from the original due date. You may request one additional extension of not more than 30 days by submitting a second Form 8809 before the end of the first extension period (see Line 7 below). Requests for an additional extension of time to file information returns are **not** automatically granted. Generally requests for additional time are granted only in cases of extreme hardship or catastrophic event. The IRS will send you a letter of explanation approving or denying your request for an additional extension only.

Note. The automatic and any approved additional request will only extend the due date for filing the returns. It will not extend the due date for furnishing statements to recipients.

Penalty. If you file required information returns late and you have not applied for and received an approved extension of time to file, you may be subject to a late filing penalty. The amount of the penalty is based on when you file the correct information return. For more information on penalties, see the General Instructions for Forms 1099, 1098, 5498, and W-2G.

Specific Instructions

Tax year. You may request an extension for only 1 tax year on this form. If no tax year is shown, the IRS will assume you are requesting an extension for the returns currently due to be filed.

Line 1. Enter the name and complete mailing address, including room or suite number of the filer or transmitter requesting the extension of time. Use the name and address where you want the response sent. For example, if you are a preparer and want to receive the response, enter your client's complete name, care of (c/o) your firm, and your complete mailing address. Enter the name of someone who is familiar with this request whom the IRS can contact if additional information is required. Please provide your telephone number and e-mail address. If you act as transmitter for a group of filers, enter your name and address here, and see *How to file* on page 1.

Note. Approval or denial notification will be sent only to the person who requested the extension (filer or transmitter).

Line 2. Enter your nine-digit employer identification number (EIN) or qualified intermediary employer identification number (QI-EIN). If you are not required to have an EIN or QI-EIN, enter your social security number. Do not enter hyphens. Failure to provide this number, and the list of numbers if you are acting as a transmitter as explained under Line 1, will result in automatic denial of the extension request.

Line 3. For electronic or magnetic media only. If you filed Form 4419, Application for Filing Information Returns Electronically/ Magnetically, to file Forms 1042-S, 1098, 1099, 5498, W-2G, or 8027, and it was approved, the IRS-Martinsburg Computing Center assigned you a five-character Transmitter Control Code (TCC). Enter that TCC here. Leave this line blank if you (1) are requesting an extension to file any Forms W-2, (2) are requesting an extension to file forms on paper, or (3) have not yet received your TCC.

Line 7. Check this box if you have already received the automatic 30-day extension, but you need an additional extension for the same year and for the same forms. Do not check this box unless you received an original extension.

If you check this box, be sure to complete line 9. Then, sign and date the request.

Signature. No signature is required for the automatic 30-day extension. For an additional extension, Form 8809 must be signed by you or a person who is duly authorized to sign a return, statement, or other document.

Privacy Act and Paperwork Reduction Act Notice. We ask for the information on this form to carry out the Internal Revenue laws of the United States. Form 8809 is provided by the IRS to request an extension of time to file information returns. Regulations section 1.6081-1 requires you to provide the requested information if you desire an extension of time for filing an information return. If you do not provide the requested information, an extension of time for filing an information return may not be granted. Section 6109 requires you to provide your taxpayer identification number (TIN). Routine uses of this information include giving it to the Department of Justice for civil and criminal litigation, and cities, states, and the District of Columbia for use in administering their tax laws. We may also disclose this information to other countries under a tax treaty, or Federal, state, or local agencies to enforce Federal nontax criminal laws and to combat terrorism. The authority to disclose information to combat terrorism expired on December 31, 2003. Legislation is pending that would reinstate this authority.

You are not required to provide the information requested on a form that is subject to the Paperwork Reduction Act unless the form displays a valid OMB control number. Books or records relating to a form or its instructions must be retained as long as their contents may become material in the administration of any Internal Revenue law. Generally, tax returns and return information are confidential, as required by Code section 6103.

The time needed to complete and file this form will vary depending on individual circumstances. The estimated average time is: Recordkeeping, 2 hrs., 10 min.; Learning about the law or the form, 36 min.; Preparing and sending the form to the IRS, 28 min.

If you have comments concerning the accuracy of these time estimates or suggestions for making this form simpler, we would be happy to hear from you. You can write to the Tax Products Coordinating Committee, Western Area Distribution Center, Rancho Cordova, CA 95743-0001. Do not send the form to this address. Instead, see *Where to file* on page 1.

✿ *Printed on recycled paper*

When Are 1099s Issued?

1099-MISC forms must be issued when paying $600 per year or more to anyone for services rendered or rents. The forms must be distributed to payees by January 31. You then have until the last day of February to file them with the IRS. (Forms may be filed on the following Monday when the due date falls on a weekend.)

I recommend that you mail out all the forms in January. Then, hold off filing them until you get the address corrections back from the post office or the payees. During this time, you'll probably hear from people if their earnings records are different from your records. This will give you the time to reconcile the amounts before you send in the final 1099s.

When you find errors, naturally, you may send in corrected 1099s, but those attract attention. Try to get it right the first time.

Oh, and if you're holding them until the end of February, don't forget to mail them in.

Payroll and Payroll Taxes

To avoid complications and painful audits, once you start using regular help, go ahead and put them on payroll. In the short run, this may cost you a little more than using contractors. In the long run, though, you'll be better off. Depending on the form your business takes, you may even end up putting yourself, your spouse, or your children on payroll.

Payroll Across Entities

Before we get into the mechanics of payrolls, you'll need to know whether or not you're required to be paid wages. Let's look at a quick outline of personal and family compensation for the different forms of businesses you learned about in Chapter 3.

- **Sole proprietorships.** The owner may never be on payroll. The spouse and children may be—if they perform services for the company.
- **Partnerships, LLPs, and LLCs taxed as partnerships.** The rules are the same as for sole proprietorships. However, partners may receive guaranteed

payments. These are specific allocations, such as a monthly stipend. Partners may receive different amounts, based on the time or resources they contribute to the business. Be sure to allocate reasonable guaranteed payments to working partners. If you don't, as explained in Chapter 3, the IRS will assign a compensation level to you.

- **Corporations and LLCs taxed as corporations.** The shareholders and officers must be on the payroll, and reasonable compensation must be paid based on profits, time devoted to the business, and industry standards. Family members may be hired. Children's payroll is fully taxed. Officers are entitled to receive benefits like any employee. When it comes to profit-sharing and retirement plans, there are special rules to avoid discriminating in favor of highly compensated employees. Those rules won't affect you if you have no employees outside your family. If you have employees outside your family, this is where your advisory board will become really helpful. We won't be covering the details in this book—that's advanced tax planning. I just wanted you to be aware of the issue.
- **S-corporations.** Working shareholders must receive wages. The IRS has just started an audit campaign to catch omissions in this area. People who own more than 2 percent of the company are excluded from benefits.

With this in mind, let's start with the very touchy issue of hiring family members.

Hiring Family Members

Your e-mail is likely full of messages from scamsters wanting to sell you tax-cutting kits. One of the tax loopholes they push most aggressively is the practice of hiring family members. The IRS has shut down a number of operations whose primary focus is encouraging people to take fraudulent deductions for home and family expenses, including The Tax People and Tax Toolbox. The IRS has filed civil and/or criminal charges against tax professionals promoting this practice fraudulently.

Does that mean you should completely avoid hiring your spouse and children? Nonsense! There would be no Rothschild dynasty, or Ford Motor Company, or Disney, or Wal-Mart, or Harry and David, or any number of great companies if people had been afraid to build family businesses. To the contrary, many founders nurture dreams of having their children take over the family business. Some of today's major corporations started out as family businesses. Many publicly traded companies still have significant family leadership and ownership.[2]

So, please, don't let fear of the IRS prevent you from establishing your own dynasty. Besides, so much good comes from getting your family involved—and some of the benefits have nothing to do with taxes.

Intangible Benefits of Hiring Family

- Your spouse and children understand the time requirements and pressures you face. This reduces familial conflict.
- You see your family more often. You don't just see them rushing out in the morning or wolfing down dinner on the way out to the library or to meet friends.
- You have things to talk about together, rather than the vacuous, "So, how was your day?"
- Being in the same office or business location, you're apt to overhear conversations with their friends and be more tuned in to the good and bad things in their lives.
- Working with you, your family members have less time to get into the kind of trouble that comes from boredom, or too much time and money.
- They actually earn their "allowances." This is so important in eliminating that attitude of entitlement. You see other people's children growing up rude and demanding, without consideration for their parents. Your children won't act this way if they work for their spending money.
- When you are your family's employer, you know how much money they have available to spend. If your children suddenly come home with something unreasonably expensive, you won't fall for "I got a bonus at work." You'll know it's a warning sign.
- Your family knows the details of your business and where the important files and documents are. If anything happens to you, they can carry on.
- Each of your family members develops marketable skills. If your business fails, your spouse and kids will be able to get jobs and earn decent money. When your children head off to college, they'll be able to score higher-paying jobs because of their skills and experience.

---

2. *Family Business* magazine lists 250 of the world's top family-owned businesses grossing over $1.2 billion each: www.familybusinessmagazine.com/topglobal.html.

- Maintaining all the records and time sheets needed to prove your family members are working in the business develops discipline, organization skills, and reporting skills—all of which will be important in the business world.
- Finally, growing up together in the business, they may become passionate about getting an education they can bring back home to enhance the family's business.

Doing everything right, just the way the IRS demands, could be the glue that holds your family together.

See, it's in your best interest to avoid the temptation to take shortcuts and to pay your family members from the business without their earning the money. Think about the kind of message you will be sending them if you cheat. You would be telling them it's all right to lie; to operate outside the rules; to avoid your responsibility to your community; to shrug off authority.

Sure, we could get into long arguments about what your tax money pays for and how often it's wasted. But the bottom line: it does go toward maintaining a measure of sanity, safety, comfort, and predictability in a community of millions of passionate individualists.

Tax Benefits of Hiring Family

In Chapter 10 you'll learn all about the health care, insurance, and retirement benefits available to small business owners and their families. Right now, we're going to cover the payroll tax and compensation benefits available to you.

Special Tax Benefits of Hiring Your Child(ren) for Proprietorships and Partnerships

- Wages paid to your children are fully deductible to your business. Allowances are not. You can give your children more money than you give them now—but have them earn it. All of it will be deductible to you.
- If you are a sole proprietorship or partnership, the wages you pay your children who are under 18 are not subject to Social Security, Medicare, or federal unemployment taxes. Most states also waive payroll taxes—but not all, so be sure to check with your state's payroll tax authority. The website www .taxadmin.org/fta/link/forms.html has more information. On wages of $7,000, this strategy would save you nearly $1,100 (15.3 percent) worth of your self-employment taxes and $2,100 (30 percent) of federal and state income taxes. You've just cut $3,200 off your tax bill.

- If you had hired a nonchild employee, you'd be paying half the Social Security/Medicare, all the federal and state unemployment taxes, workers' compensation insurance, holidays, sick days, and, possibly, benefits. Those additional expenses would add more than $1,000 to your business overhead. Paying your child, you're just converting money you'd give to your child anyway into a deduction. Even when you spend twice as much on your child as before, the government pays for nearly half the money you give him or her.

Tax Benefits of Hiring Family in General

- For jobs requiring the use of cars, you may pay your spouse, your child, or yourself a mileage allowance or auto expenses. Be sure to get a mileage report and a copy of auto expenses to support your checks. The tax court just issued a ruling in support of the IRS's position. The IRS determined payments Continental Express, Inc.[3] made to its drivers were subject to the meals and entertainment rules. Continental Express didn't require substantiation of the expenses from its drivers. That ruling cut the company's deduction by 50 percent. Expect this same logic to be applied to other businesses. Warnings aside, paying your child $100 per month for deliveries and errands cuts your taxes by about $550 per year (15.3 percent self-employment taxes, 30 percent federal and state taxes). If your child submits expense reports, he or she doesn't report this income at all. You don't have to pay your spouse or child's auto upkeep from your own pocket.
- The money you pay your spouse or child doesn't need to go into their pockets. Arrange to set up IRAs or other retirement plans, to save $3,000–$3,500 of those wages each year. They will get a deduction for the contribution. Your child may end up paying no tax at all on that money, and your personal taxes are reduced. Chapter 10 describes the types of plans available.
- Chapter 10 explains how medical expenses may be deducted by small businesses. This could convert $5,000–$10,000 of unusable deductions into business deductions.

The financial and emotional rewards of hiring family are substantial. Only don't push it. If your family resists, don't force the issue relentlessly. You'll only

---

3. *Boyd v. Commissioner*, 122 T.C. No. 18 (4/24/04)—an S-corporation's shareholders were not entitled to a 100 percent deduction for the portion of the per diem allowance paid to drivers for non-meal expenses, including mileage.

take a good thing and turn in into something nasty. Knowing that you're doing it for their own good won't make them resent you less. Know when not to push. Just leave the door open for whenever they're ready to join you.

Better yet, sucker them into it. Just ask for a little help with some minor thing. Be sure to thank them and praise them. Once they get used to doing that, add one more little thing. As they do the small things automatically, and well . . . gradually add a few more tasks. Pretty soon, they'll be working by your side. Shhh, don't tell them I told you.

Now it's time to work on the payroll.

Paying Payroll

First of all, whenever you hire someone have them fill out two forms before they start working. The first is Form W-4, Employee's Withholding Allowance Certificate. (See Figure 9.4.) You've seen W-4s before. The second form is the I-9. (See Figure 9.5, which includes the form and instructions.) It's important that all your employees fill out this form for the benefit of immigration, even if they are citizens.

Compensation Methods

You may pay your employees in a variety of ways. Each one is acceptable, as long as you're consistent, using the same method for all people in the same position. If you pay people doing the same job at different rates, or using different methods, it won't be the IRS you'll have to face. Most likely it will be the wrath of the employee, in front of a labor judge. So, if you're going to discriminate in favor of friends or family members—give them a higher title or additional duties to justify the higher pay rate.

These are common compensation methods:

- **Hourly.** Your employees keep a time sheet or punch a time card. Multiply their hours worked by their hourly pay rate. If they work overtime, multiply the pay rate by 1.5 to get the overtime rate. For example, if the base hourly rate is $10, overtime is paid at $15 (10 × 1.5). A weekly payroll for fifty hours of work including ten hours of overtime would look like this:

  Base pay: 40 hours × $10 = $400
  Overtime pay: 10 hours × $15 = $150
  Total wages = $550

FIGURE 9.4 Form W-4, Employee's Withholding Allowance Certificate

Form W-4 (2004)

Purpose. Complete Form W-4 so that your employer can withhold the correct Federal income tax from your pay. Because your tax situation may change, you may want to refigure your withholding each year.

Exemption from withholding. If you are exempt, complete only lines 1, 2, 3, 4, and 7 and sign the form to validate it. Your exemption for 2004 expires February 16, 2005. See **Pub. 505,** Tax Withholding and Estimated Tax.

Note: *You cannot claim exemption from withholding if:* **(a)** *your income exceeds $800 and includes more than $250 of unearned income (e.g., interest and dividends) and* **(b)** *another person can claim you as a dependent on their tax return.*

Basic instructions. If you are not exempt, complete the **Personal Allowances Worksheet** below. The worksheets on page 2 adjust your withholding allowances based on itemized

deductions, certain credits, adjustments to income, or two-earner/two-job situations. Complete all worksheets that apply. **However, you may claim fewer (or zero) allowances.**

Head of household. Generally, you may claim head of household filing status on your tax return only if you are unmarried and pay more than 50% of the costs of keeping up a home for yourself and your dependent(s) or other qualifying individuals. See line **E** below.

Tax credits. You can take projected tax credits into account in figuring your allowable number of withholding allowances. Credits for child or dependent care expenses and the child tax credit may be claimed using the **Personal Allowances Worksheet** below. See **Pub. 919,** How Do I Adjust My Tax Withholding? for information on converting your other credits into withholding allowances.

Nonwage income. If you have a large amount of nonwage income, such as interest or dividends, consider making estimated tax payments using

Form 1040-ES, Estimated Tax for Individuals. Otherwise, you may owe additional tax.

Two earners/two jobs. If you have a working spouse or more than one job, figure the total number of allowances you are entitled to claim on all jobs using worksheets from only one Form W-4. Your withholding usually will be most accurate when all allowances are claimed on the Form W-4 for the highest paying job and zero allowances are claimed on the others.

Nonresident alien. If you are a nonresident alien, see the **Instructions for Form 8233** before completing this Form W-4.

Check your withholding. After your Form W-4 takes effect, use Pub. 919 to see how the dollar amount you are having withheld compares to your projected total tax for 2004. See Pub. 919, especially if your earnings exceed $125,000 (Single) or $175,000 (Married).

Recent name change? If your name on line 1 differs from that shown on your social security card, call 1-800-772-1213 to initiate a name change and obtain a social security card showing your correct name.

Personal Allowances Worksheet (Keep for your records.)

A Enter "1" for **yourself** if no one else can claim you as a dependent . . . . **A** _____

B Enter "1" if:
- You are single and have only one job; or
- You are married, have only one job, and your spouse does not work; or
- Your wages from a second job or your spouse's wages (or the total of both) are $1,000 or less.

. . **B** _____

C Enter "1" for your **spouse.** But, you may choose to enter "-0-" if you are married and have either a working spouse or more than one job. (Entering "-0-" may help you avoid having too little tax withheld.) . . . . . . **C** _____

D Enter number of **dependents** (other than your spouse or yourself) you will claim on your tax return . . . . . . **D** _____

E Enter "1" if you will file as **head of household** on your tax return (see conditions under **Head of household** above) . **E** _____

F Enter "1" if you have at least $1,500 of **child or dependent care expenses** for which you plan to claim a credit . . **F** _____

(**Note:** *Do* **not** *include child support payments. See* **Pub. 503,** *Child and Dependent Care Expenses, for details.*)

G **Child Tax Credit** (including additional child tax credit).
- If your total income will be less than $52,000 ($77,000 if married), enter "2" for each eligible child.
- If your total income will be between $52,000 and $84,000 ($77,000 and $119,000 if married), enter "1" for each eligible child plus "1" **additional** if you have four or more eligible children. . . . . **G** _____

H Add lines A through G and enter total here. **Note:** *This may be different from the number of exemptions you claim on your tax return.* ▶ **H** _____

For accuracy, complete all worksheets that apply.
- If you plan to **itemize or claim adjustments to income** and want to reduce your withholding, see the **Deductions and Adjustments Worksheet** on page 2.
- If you have **more than one job** or are **married and you and your spouse both work** and the combined earnings from all jobs exceed $35,000 ($25,000 if married) see the **Two-Earner/Two-Job Worksheet** on page 2 to avoid having too little tax withheld.
- If **neither** of the above situations applies, **stop here** and enter the number from line H on line 5 of Form W-4 below.

- **Cut here and give Form W-4 to your employer. Keep the top part for your records.** - - - - - - - - - - - - - - - - - - -

Form **W-4**	**Employee's Withholding Allowance Certificate**	OMB No. 1545-0010
Department of the Treasury Internal Revenue Service	▶ **Your employer must send a copy of this form to the IRS if: (a) you claim more than 10 allowances or (b) you claim "Exempt" and your wages are normally more than $200 per week.**	2004

1 Type or print your first name and middle initial | Last name | **2** Your social security number

Home address (number and street or rural route)

3 ☐ Single ☐ Married ☐ Married, but withhold at higher Single rate.
Note: *If married, but legally separated, or spouse is a nonresident alien, check the "Single" box.*

City or town, state, and ZIP code

4 **If your last name differs from that shown on your social security card, check here. You must call 1-800-772-1213 for a new card.** ▶ ☐

5 Total number of allowances you are claiming (from line **H** above **or** from the applicable worksheet on page 2) | **5** _____

6 Additional amount, if any, you want withheld from each paycheck . . . . | **6** $ _____

7 I claim exemption from withholding for 2004, and I certify that I meet **both** of the following conditions for exemption:
- Last year I had a right to a refund of **all** Federal income tax withheld because I had **no** tax liability **and**
- This year I expect a refund of **all** Federal income tax withheld because I expect to have **no** tax liability.

If you meet both conditions, write "Exempt" here . . . . ▶ | **7** _____

Under penalties of perjury, I certify that I am entitled to the number of withholding allowances claimed on this certificate, or I am entitled to claim exempt status.

Employee's signature
(Form is not valid unless you sign it.) ▶ _____ | Date ▶ _____

8 Employer's name and address (Employer: Complete lines 8 and 10 only if sending to the IRS.) | **9** Office code (optional) | **10** Employer identification number (EIN)

For Privacy Act and Paperwork Reduction Act Notice, see page 2. | Cat. No. 10220Q | Form **W-4** (2004)

continued

FIGURE 9.4 *continued*

Form W-4 (2004)   Page **2**

Deductions and Adjustments Worksheet

Note: *Use this worksheet **only** if you plan to itemize deductions, claim certain credits, or claim adjustments to income on your 2004 tax return.*

1 Enter an estimate of your 2004 itemized deductions. These include qualifying home mortgage interest, charitable contributions, state and local taxes, medical expenses in excess of 7.5% of your income, and miscellaneous deductions. (For 2004, you may have to reduce your itemized deductions if your income is over $142,700 ($71,350 if married filing separately). See **Worksheet 3** in Pub. 919 for details.) . . . **1** $ _____

2 Enter: $9,700 if married filing jointly or qualifying widow(er)
$7,150 if head of household
$4,850 if single
$4,850 if married filing separately . . . . **2** $ _____

3 **Subtract** line 2 from line 1. If line 2 is greater than line 1, enter "-0-" . . . . **3** $ _____

4 Enter an estimate of your 2004 adjustments to income, including alimony, deductible IRA contributions, and student loan interest **4** $ _____

5 **Add** lines 3 and 4 and enter the total. (Include any amount for credits from **Worksheet 7** in Pub. 919) . **5** $ _____

6 Enter an estimate of your 2004 nonwage income (such as dividends or interest) . . . . **6** $ _____

7 **Subtract** line 6 from line 5. Enter the result, but not less than "-0-" . . . . **7** $ _____

8 **Divide** the amount on line 7 by $3,000 and enter the result here. Drop any fraction . . . . . . **8** _____

9 Enter the number from the **Personal Allowances Worksheet,** line H, page 1 . . . . **9** _____

10 **Add** lines 8 and 9 and enter the total here. If you plan to use the **Two-Earner/Two-Job Worksheet,** also enter this total on line 1 below. Otherwise, **stop here** and enter this total on Form W-4, line 5, page 1 . **10** _____

Two-Earner/Two-Job Worksheet (See **Two earners/two jobs** on page 1.)

Note: *Use this worksheet **only** if the instructions under line H on page 1 direct you here.*

1 Enter the number from line H, page 1 (or from line 10 above if you used the **Deductions and Adjustments Worksheet**) **1** _____

2 Find the number in **Table 1** below that applies to the **LOWEST** paying job and enter it here . . . . **2** _____

3 If line 1 is **more than or equal to** line 2, subtract line 2 from line 1. Enter the result here (if zero, enter "-0-") and on Form W-4, line 5, page 1. **Do not** use the rest of this worksheet . . . . **3** _____

Note: *If line 1 is **less than** line 2, enter "-0-" on Form W-4, line 5, page 1. Complete lines 4–9 below to calculate the additional withholding amount necessary to avoid a year-end tax bill.*

4 Enter the number from line 2 of this worksheet . . . . **4** _____

5 Enter the number from line 1 of this worksheet . . . . **5** _____

6 **Subtract** line 5 from line 4 . . . . **6** _____

7 Find the amount in **Table 2** below that applies to the **HIGHEST** paying job and enter it here . . . . **7** $ _____

8 **Multiply** line 7 by line 6 and enter the result here. This is the additional annual withholding needed . . **8** $ _____

9 Divide line 8 by the number of pay periods remaining in 2004. For example, divide by 26 if you are paid every two weeks and you complete this form in December 2003. Enter the result here and on Form W-4, line 6, page 1. This is the additional amount to be withheld from each paycheck . . . . **9** $ _____

Table 1: Two-Earner/Two-Job Worksheet

Married Filing Jointly			Married Filing Jointly			All Others	
If wages from **HIGHEST** paying job are—	AND, wages from **LOWEST** paying job are—	Enter on line 2 above	If wages from **HIGHEST** paying job are—	AND, wages from **LOWEST** paying job are—	Enter on line 2 above	If wages from **LOWEST** paying job are—	Enter on line 2 above
$0 - $40,000	$0 - $4,000	0	$40,001 and over	31,001 - 38,000	6	$0 - $6,000	0
	4,001 - 8,000	1		38,001 - 44,000	7	6,001 - 11,000	1
	8,001 - 17,000	2		44,001 - 50,000	8	11,001 - 18,000	2
	17,001 and over	3		50,001 - 55,000	9	18,001 - 25,000	3
				55,001 - 65,000	10	25,001 - 31,000	4
$40,001 and over	$0 - $4,000	0		65,001 - 75,000	11	31,001 - 44,000	5
	4,001 - 8,000	1		75,001 - 85,000	12	44,001 - 55,000	6
	8,001 - 15,000	2		85,001 - 100,000	13	55,001 - 70,000	7
	15,001 - 22,000	3		100,001 - 115,000	14	70,001 - 80,000	8
	22,001 - 25,000	4		115,001 and over	15	80,001 - 100,000	9
	25,001 - 31,000	5				100,001 and over	10

Table 2: Two-Earner/Two-Job Worksheet

Married Filing Jointly		All Others	
If wages from **HIGHEST** paying job are—	Enter on line 7 above	If wages from **HIGHEST** paying job are—	Enter on line 7 above
$0 - $60,000	$470	$0 - $30,000	$470
60,001 - 110,000	780	30,001 - 70,000	780
110,001 - 150,000	870	70,001 - 140,000	870
150,001 - 270,000	1,020	140,001 - 320,000	1,020
270,001 and over	1,090	320,001 and over	1,090

FIGURE 9.5 Form I-9, Employment Eligibility Verification

U.S. Department of Justice
Immigration and Naturalization Service

OMB No. 1115-0136

Employment Eligibility Verification

Please read instructions carefully before completing this form. The instructions must be available during completion of this form. ANTI-DISCRIMINATION NOTICE: It is illegal to discriminate against work eligible individuals. Employers CANNOT specify which document(s) they will accept from an employee. The refusal to hire an individual because of a future expiration date may also constitute illegal discrimination.

Section 1. Employee Information and Verification. To be completed and signed by employee at the time employment begins.

Print Name: Last	First	Middle Initial	Maiden Name

Address (Street Name and Number)	Apt. #	Date of Birth (month/day/year)

City	State	Zip Code	Social Security #

I am aware that federal law provides for imprisonment and/or fines for false statements or use of false documents in connection with the completion of this form.

I attest, under penalty of perjury, that I am (check one of the following):
- [ ] A citizen or national of the United States
- [ ] A Lawful Permanent Resident (Alien # A_____)
- [ ] An alien authorized to work until ___ ___/___
  (Alien # or Admission #) _____

Employee's Signature   Date (month/day/year)

Preparer and/or Translator Certification. (To be completed and signed if Section 1 is prepared by a person other than the employee.) I attest, under penalty of perjury, that I have assisted in the completion of this form and that to the best of my knowledge the information is true and correct.

Preparer's/Translator's Signature   Print Name

Address (Street Name and Number. City. State. Zip Code)   Date (month/day/year)

Section 2. Employer Review and Verification. To be completed and signed by employer. Examine one document from List A OR examine one document from List B and one from List C, as listed on the reverse of this form, and record the title, number and expiration date, if any, of the document(s)

List A	OR	List B	AND	List C

Document title: _____
Issuing authority: _____
Document #: _____
Expiration Date (if any): ___/___/___
Document #: _____
Expiration Date (if any): ___/___/___

CERTIFICATION - I attest, under penalty of perjury, that I have examined the document(s) presented by the above-named employee, that the above-listed document(s) appear to be genuine and to relate to the employee named, that the employee began employment on (month/day/year) ___/___/___ and that to the best of my knowledge the employee is eligible to work in the United States. (State employment agencies may omit the date the employee began employment.)

Signature of Employer or Authorized Representative   Print Name   Title

Business or Organization Name   Address (Street Name and Number, City, State, Zip Code)   Date (month/day/year)

Section 3. Updating and Reverification. To be completed and signed by employer.

A. New Name (if applicable)   B. Date of rehire (month/day/year) (if applicable)

C. If employee's previous grant of work authorization has expired, provide the information below for the document that establishes current employment eligibility.

Document Title: _____   Document #: _____   Expiration Date (if any) ___/___/___

I attest, under penalty of perjury, that to the best of my knowledge, this employee is eligible to work in the United States, and if the employee presented document(s), the document(s) I have examined appear to be genuine and to relate to the individual.

Signature of Employer or Authorized Representative   Date (month/day/year)

Form I-9 (Rev. 11-21-91)N Page 2

continued

FIGURE 9.5 *continued*

U.S. Department of Justice
Immigration and Naturalization Service

OMB No. 1115-0136

Employment Eligibility Verification

INSTRUCTIONS
PLEASE READ ALL INSTRUCTIONS CAREFULLY BEFORE COMPLETING THIS FORM.

Anti-Discrimination Notice. It is illegal to discriminate against any individual (other than an alien not authorized to work in the U.S.) in hiring, discharging, or recruiting or referring for a fee because of that individual's national origin or citizenship status. It is illegal to discriminate against work eligible individuals. Employers **CANNOT** specify which document(s) they will accept from an employee. The refusal to hire an individual because of a future expiration date may also constitute illegal discrimination.

Section 1 - Employee. All employees, citizens and noncitizens, hired after November 6, 1986, must complete Section 1 of this form at the time of hire, which is the actual beginning of employment. **The employer is responsible for ensuring that Section 1 is timely and properly completed.**

Preparer/Translator Certification. The Preparer/Translator Certification must be completed if Section 1 is prepared by a person other than the employee. A preparer/translator may be used only when the employee is unable to complete Section 1 on his/her own. However, the employee must still sign Section 1.

Section 2 - Employer. For the purpose of completing this form, the term "employer" includes those recruiters and referrers for a fee who are agricultural associations, agricultural employers or farm labor contractors.

Employers must complete Section 2 by examining evidence of identity and employment eligibility within three (3) business days of the date employment begins. If employees are authorized to work, but are unable to present the required document(s) within three business days, they must present a receipt for the application of the document(s) within three business days and the actual document(s) within ninety (90) days. However, if employers hire individuals for a duration of less than three business days, Section 2 must be completed at the time employment begins. **Employers must record: 1)** document title; **2)** issuing authority; **3)** document number, **4)** expiration date, if any; and **5)** the date employment begins. Employers must sign and date the certification. Employees must present original documents. Employers may, but are not required to, photocopy the document(s) presented. These photocopies may only be used for the verification process and must be retained with the I-9. **However, employers are still responsible for completing the I-9.**

Section 3 - Updating and Reverification. Employers must complete Section 3 when updating and/or reverifying the I-9. Employers must reverify employment eligibility of their employees on or before the expiration date recorded in Section 1. Employers **CANNOT** specify which document(s) they will accept from an employee.

- If an employee's name has changed at the time this form is being updated/ reverified, complete Block A.

- If an employee is rehired within three (3) years of the date this form was originally completed and the employee is still eligible to be employed on the same basis as previously indicated on this form (updating), complete Block B and the signature block.

- If an employee is rehired within three (3) years of the date this form was originally completed and the employee's work authorization has expired **or** if a current employee's work authorization is about to expire (reverification), complete Block B and:
  - examine any document that reflects that the employee is authorized to work in the U.S. (see List A or C),
  - record the document title, document number and expiration date (if any) in Block C, and complete the signature block.

Photocopying and Retaining Form I-9. A blank I-9 may be reproduced, provided both sides are copied. The Instructions must be available to all employees completing this form. Employers must retain completed I-9s for three (3) years after the date of hire or one (1) year after the date employment ends, whichever is later.

For more detailed information, you may refer to the INS Handbook for Employers, (Form M-274). You may obtain the handbook at your local INS office.

Privacy Act Notice. The authority for collecting this information is the Immigration Reform and Control Act of 1986, Pub. L. 99-603 (8 USC 1324a).

This information is for employers to verify the eligibility of individuals for employment to preclude the unlawful hiring, or recruiting or referring for a fee, of aliens who are not authorized to work in the United States.

This information will be used by employers as a record of their basis for determining eligibility of an employee to work in the United States. The form will be kept by the employer and made available for inspection by officials of the U.S. Immigration and Naturalization Service, the Department of Labor and the Office of Special Counsel for Immigration Related Unfair Employment Practices.

Submission of the information required in this form is voluntary. However, an individual may not begin employment unless this form is completed, since employers are subject to civil or criminal penalties if they do not comply with the Immigration Reform and Control Act of 1986.

Reporting Burden. We try to create forms and instructions that are accurate, can be easily understood and which impose the least possible burden on you to provide us with information. Often this is difficult because some immigration laws are very complex. Accordingly, the reporting burden for this collection of information is computed as follows: **1)** learning about this form, 5 minutes; **2)** completing the form, 5 minutes; and **3)** assembling and filing (recordkeeping) the form, 5 minutes, for an average of 15 minutes per response. If you have comments regarding the accuracy of this burden estimate, or suggestions for making this form simpler, you can write to the Immigration and Naturalization Service, HQPDI, 425 I Street, N.W., Room 4034, Washington, DC 20536. OMB No. 1115-0136.

EMPLOYERS MUST RETAIN COMPLETED FORM I-9
PLEASE DO NOT MAIL COMPLETED FORM I-9 TO INS

Form I-9 (Rev. 11-21-91)N

FIGURE 9.5 *continued*

LISTS OF ACCEPTABLE DOCUMENTS

LIST A		LIST B		LIST C
Documents that Establish Both Identity and Employment Eligibility	**OR**	**Documents that Establish Identity**	**AND**	**Documents that Establish Employment Eligibility**

LIST A — Documents that Establish Both Identity and Employment Eligibility

1. U.S. Passport (unexpired or expired)

2. Certificate of U.S. Citizenship *(INS Form N-560 or N-561)*

3. Certificate of Naturalization *(INS Form N-550 or N-570)*

4. Unexpired foreign passport, with *I-551 stamp or* attached *INS Form I-94* indicating unexpired employment authorization

5. Alien Registration Receipt Card with photograph *(INS Form I-151 or I-551)*

6. Unexpired Temporary Card *(INS Form I-688)*

7. Unexpired Employment Authorization Card *(INS Form I-688A)*

8. Unexpired Reentry Permit *(INS Form I-327)*

9. Unexpired Refugee Travel Document *(INS Form I-571)*

10. Unexpired Employment Authorization Document issued by the INS which contains a photograph *(INS Form I-688B)*

LIST B — Documents that Establish Identity

1. Driver's license or ID card issued by a state or outlying possession of the United States provided it contains a photograph or information such as name, date of birth, sex, height, eye color and address

2. ID card issued by federal, state or local government agencies or entities, provided it contains a photograph or information such as name, date of birth, sex, height, eye color and address

3. School ID card with a photograph

4. Voter's registration card

5. U.S. Military card or draft record

6. Military dependent's ID card

7. U.S. Coast Guard Merchant Mariner Card

8. Native American tribal document

9. Driver's license issued by a Canadian government authority

For persons under age 18 who are unable to present a document listed above:

10. School record or report card

11. Clinic, doctor or hospital record

12. Day-care or nursery school record

LIST C — Documents that Establish Employment Eligibility

1. U.S. social security card issued by the Social Security Administration *(other than a card stating it is not valid for employment)*

2. Certification of Birth Abroad issued by the Department of State *(Form FS-545 or Form DS-1350)*

3. Original or certified copy of a birth certificate issued by a state, county, municipal authority or outlying possession of the United States bearing an official seal

4. Native American tribal document

5. U.S. Citizen ID Card *(INS Form I-197)*

6. ID Card for use of Resident Citizen in the United States *(INS Form I-179)*

7. Unexpired employment authorization document issued by the INS *(other then those listed under List A)*

Illustrations of many of these documents appear in Part 8 of the Handbook for Employers (M-274)

Form I-9 (Rev. 11-21-91)N Page 3

- **Salary.** Your employee gets paid the same amount each pay period, regardless of the hours worked. For instance, Nancy gets $50,000 per year, paid every two weeks. (Note: That does not mean twice a month. Twice a month is 24 pay periods.) Fifty-two weeks divided by two weeks results in twenty-six pay periods. Divide $50,000 by twenty-six weeks. That gives Nancy $1,923 per pay period. Often, when paying salaries, there is no overtime.[4]
- **Commission.** Employees are paid on a percentage of their sales or unit's revenues. Often, to equalize the compensation, they are paid some fixed rate against commission. That means they get a base pay of, let's say, $1,000 per month, before they earn commissions. When they earn the commissions, their advance payments get deducted from their commission checks. Josey's sales netted her a commission of $25,000 in December. She had been with the company since June and had received $9,000 in advances. When she gets paid her commissions in December, her employer will deduct the $9,000 from her net check, after taxes are taken out. The taxes will be computed on the full $25,000.
- **Bonus.** Regardless of the other compensation methods, there is nothing to prevent you from giving your employees bonuses at any time you choose. Bonuses may be rewards for individuals or teams hitting targets or goals. They may simply be split among all employees because you had a great month. Even small bonuses, given to everyone to celebrate, can really boost morale and build team spirit. The bonus is taxable, just like payroll.

Payroll Taxes

Along with a payroll come payroll taxes. When you cut the check to the IRS at the end of each payroll period, it looks like you're paying the IRS a ton of money. Actually, your payroll taxes are lower than you think. Most of the money you're sending to the IRS is the employees' own money, deducted from their paychecks. The only things the employer pays are:

Social Security 6.2 percent	Up to annual limit ($87,900 in 2004)
Medicare 1.45 percent	No limit

---

4. As we write this the new overtime law passed as the Fair Labor Standards Act, and the April 23, 2004, revisions have become effective on August 23, 2004, available at www.cch.com/press/news /2004/EmploymentLawBriefing.pdf. The Senate attempted to block implementations of the new rules, available at http://news.findlaw.com/politics/s/20040505/congressovertimedc.html.

| Federal Unemployment 8 percent | Up to $7,000 in wages |
| Total Federal Employer Taxes | 8.45 percent |

Add in your state unemployment taxes and other minor local taxes as well as mandatory workers' compensation, and you're paying about 10 percent of the employees' wages.

Preparing Payroll: Checks, Journals, Reports

You have several options when it comes to the accounting involved with payroll. You can do it the old-fashioned way, by hand, on paper, on columnar pads, or on journals. You can do it by hand using preprinted manual systems. One-Write is a very popular manual system. You also can use software that either integrates into your accounting system or stands alone. Or you can do the really smart thing—don't do it yourself.

Payroll record keeping is fraught with danger. There are so many little things that go wrong all the time, due to errors on your part, program glitches, or tax law changes you didn't get. Messing up on payroll tax forms unleashes a gusher of notices. Your time is worth more than that.

Make it all go away. Turn your payroll processing over to a professional. It will cost $30–$50 per month for a small company, but it's really worth it. A good payroll processing house will make your life so easy. Once you set up your employees, all you have to do is call in with their hours. Many companies let you log in and enter the hours yourself online, to be sure there are no errors. All the major companies have toll-free customer service centers. They prepare your payroll, cut payroll checks on your account, file all the tax returns, issue the W-2s, and—for a small extra fee—arrange to make your tax agency payments directly from your account. This will give you proof your payments were made on time. If they make an error, the payroll service must pay any penalties incurred, not you. (But if you don't have funds in your bank account on payroll day—that's your error, not theirs.)

The best thing about a payroll service is that if the IRS sends correspondence, the payroll services will handle all the responses. You don't need to be bothered. If you're the kind of person who cringes every time you see one of those white envelopes with the IRS eagle . . . a payroll service is for you.

Here are the top two companies in the industry:

- **Intuit's Complete Payroll (used to be CBS Payroll).** They are one of the few companies who will send your tax professional a copy of all reports, if you request this service. (Only one of my clients has ever had a problem with them in more than ten years.) They have additional services, including background checks before hiring, integration into QuickBooks, cafeteria plans, and retirement plans. Reach them at www.payroll.com/complete payroll.

- **Paychex.** Though geared toward companies with fifty employees or more, they will still work with mom-and-pop businesses. Their service reps are a joy to work with. While I have heard some grumbling from other tax professionals about their error rate, the last time was more than four years ago. (Only one of my clients had a problem with them, the same client who then went to Complete Payroll. Could that single client have been the problem?) Check them out at www.paychex.com.

For more options, visit the IRS's list of payroll providers, available at www.irs.gov/efile/lists/0,,id=101120,00.html.

Tips on Using Payroll Service Bureaus
- Be sure to get yourself assigned to a local personal account manager. He or she will be a big help to you at any time there is a problem or you have a question.
- Give your tax preparers online access so they can look up information and print out forms and reports when working on your business return, without ever bothering you.
- Using a payroll service will make it possible to offer your employees and yourself the ability to deposit paychecks directly into your accounts.
- You will be able to offer employee benefits economically, even if you're a small company.

Regardless of who prepares your payroll, it pays for you to get educated about it. The IRS provides detailed information on their Employment Taxes for Small Business website, available at www.irs.gov/businesses/small/content/0,,id=98942,00.html.

The IRS, SCORE, and your state government frequently offer free workshops on how to handle payroll and employee issues. Take advantage of the free information. It's important that you understand your responsibilities and how things work. It also will help you catch errors or oversights on the part of your staff, service bureau, or tax preparer. It's important that you know what forms must be filed and when.

FIGURE 9.6 Quarterly Payroll Tax Return Due Dates

When the last day of the month falls on a weekend or holiday, the forms and payments are due on the following business day.

Quarter	Date	Forms Due
1st Quarter (Q1)	April 30	941 and State
2nd Quarter (Q2)	July 31	941 and State
3rd Quarter (Q3)	October 31	941 and State
4th Quarter (Q4)	January 31 of following year	940, 941, 1099s, W-2s, and State

Reporting Payroll

Payroll tax returns are filed quarterly and annually. Figure 9.6 provides the due dates and lists the forms that are due. For the final quarter of the year, you must file both the quarterly reports and the annual summaries, for both the IRS and state, along with the W-2s and 1099s.

Form 941, as seen in Figure 9.7, is the quarterly report. You can also find this form on the IRS's website at www.irs.gov/pub/irs-pdf/f941.pdf.

Do you see that arrow and box next to line 8? If you've hired your children who are under age 18, check that box. That alerts the IRS that you didn't omit the Social Security and Medicare wages by accident. Remember, your children's wages are *not* subject to those taxes. Be prepared to get a flurry of mail from the IRS. It usually takes them three letters before they accept your explanation about having hired your child. But keep replying to them. You will get them to accept it—and next quarter the letters will start again.

You must send in your payroll tax payments within three business days after each payroll. (Some people have more time, but it's a good habit to get into.) When you file the returns at the end of the quarter, you should owe no more than $2,500. If you do owe more than that, send the payment in using the vouchers in that thin yellow book the IRS sent you when you got your employer identification number. The vouchers are the Form 8109s. Looking at Figure 9.8, you can see where you blacken the quarter and the type of tax; then take it to the bank with your check.

Form 941-V, shown in Figure 9.9, is the payment coupon for Form 941. If you are making payment by check, fill it in and send the check with it. Be sure to

FIGURE 9.7 Form 941, Employer's Quarterly Federal Tax Return

Form **941**
(Rev. January 2004)
Department of the Treasury
Internal Revenue Service (99)

Employer's Quarterly Federal Tax Return

▶ See separate instructions revised January 2004 for information on completing this return.
Please type or print.

Enter state code for state in which deposits were made **only** if different from state in address to the right ▶ | | (see page 2 of separate instructions).

Name (as distinguished from trade name)   Date quarter ended

Trade name, if any   Employer identification number

Address (number and street)   City, state, and ZIP code

OMB No. 1545-0029

T
FF
FD
FP
I
T

If address is different from prior return, check here ▶

IRS Use

1 1 1 1 1 1 1 1 1 1   2   3 3 3 3 3 3 3   4 4 4   5 5 5

6 7   8 8 8 8 8 8 8   9 9 9 9   10 10 10 10 10 10 10 10 10 10

A If you **do not have to file** returns in the future, check here ▶ | | and enter date final wages paid ▶
B If you are a seasonal employer, see **Seasonal employers** on page 1 of the instructions and check here ▶ | |

| 1 | Number of employees in the pay period that includes March 12th ▶ | **1** | |

2	Total wages and tips, plus other compensation (see separate instructions)	**2**	
3	Total income tax withheld from wages, tips, and sick pay	**3**	
4	Adjustment of withheld income tax for preceding quarters of **this calendar year**	**4**	
5	Adjusted total of income tax withheld (line 3 as adjusted by line 4)	**5**	
6	Taxable social security wages	**6a**		× 12.4% (.124) =	**6b**	
	Taxable social security tips	**6c**		× 12.4% (.124) =	**6d**	
7	Taxable Medicare wages and tips . . .	**7a**		× 2.9% (.029) =	**7b**	
8	Total social security and Medicare taxes (add lines 6b, 6d, and 7b). **Check here if wages are not subject to social security and/or Medicare tax** . . . . ▶			**8**	
9	Adjustment of social security and Medicare taxes (see instructions for required explanation) Sick Pay $_____ ± Fractions of Cents $_____ ± Other $_____ =	**9**	
10	Adjusted total of social security and Medicare taxes (line 8 as adjusted by line 9)	**10**	
11	**Total taxes** (add lines 5 and 10)	**11**	
12	Advance earned income credit (EIC) payments made to employees (see instructions) . . .	**12**	
13	Net taxes (subtract line 12 from line 11). **If $2,500 or more, this must equal line 17, column (d) below (or line D of Schedule B (Form 941))**	**13**	
14	Total deposits for quarter, including overpayment applied from a prior quarter	**14**	
15	**Balance due** (subtract line 14 from line 13). See instructions	**15**	
16	**Overpayment.** If line 14 is more than line 13, enter excess here ▶ $ _____		

and check if to be: | | Applied to next return **or** | | Refunded.

• **All filers:** If line 13 is less than $2,500, **do not** complete line 17 or Schedule B (Form 941).
• **Semiweekly schedule depositors:** Complete Schedule B (Form 941) and check here . . . . ▶ | |
• **Monthly schedule depositors:** Complete line 17, columns (a) through (d), and check here. . . . . ▶ | |

17	**Monthly Summary of Federal Tax Liability.** (Complete **Schedule B (Form 941)** instead, if you were a semiweekly schedule depositor.)			
	(a) First month liability	**(b)** Second month liability	**(c)** Third month liability	**(d)** Total liability for quarter

Third Party Designee

Do you want to allow another person to discuss this return with the IRS (see separate instructions)? | | **Yes. Complete the following.** | | **No**

Designee's name ▶   Phone no. ▶ ( )   Personal identification number (PIN) ▶ | | | | | |

Sign Here

Under penalties of perjury, I declare that I have examined this return, including accompanying schedules and statements, and to the best of my knowledge and belief, it is true, correct, and complete.

Signature ▶   Print Your Name and Title ▶   Date ▶

For Privacy Act and Paperwork Reduction Act Notice, see back of Payment Voucher.   Cat. No. 17001Z   Form **941** (Rev. 1-2004)

FIGURE 9.8 Form 8109-B, Federal Tax Deposit Coupon

AMOUNT OF DEPOSIT (Do NOT type, please print.)

DOLLARS — CENTS

MONTH TAX YEAR ENDS →

EMPLOYER IDENTIFICATION NUMBER →

BANK NAME/ DATE STAMP

Name _____

Address _____

City _____

State _____ ZIP _____

Telephone number ( )

Darken only one **TYPE OF TAX**

- 941
- 990-C
- 943
- 720
- CT-1
- 940

- 945
- 1120
- 990-T
- 990-PF
- 1042

Darken only one **TAX PERIOD**

- 1st Quarter
- 2nd Quarter
- 3rd Quarter
- 4th Quarter

IRS USE ONLY

35

FOR BANK USE IN MICR ENCODING

Federal Tax Deposit Coupon
Form 8109-B (Rev. 12-2002)

⤒ SEPARATE ALONG THIS LINE AND SUBMIT TO DEPOSITARY WITH PAYMENT ⤒ OMB NO. 1545-0257

Note: Except for the name, address, and telephone number, entries must be made in pencil. **Use soft lead** *(for example, a #2 pencil) so that the entries can be read more accurately by optical scanning equipment. The name, address, and telephone number may be completed other than by hand.* **You cannot use photocopies of the coupons to make your deposits. Do not** *staple, tape, or fold the coupons.*

Purpose of form. Use Form 8109-B to make a tax deposit **only** in the following two situations:

1. You have not yet received your resupply of preprinted deposit coupons (Form 8109); or

2. You are a new entity and have already been assigned an employer identification number (EIN), but you have not received your initial supply of preprinted deposit coupons (Form 8109). If you have not received your EIN, see **Exceptions** below.

Note: If you do not receive your resupply of deposit coupons and a deposit is due or you do not receive your initial supply within 5–6 weeks of receipt of your EIN, call 1-800-829-4933.

How to complete the form. Enter your name as shown on your return or other IRS correspondence, address, and EIN in the spaces provided. **Do not** make a name or address change on this form (see **Form 8822,** Change of Address). If you are required to file a Form 1120, 990-C, 990-PF (with net investment income), 990-T, enter the month in which your tax year ends in the MONTH TAX YEAR ENDS boxes. For example, if your tax year ends in January, enter 01; if it ends in December, enter 12. Make your entries for EIN and MONTH TAX YEAR ENDS (if applicable) as shown in **Amount of deposit** below.

Exceptions. If you have applied for an EIN, have not received it, and a deposit must be made, **do not** use Form 8109-B. Instead, send your payment to the IRS address where you file your return. Make your check or money order payable to the United States Treasury and show on it your name (as shown on **Form SS-4,** Application for Employer Identification Number), address, kind of tax, period covered, and date you applied for an EIN. **Do not** use Form 8109-B to deposit delinquent taxes assessed by the IRS. Pay those taxes directly to the IRS. See **Circular E,** Employer's Tax Guide, for information on depositing by electronic funds transfer.

Amount of deposit. Enter the amount of the deposit in the space provided. Enter the amount legibly, forming the characters as shown below:

Hand print money amounts without using dollar signs, commas, a decimal point, or leading zeros. If the deposit is for whole dollars only, enter "00" in the CENTS boxes. For example, a deposit of $7,635.22 would be entered like this:

DOLLARS — CENTS

7 6 3 5 2 2

Caution: *Darken one space each in the TYPE OF TAX and TAX PERIOD columns as explained below. Darken the space to the left of the applicable tax form and tax period. Darkening the wrong space may delay proper crediting of your account.*

Types of Tax

Form 941 Employer's Quarterly Federal Tax Return (includes Forms **941-M, 941-PR,** and **941-SS**)

Form 943 Employer's Annual Tax Return for Agricultural Employers

Form 945 Annual Return of Withheld Federal Income Tax

Form 720 Quarterly Federal Excise Tax Return

Form CT-1 Employer's Annual Railroad Retirement Tax Return

Form 940 Employer's Annual Federal Unemployment (FUTA) Tax Return (includes Forms **940-EZ** and **940-PR**)

Form 1120 U.S. Corporation Income Tax Return (includes Form **1120** series of returns and Form **2438**)

Form 990-C Farmers' Cooperative Association Income Tax Return

Form 990-T Exempt Organization Business Income Tax Return

Form 990-PF Return of Private Foundation or Section 4947(a)(1) Nonexempt Charitable Trust Treated as a Private Foundation

Form 1042 Annual Withholding Tax Return for U.S. Source Income of Foreign Persons

Marking the Proper Tax Period

Payroll taxes and withholding. For Forms 941, 940, 943, 945, CT-1, and 1042, if your liability was incurred during:

- January 1 through March 31, darken the 1st quarter space
- April 1 through June 30, darken the 2nd quarter space
- July 1 through September 30, darken the 3rd quarter space
- October 1 through December 31, darken the 4th quarter space

Note: If the liability was incurred during one quarter and deposited in another quarter, darken the space for the quarter in which the tax liability was incurred. For example, if the liability was incurred in March and deposited in April, darken the 1st quarter space.

Excise taxes. For Form 720, follow the instructions above for Forms 941, 940, etc. For Form 990-PF, with net investment income, follow the instructions below for Form 1120, 990-C, etc.

Income Taxes (Form 1120, 990-C, 990-T, and 2438). To make an estimated tax deposit for any quarter of the current tax year, **darken only the 1st quarter space.**

Example 1. If your tax year ends on December 31, 2003, and a deposit for 2003 is being made between January 1 and December 31, 2003, darken the 1st quarter space.

Department of the Treasury
Internal Revenue Service

Cat. No. 61042S

Form **8109-B** (Rev. 12-2002)

FIGURE 9.9 Form 941-V, Payment Voucher

Form 941-V
Payment Voucher

Purpose of Form

Complete Form 941-V if you are making a payment with **Form 941,** Employer's Quarterly Federal Tax Return. We will use the completed voucher to credit your payment more promptly and accurately, and to improve our service to you.

If you have your return prepared by a third party and make a payment with that return, please provide this payment voucher to the return preparer.

Making Payments With Form 941

Make your payment with Form 941 **only if:**

• Your net taxes for the quarter (line 13 on Form 941) are less than $2,500 and you are paying in full with a timely filed return or

• You are a monthly schedule depositor making a payment in accordance with the **Accuracy of Deposits Rule.** (See section 11 of **Circular E (Pub. 15),** Employer's Tax Guide, for details.) This amount may be $2,500 or more.

Otherwise, you must deposit the amount at an authorized financial institution or by electronic funds transfer. (See section 11 of Circular E (Pub. 15) for deposit instructions.) Do not use the Form 941-V payment voucher to make Federal tax deposits.

Caution: *If you pay amounts with Form 941 that should have been deposited, you may be subject to a penalty. See* **Deposit Penalties** *in section 11 of Circular E (Pub. 15).*

Specific Instructions

Box 1—Employer identification number (EIN). If you do not have an EIN, apply for one on **Form SS-4,** Application for Employer Identification Number, and write "Applied For" and the date you applied in this entry space.

Box 2—Amount paid. Enter the amount paid with Form 941.

Box 3—Tax period. Darken the capsule identifying the quarter for which the payment is made. Darken only one capsule.

Box 4—Name and address. Enter your name and address as shown on Form 941.

• Enclose your check or money order made payable to the "United States Treasury." Be sure also to enter your EIN, "Form 941," and the tax period on your check or money order. Do not send cash. Please do not staple this voucher or your payment to the return (or to each other).

• Detach the completed voucher and send it with your payment and Form 941 to the address provided on the back of Form 941.

Note: *You* **must** *also complete the entity information above line A on Form 941.*

▼ Detach Here and Mail With Your Payment and Tax Return. ▼ Form **941-V** (2004)

Form **941-V** Department of the Treasury Internal Revenue Service (99)	**Payment Voucher** ▶ Do not staple or attach this voucher to your payment.	OMB No. 1545-0029 2004

1 Enter your employer identification number (EIN).	2 Enter the amount of your payment. ▶	Dollars	Cents

3 Tax period	4 Enter your business name (individual name if sole proprietor).

O 1st Quarter	O 3rd Quarter	Enter your address.
O 2nd Quarter	O 4th Quarter	Enter your city, state, and ZIP code.

FIGURE 9.10 Form 940, Employer's Annual Federal Unemployment Tax Return

Form **940**	**Employer's Annual Federal Unemployment (FUTA) Tax Return**	OMB No. 1545-0028
Department of the Treasury Internal Revenue Service (99)	▶ See separate Instructions for Form 940 for information on completing this form.	20**03**

	T	
	FF	
	FD	
	FP	
	I	
	T	

You must complete this section. ▶

Name (as distinguished from trade name)   Calendar year

Trade name, if any   Employer identification number (EIN)

Address (number and street)   City, state, and ZIP code

A Are you required to pay unemployment contributions to only one state? (If "No," skip questions B and C.) ☐ Yes ☐ No

B Did you pay all state unemployment contributions by February 2, 2004? ((1) If you deposited your total FUTA tax when due, check "Yes" if you paid all state unemployment contributions by February 10, 2004. (2) If a 0% experience rate is granted, check "Yes." (3) If "No," skip question C.) . . . . ☐ Yes ☐ No

C Were all wages that were taxable for FUTA tax also taxable for your state's unemployment tax? . . . . . ☐ Yes ☐ No

If you answered "No" to any of these questions, you must file Form 940. If you answered "Yes" to all the questions, you may file Form 940-EZ, which is a simplified version of Form 940. (Successor employers, see **Special credit for successor employers** on page 3 of the separate instructions.) You can get Form 940-EZ by calling 1-800-TAX-FORM (1-800-829-3676) or from the IRS website at **www.irs.gov.**

If you will not have to file returns in the future, check here (see **Who Must File** in the separate instructions) **and complete and sign the return** . . . . ▶ ☐

If this is an Amended Return, check here (see **Amended Returns** in the separate instructions) . . . . ▶ ☐

Part I	**Computation of Taxable Wages**

1 Total payments (including payments shown on lines 2 and 3) during the calendar year for services of employees **1**

2 Exempt payments. (Explain all exempt payments, attaching additional sheets if necessary.) ▶ -- **2**

3 Payments of more than $7,000 for services. Enter only amounts over the first $7,000 paid to each employee (see separate instructions). Do not include any exempt payments from line 2. The $7,000 amount is the Federal wage base. Your state wage base may be different. **Do not use your state wage limitation** **3**

4 Add lines 2 and 3 . . . . ▶ **4**

5 **Total taxable wages** (subtract line 4 from line 1) . . . . ▶ **5**

Be sure to complete both sides of this form, and sign in the space provided on the back.

For Privacy Act and Paperwork Reduction Act Notice, see separate instructions. ▼ **DETACH HERE** ▼   Cat. No. 11234O   Form **940** (2003)

Form **940-V**	**Payment Voucher**	OMB No. 1545-0028
Department of the Treasury Internal Revenue Service	**Use this voucher only when making a payment with your return.**	20**03**

Complete boxes 1, 2, and 3. Do not send cash, and do not staple your payment to this voucher. Make your check or money order payable to the "United States Treasury." Be sure to enter your employer identification number (EIN), "Form 940," and "2003" on your payment.

1 Enter your employer identification number (EIN).	**2** **Enter the amount of your payment.** ▶	Dollars	Cents
	3 Enter your business name (individual name for sole proprietors).		
	Enter your address.		
	Enter your city, state, and ZIP code.		

continued

FIGURE 9.10 *continued*

Form 940 (2003)   Page **2**

Part II   **Tax Due or Refund**

1   Gross FUTA tax. (Multiply the wages from Part I, line 5, by .062) . . . . | 1
2   Maximum credit. (Multiply the wages from Part I, line 5, by .054) . | 2 |
3   Computation of tentative credit (**Note:** *All taxpayers must complete the applicable columns.*)

(a) Name of state	(b) State reporting number(s) as shown on employer's state contribution returns	(c) Taxable payroll (as defined in state act)	(d) State experience rate period		(e) State experience rate	(f) Contributions if rate had been 5.4% (col. (c) x .054)	(g) Contributions payable at experience rate (col. (c) x col. (e))	(h) Additional credit (col. (f) minus col.(g)) If 0 or less, enter -0-.	(i) Contributions paid to state by 940 due date
			From	To					

3a   Totals . . . ▶

3b   **Total tentative credit** (add line 3a, columns (h) and (i) only—for late payments, also see the instructions for Part II, line 6) . . . . ▶ | 3b

4
5

6   **Credit:** Enter the smaller of the amount from Part II, line 2 or line 3b; or the amount from the worksheet on page 5 of the separate instructions . . . . | 6
7   **Total FUTA tax** (subtract line 6 from line 1). If the result is over $100, also complete Part III . . | 7
8   Total FUTA tax deposited for the year, including any overpayment applied from a prior year . . | 8
9   **Balance due** (subtract line 8 from line 7). Pay to the "United States Treasury." If you owe more than $100, see **Depositing FUTA Tax** on page 3 of the separate instructions . . . . . ▶ | 9
10   **Overpayment** (subtract line 7 from line 8). Check if it is to be: ☐ **Applied to next return** or ☐ **Refunded** . . . . ▶ | 10

Part III   **Record of Quarterly Federal Unemployment Tax Liability** (Do not include state liability.) **Complete only if line 7 is over $100.** See page 6 of the separate instructions.

Quarter	First (Jan. 1–Mar. 31)	Second (Apr. 1–June 30)	Third (July 1–Sept. 30)	Fourth (Oct. 1–Dec. 31)	Total for year
Liability for quarter					

Third Party Designee   Do you want to allow another person to discuss this return with the IRS (see separate instructions)? ☐ **Yes.** Complete the following.   ☐ **No**

Designee's name ▶   Phone no. ▶ ( )   Personal identification number (PIN) ▶ ☐☐☐☐☐

Under penalties of perjury, I declare that I have examined this return, including accompanying schedules and statements, and, to the best of my knowledge and belief, it is true, correct, and complete, and that no part of any payment made to a state unemployment fund claimed as a credit was, or is to be, deducted from the payments to employees.

Signature ▶   Title (Owner, etc.) ▶   Date ▶

✹

Form **940** (2003)

include FYTIN (form number, year, and taxpayer ID number). If the balance due is more than $2,500, pay it via the online EFTPS system, or take Form 8109 to the bank with a check.

Form 940, which you can see in Figure 9.10, is the annual unemployment tax return. The final tax rate only ends up being 0.8 percent if you file the return on time and pay your state unemployment taxes on time. If you default on the state tax, you end up paying 6.2 percent for federal unemployment.

W-2s must be mailed out to employees by January 31. No payment goes with these forms. They must be sent to the Social Security Administration by February

28 or 29, if applicable. Do the same thing you did with the 1099s; hold off filing them until the last minute. That way, you'll have time to update addresses and correct any errors employees find.

Form W-3 is the summary of all the W-2s. Be sure all the boxes on the W-2s add up to the totals on the W-3. Included on the W-2 is the information about employee benefits, which we'll discuss in the next section.

Employee Benefits

Companies may offer their employees an array of benefits. Owners can only participate if they are incorporated. On the other hand, S-corporation shareholders who own 2 percent or more of the company are excluded from most benefits.

Two of the common benefits employees receive are sick pay and vacations. Were you aware these benefits are not a legal requirement in all states—particularly for small companies? Paying for these for employees is more custom than law. Check with your own state's labor commission to learn the standards in your state.

You can offer some fringe benefit plans for employees that they pay for themselves—and would gladly. When it comes to medical and insurance plans, even if you don't pay the premiums, your employees could get some terrific tax savings. You pay a small administrative fee, offset by the tax savings from the plan, and for your employees it's like a small raise. They save nearly 40 percent of the amount they spend anyway on things such as medical insurance, medical costs, or dependent care (7.65 percent Social Security/Medicare + 25 percent federal tax + 5 percent state tax). For the average family paying $3,000 in medical premiums, that's at least $100 per month into their pockets, perhaps double if they have dependent care. As the employer, you save about 12 percent of the cost of those premiums because the employer's taxes don't apply to that money either. That savings will more than cover your administrative costs for the plan.

Plans Where Employees' Money Is Spent

Here are two popular fringe benefit plans employees pay for.

- **Premium Only Plans (POPs).** The employees pay their medical insurance premiums. Premiums are deducted from their wages before taxes are computed.

- **Flexible Spending Accounts (FSAs).**[5] These accounts let your staff deduct their medical, dental, optical, and therapy costs, as well as dependent care expenses (child or elder care). Dependent care is limited to $5,000 per year. Employers, or your payroll service, sets up limits on the medical spending.

Plans Where Your Money Is Spent

Setting up employee plans for small companies has been complicated and expensive. Now that the payroll services are offering complete administration packages, even a small employer can offer these benefits. It only costs a few extra dollars per employee per month for the administration.

- **Group term life insurance.** Employee benefits up to $50,000 are free to the employee. The premiums for coverage exceeding $50,000 are added back to their wages. Have the insurance expert on your advisory team help you find the right plan.
- **Education benefits.** You may reimburse employees for up to $5,250 per year. It's tax-free to them and a full deduction to you.
- **Employee death benefits.** Employee death benefits may be paid to the employee's family to help out with the funeral and other related costs. It would be a deduction to the employer. And it would be income to the employee if the benefit is based on the employee's past service or other economic benefit due to the employee.
- **Meals and lodging.** Some companies set up a cafeteria offering free meals to all employees to save time off from work or to ensure they get some nutritious meals. When you offer it to all employees, the company may deduct the costs without charging the employees. I'd be careful about this if you're working from home and it's just you and your family. Lodging is a bit more interesting. When your employee (such as an apartment manager) must live on the premises so they are available full-time, the lodging is free, without tax consequences to the employee.

Companies providing fringe benefits to qualified employees may deduct the costs of the benefits and administration. You'll want to think carefully about setting up these plans, because once you start, employees expect them. To keep

---

5. The FSA Feds site's FAQs page provides a comprehensive set of answers to most FSA questions, available at www.fsafeds.com/fsafeds/faq.asp.

employees for the long term, you'll need to be generous. Be sure to build the costs of the perquisites into your product or service costs. On the other hand, many of these benefits reduce your tax and insurance costs and you can use that savings to pay for the benefits.

There are a variety of retirement plans and profit-sharing plans you can offer your employees. Chapter 10 describes most of them as they apply to business owners and related parties. The spreadsheets in Tables 10.1 and 10.2 in Chapter 10 will give you an overview of each plan, with the limits, set-up dates, and funding dates as well as the pros and cons of each plan.

Employee Ownership and Stock Options

Whether for tax planning or retention, employee ownership is an appealing option. Since the IPO craze of the 1990s, highly skilled employees are starting to expect a share of the equity and growth of a company.

Using stock is an excellent lure to hire an employee whose price you couldn't otherwise afford. Giving up stock, you can offer a salary you can presently afford, with a promise of riches as the company grows. The right highly talented employee, who isn't also highly strung, will make the difference between growing slowly or explosively. Which is better, giving up 5 percent of a company worth $10 million, or owning 100 percent of a company worth $250,000? That's the kind of difference the right employee(s) can make.

You can also use employee stock ownership plans (ESOPs)[6] to avoid paying taxes. When you turn over 100 percent of the company's stock to an ESOP, the ESOP pays no taxes on the company's profits. It does mean giving up stock to each employee as they become eligible and you will own less of the company. But you will also own a share of the ESOP. However, with all the tax money available to the company for growth, what you've given up may earn you a greater reward—allowing you to build a bigger company.

Companies such as JetBlue and United Airlines have substantial employee ownership. You don't have to be a large company to do this. Kinko's started out quite small and was entirely employee-owned. With great employee training and participation, they grew dramatically. In February 2004, Federal Express paid $2.4 billion for the company. You can just bet those Kinko's employees' retirement plans

---

6. The National Center for Employee Ownership (NCEO) has an extensive ESOP resource section, available at www.nceo.org/esops/esop_articles.html.

look healthy. All the profit is sitting in their ESOP accounts, ready to be drawn whenever they want to retire.

You can also offer stock options.[7] The rules on when the options are taxable, when the employee can exercise them, and what taxes get paid when are very complex. I prefer to leave all that in the hands of the tax and labor attorneys. If you want to study this in depth, you'll find a feast at the National Center for Employee Ownership's website at www.nceo.org.

Summing Up Employees

Overall, you and your family can gain great benefits by having eligible family members go on the payroll. The trick is to pay wages only for valuable services performed on behalf of the business. Do what the IRS asks of you—your family will be closer-knit and your business will grow in leaps and bounds.

Just as the benefits are good for your family, think of how treating your employees well affects them. Seeing you extend yourself to provide them with ways to make their money go further will increase their loyalty to you.

At tax educational seminars I often hear the presenters speak about how to devise retirement and benefit plans that cut the employees out. Isn't that the silliest thing you've ever heard? Why would you not want to give your employees benefits? Cost? Sure, cost is a factor. But think of the cost of hiring, training, and teaching a new employee because you didn't value the previous employee enough. Cheap labor is not cheap! New hires make mistakes—sometimes mistakes big enough to cost you important clients.

So, as you prosper, see to it that your employees do, too. Get some good planning with the help of the employee benefit specialist on your advisory team—and you'll ensure being able to retire in style.

Employee and Independent Contractor Resources

- **Form I-9, Employment Eligibility Verification.** http://uscis.gov /graphics/formsfee/forms/files/i-9.pdf
- **Form SS-8, Determination of Worker Status.** www.irs.gov/pub/irs-pdf /fss8.pdf

---

7. NCEO also provides an extensive stock options resource at www.nceo.org/options/option_articles .html.

- **Form W-4, Employee's Withholding Allowance Certificate.** www.irs .gov/pub/irs-pdf/fw4.pdf
- **Form W-9, Request for Taxpayer Identification Number and Certification.** www.irs.gov/pub/irs-pdf/fw9.pdf
- **Form 940, Employer's Annual Federal Unemployment (FUTA) Tax Return and Form 940-V Payment Voucher.** www.irs.gov/pub/irs-pdf /f940.pdf
- **Form 941, Employer's Quarterly Federal Tax Return and Form 941-V Payment Voucher.** www.irs.gov/pub/irs-pdf/f941.pdf
- **Form 8109, Federal Tax Deposit Coupon.** www.irs.gov/pub/irs-pdf /f8109b.pdf
- **Form 8809, Request for Extension of Time to File Information Returns.** www.irs.gov/pub/irs-pdf/f8809.pdf
- **Links to State Tax Agencies.** www.taxadmin.org/fta/link/forms.html
- **Intuit's Complete Payroll (used to be CBS Payroll).** www.payroll.com /completepayroll
- **Paychex.** www.paychex.com
- **IRS's list of payroll providers.** www.irs.gov/efile/lists/0,,id=101120,00 .html
- **Service Corps of Retired Executives (SCORE).** www.score.org
- *Family Business* **Magazine.** www.familybusinessmagazine.com: An excellent collection of articles, resources, and information for small family businesses intending to become major businesses.
- **National Center for Employee Ownership.** www.nceo.org: A private, nonprofit membership and research organization providing unbiased information on employee stock ownership plans (ESOPs), broadly granted employee stock options and related programs, and ownership culture.

10

OWNERS' FRINGE BENEFITS, RETIREMENT, AND DEFERRING TAXES

Income tax is the fine you pay for thriving so fast.

—TOM ANTION

There are wonderful benefits to being in business for yourself. You may spend as much as you like to improve yourself, educate yourself, care for your health, and plan for your ultimate triumphant retirement. While I won't cover all the potential benefits here, I will include some options you won't find anywhere else. For the ones everyone covers—you know the usual suspects—simply go to an Internet search engine (such as www.google.com) and type in "fringe benefits."

Fringe Benefits and Reimbursements

When you're an employee in a responsible position, you are always offered an array of fringe benefits to induce you to take the job. You get vacation, sick time, bonuses, stock options, medical plans, and various reimbursement plans for things like child care, education, auto, and meals. Your employer pays for all that.

Having your own company means you may offer those things to your employees. (See Chapter 9.) But if you get them, the cost for them comes out of your own pocket. On the other hand, if you handle the benefits properly, Uncle Sam will pick up a nice part of the freight.

Health Insurance

The form of business you've chosen (see Chapter 3) will govern whether or not your insurance expenses are deductible in your business. C-corporations get to deduct all employee fringe benefits, and as an employee of your own C-corporation, you're treated the same way as other employees. On the other hand, when you're self-employed, in a partnership, or in an S-corporation, you don't get a business deduction.[1] You may deduct your family's health insurance costs on page 1 of your tax return, as an adjustment to income. If you have an S-corporation, this doesn't matter as much, because you're not paying self-employment taxes on your profits. But, when your income is on your Schedule C or through a partnership (or LLC filing as a partnership), all your profit is subject to an extra 15.3 percent levy for Social Security/Medicare taxes.

Not being able to deduct your family's medical insurance costs of $300 per month from your business costs you an extra $550 in taxes each year. Toss in the cost of routine out-of-pocket medical expenses (braces, contacts, eyeglasses, annual checkups, co-pays), which might average another $1,200 for a family of three, and your extra taxes go up more than $700 per year.

Health Savings Accounts (HSAs)

Congress voted Health Savings Accounts into law on December 8, 2003, and insurance companies are still scrambling to provide these plans. So coverage has been hard to find. To help you find insurance carriers for these plans in your state, eHealthInsurance.com put a special section up on their website.

What's so special about these accounts? Your medical insurance costs are cut because your deductible must be at least $1,000. Your medical expenses drop because no co-pays are permitted. A Health Savings Account is something like an IRA. The money you deposit is deductible in the current year. You can draw that money out to pay for medical expenses, tax-free. Or, you can leave it invested for years, until you really need the money to cover medical expenses or until you get old and infirm—and need to spend money on in-home care or long-term care. Or, you can just draw it out and pay taxes, like an IRA. For more information, refer to my website at www.taxmama.com/Articles/HSA1.html.

---

1. You may have seen a company pay the officers' medical insurance or expenses in an S-corporation. The money is added to the wages as additional compensation. Or it is treated as dividends or as repayments of the officer's loan.

Code Section 105 Medical Reimbursement Plans

Created for farming families whose lives are so closely tied to their businesses, this is a special provision of the tax code. It provides a way for family businesses to deduct all the medical insurance and medical expenses for family members from their business returns, just the way you can for your employees. The plan is based on the premise that you can hire your spouse, paying him or her a salary. The family medical plan is part of the compensation. There are stringent rules to follow, including a plan document and keeping records of all the expenses and reimbursements. You could do it yourself or with the help of your tax professional. You can also contact the Agri-BizPlan folks at (800) 422-4661. They pretty much own this niche, so they are quite efficient and reasonably priced. For more information, go to www.tasconline.com/html/frameset.html?agriplan_bizplan.html.

If you prefer to do it yourself, you will need a plan document. You may adapt the one on A/N Group, Inc.'s website for your own company (www.smbiz.com /sbfrm002.html). Make sure you don't issue reimbursement checks to your spouse or your employees unless you have a copy of the medical receipt in your hands—

The Section 105 Plan in Action

Ward Cleaver is self-employed by his California business. He hires his wife, June, to answer his phones at his office. He pays her a modest salary, so she has some spending money—$500 per month. In addition to the salary, he sets up a Section 105 plan, giving their entire family full medical coverage. The insurance premiums are $400 per month for the family of four ($4,800 per year). They pay another $125 per person for dental and visual insurance ($500 per year). Even with the dental insurance providing $1,500 toward Beaver's braces, the Cleavers are still paying $3,000 out of their pockets. Beaver's scrapes and Wally's sports activities usually result in a few hospital visits, generally at least $500 per year. Ward and June's annual checkups and co-pays usually add up to $500 per year. In addition, they spend an additional $500 on Ward's eyeglasses and prescription sunglasses and June's contacts each year. The medical benefits added $9,800 to June's compensation. Since the $9,800 was not subject to employment tax, it saves the Cleaver family $4,860 in taxes (15.3 percent self-employment tax, 25 percent IRS tax, 9.3 percent state tax = 49.6 percent).

Without the Section 105 plan, they would only have been able to deduct the medical insurance, on page 1 of Form 1040. This reduces the Cleavers' taxes by $1,650 ($4,800 × 34.3 percent, rounded). As to the other $5,000 of medical expenses, Ward's income was too high (more than $66,000) to itemize any of it. The Section 105 plan saved the Cleavers more than $3,200.

---

and it qualifies as a medical deduction.[2] Keep separate files for each employee and separate each year—either with tabs or using different folders for each year.

Since Section 105 lets your business deduct all the family medical expenses, not just the insurance premiums, the savings are substantial.

Employer-Provided Child-Care Facilities Credit

Hardly any small businesses even know about this excellent way to reduce your taxes if you have a child. The IRS will give you up to 25 percent of the cost of a qualified child-care facility for your children—or your employees' children—to a maximum of $150,000 per year. Unused credits may be carried to the future—for up to twenty years. That doesn't mean you have to set up your own child-care facility. You can get the credit for paying an existing facility for child care, as long as it's licensed and meets all of the IRS's rules for such facilities. The employer must pay the facility directly; reimbursements are not permitted. Use Form 8882, available at www.irs.gov/pub/irs-pdf/f8882.pdf.

Your state might also have similar credits. For instance, California has a 30 percent credit. Just think, if you lived in California and paid $300 per month for your child's care, your tax credit would be $1,080. In addition, the business gets the deduction of $2,520 (total cost of $3,600, credit of $1,980). That's worth about $1250 more (15.3 percent SE tax, 25 percent IRS tax, and 9.3 percent California tax). You've just saved over $2,300 of the $3,600 costs of your child's day care.

Life Insurance

Typically, life insurance is not a deductible expense. Certainly not when it is for the benefit of the owner of the business. In a C-corporation, though, you may deduct the cost of up to $50,000 coverage for each employee, including the primary shareholder. Check with your tax professional to see if there are other ways to include life insurance in your business and make it deductible. There are ways to use trusts and employee leasing arrangements to generate substantial deductions. But, that's advanced tax planning, often requiring the services of a sophisticated tax attorney.

---

2. For medical expenses, see IRS Publication 502 at www.irs.gov/publications/p502/index.html.

Education

Naturally, your business may deduct the cost of all courses you or your staff take to increase your professional or trade expertise related to your business or industry. Management and business courses and seminars are deductible. When it comes to courses taken in order to get a college degree, you may have to fight to win those deductions. Individual courses related directly to what you need to know for your business can probably be deducted. But, those anthropology courses? For a plumber . . . well, I don't think so. You get the idea.

Your company may offer an education assistance plan, reimbursing employees for up to $5,250 of annual education expenses.[3] Since January 1, 2002, graduate-level courses qualify. In the past, only courses up to a bachelor's degree or a certificate program were included. If you are a C-corporation, the cost of your education expenses for a degree may be reimbursed, along with those taken by other employees. However, in an S-corporation, or other entity, nope. You may, of course, deduct the cost of specific seminars or workshops for your industry—just not the cost of courses leading to a degree. You may hire your spouse or children. If they legitimately work for the business, like any other arm's-length employee, you may be able to reimburse their education expenses as part of their employee compensation. This may be iffy in an S-corporation. Since your family members are related parties, the IRS treats them as owning the business, too. Definitely clear this with your tax professional before including it in your business plan, especially because this is an area of tax law that may change soon.

What expenses are deductible when it comes to education? The cost of books, tuition, fees, tools, and supplies related to the course. Travel to the course or seminar are also included as well as meals, if you are gone overnight. There's a broad definition for *tools*. But, if you're studying construction and your class project is to build a house and you build one for yourself . . . I don't think you'll be able to deduct the costs as education expenses. So, be reasonable when you take deductions on your tax return.

Courses to qualify you for a new business or a new profession aren't deductible. For instance, if I were working for a certified public accounting firm and wanted to take a CPA review course, that wouldn't be deductible for me. Even if I took the course and passed, and I continued to do exactly the same job as before, as if nothing changed, it would *not* be deductible. The IRS considers CPAs

---

3. See IRS Publication 970 for education fringe benefits: www.irs.gov/publications/p970/ch11.html.

a different profession than simply a degreed accountant. Look at your industry and see how that relates. Education deductions can be lucrative—or they can be dangerous. However, for the next few years, even if you can't use the deductions as business expenses, you have education credits and above the line deductions available to use.

Retirement Plans

The good news is, if your business follows your business plan, you'll be making lots of money and living well. The bad news is, you won't die young. At least, so says the Centers for Disease Control (CDC).[4] Their latest projections say you'll live until age 77.2. That looks like a long time from now, doesn't it?

News flash. It sneaks up on you faster than you can imagine. I was just twenty-four last week. Or so it seems. I blinked and more than two decades passed. Looking around at friends, family, and clients, many are living well into their eighties. So, we'd better look toward saving for our own longevity.

Retirement Basics You Must Know

Each investment vehicle has contribution limits based on your income, except the SIMPLE-IRA. In general, if you, or your spouse, have a job with a retirement plan, your contribution to any IRA-related (individual retirement account) plans will be limited.

You may contribute $500 to $2,500 extra per year if you're age 50 or over, depending on the plan. They're called catch-up contributions. All contribution amounts, catch-ups, and income limits change based on inflation or congressional rules, through 2009. Then, who knows?

You may not put money into all these retirement vehicles at once. Putting money into one will generally conflict with your right to fund one of the other retirement options—so pick the optimum retirement plan(s) for your business.

A common misconception is that these plans are investments. They are not. They are vehicles into which you put money. You may open these plans with banks, brokerages, perhaps even with insurance companies. Brokerages and mutual fund companies let you diversify and manage your investments. You control the rate of

---

4. Fast stats on average life expectancy can be found at www.cdc.gov/nchs/fastats/lifexpec.htm.

the return by watching the appropriate market. You may move the funds from one company to another—as long as they stay within the same investment vehicle.

All of the plan descriptions assume you have no employees. If you have any, please see a good local tax professional who understands qualified and nonqualified plans. If they don't know what those terms mean, go somewhere else.

Tax-Free Retirement

Tax-free means you'll never have to pay tax on the money when you take it out. You also don't generally get a deduction for your deposits when you make them, though. Table 10.1 provides an overview of the tax-free plans. Here are the details of some plans available to small business owners.

Roth IRAs. For any year, contributions to Roth IRAs must be deposited by April 15 of the following year. For 2004, for example, you may contribute up to $3,000, plus a catch-up of $500 by April 15, 2005.

There is no deduction for the amount you contribute to a Roth IRA. Obey the rules—you'll get all the money out tax free when you retire. You may only draw the money out of your own account when you and your spouse are each over age 59½ and you've left the money in the account for five years. In times when investments do well, this is a very appealing investment. For young people, whose money will grow in these IRA accounts for fifteen or twenty years, this option can yield a generous source of tax-free money in the future.

Why doesn't everyone use it? Several reasons:

- The contribution allowed is low.
- The income limits to qualify are low.
- Roths are a nuisance to fix if you contribute when your income is too high.

Section 529 College Education Plans. You may contribute up to $11,000 per beneficiary, per year.[5] Or, in the first year, you may deposit up to $55,000, using up five years' contributions at once. Contributions must be made by December 31 of the plan's year. Section 529 plans are unique because, although you are gifting a fortune to your child, relative, or friend, you still have control of this asset. At

---

5. The annual contribution limit is the amount of the annual gift tax exclusion—the amount of money you may give a person as a gift without paying gift tax on it.

TABLE 10.1 Tax-Free Retirement and Savings Plans Available in 2004

If a contribution date falls on a weekend or holiday, it is due on the next business day.

Tax-Free	Roth IRA	Municipal Bonds in Your State	Sec. 529 College Plans	Employees 401(k)s, 403(b)s, 457, SAR-SEP
Basic contribution 2004	$3,000	No limit	$11,000	$13,000
Age 50 catch-up	$500	N/A	N/A	$3,000
Income limits—single	$95,000–$110,000	No limit	No limit	
Income limits—joint	$150,000–$160,000	No limit	No limit	
Date account must be opened	April 15 of the following year	N/A	December 31 of plan year	
Date contribution is due	April 15 of the following year	N/A	December 31 of plan year	
Pros	Qualified withdrawals are not taxable.	Earnings are not taxable. Draw money anytime.	Earnings are not taxable. If funds are spent on courses, supplies, room, and board, including travel or hobbies, you may use the money tax-free.	
Cons	People who deposit early may face penalties if they don't remove the funds when they prepare their tax returns and don't quality. Requires planning.	Low interest rate. Tax-free interest may be subject to AMT.	This isn't really a retirement fund. It's an education fund.	

Special Rules

	Roth IRA	Municipal Bonds in Your State	Sec. 529 College Plans	Employees 401(k)s, 403(b)s, 457, SAR-SEP
Contribution: 2005–2007	$4,000		Tied to gift tax limits	2005 is $14,000
Contribution: 2006 forward				$15,000
Age 50 catch-up 2005	$500			$4,000
Contribution: 2008 forward	$5,000			
Age 50 catch-up 2006 forward	$1,000			$5,000
Age to draw	59½			
Holding term minimum	5 years			
Investment's annual income limit	N/A	$100,000	N/A	
First year maximum contribution			$55,000 (it replaces five years of gifts)	

any time you choose, you may pull it back into your own estate and keep the money. Or, if your beneficiary doesn't use up all the money, you may either transfer it to another student—or take it back. The money may be spent on tuition, fees, books, supplies, room, and board—as long as the school is on the approved list.

You're saying 529s are not really retirement plans? My approach is indeed novel. No one else has written about this—but, it was cleared with the IRS on May 13, 2004. The IRS agrees it's legal. If you are related to the beneficiary, you may transfer the money to yourself, as the new beneficiary, even if you're a senior citizen. Once in your name, you're free to use that money to get educated—taking courses on cruise ships, traveling across Europe, or wherever, including most expenses and course supplies for accredited schools. Just think—gourmet cooking school, scuba training, professional golf college . . . what have you always wanted to learn?

Your Home: A Tax-Free Strategy. Buy a home and build equity. You may sell a home every two years and keep up to $250,000 ($500,000 for couples) tax-free. Use the proceeds to buy the next home in a rapidly appreciating area. Repeat every few years. Ten years before you plan to retire, accelerate the mortgage payments so you pay off the loan entirely. If your profits look as if they'll be more than $500,000, add your children, living at home, to the title. Each owner gets that $250,000 exclusion. Along the way, you collected lots of money to use either toward a better house, toward funding your retirement plans, or both. Once retired, you'll have no mortgage payments, so if anything goes wrong with your retirement accounts (as happened to many in April 2000), you'll still be fine. If you ever need money, simply make sure to establish a home equity line of credit. They cost little or nothing to have. You only pay interest on any money you borrow—usually at favorable rates.

Tax-Deferred Opportunities

Tax-deferred means you get a deduction or credit for your contributions now, when you deposit the money. But you'll pay tax on all the money when you take it out.

There is a whole menu of retirement savings opportunities, but they're deceptively complicated. Many have income limits and strings attached. Use Table 10.2 as a starting point. Discuss the options with your own tax pro. Table 10.2 provides an overview of tax-deferred plans. Here are the details of some plans available to small business owners.

TABLE 10.2 Tax-Deferred Retirement and Savings Plans Available in 2004

If a contribution date falls on a weekend or holiday, it is due on the next business day.

Tax Deferred	IRAs	SEPs and KEOGHs	SIMPLE IRAs
Basic contribution	$3,000	25% of income up to $41,000	$9,000
Age 50 catch-up	$500		$1,500
Income limits—single	$40,000–$50,000 (1)	$205,000 (2)	
Income limits—joint	$60,000–$70,000 (1)	$205,000 (2)	
Date account must be opened	April 15 of the following year	SEP: due date of your return KEOGH: December 31 of plan year	September 30 of plan year
Date contribution is due	April 15 of the following year	Due date of your tax return, excluding extension	30 days after the end of the month for which you're making contributions
Pros	Contributions are deductible.	Contributions are deductible. May be funded by employer or employee.	3% matching may be paid on due date of return, including extensions.
Types of Plans Available	You may invest in CDs, stocks, bonds, or mutual funds.	Money purchase, profit sharing, defined benefit	You may invest in CDs, stocks, bonds, or mutual funds.
Cons	Withdrawals are taxable.	Withdrawals are taxable.	Withdrawals are taxable.
Special Rules			
Phase-out	(1) Applies only if covered by qualified plan at work or from your own business.	(2) Income is net business profit or wages per person.	
Contribution: 2005–2007	$4,000	N/A	Increases annually by $1,000 until reaching $10,000.
Age 50 catch-up	2005–2006 is $500; 2007 forward is $1,000	N/A	Increases in increments of $500 annually; indexed
KEOGH rules		Lets you contribute up to 100% of business earnings or up to 25% of all employees' earnings.	

Savings Incentive Match Plan for Employees (SIMPLE IRAs)

You may contribute up to $9,000 plus $1,500 catch-up in 2004. You may contribute your entire profit, or wages from your own corporation or LLC, up to those limits. The money must be deposited by December 31. As your own employer, you must also make a matching contribution of 3 percent of your wages or profits. The matching contribution may be funded when you file your tax return. The plan must be opened before October 1, 2005, to use it in 2005.

Simplified Employee Pension (SEP-IRA)

You may fund 25 percent of your net profits or wages from your own business, up to $41,000, into an SEP-IRA. You may set up and fund SEP-IRAs until the due date of your tax return, including extensions.

KEOGH Plans

KEOGHs are similar to the SEP-IRA, but with two differences: (1) they must be opened by December 31 of the tax year being deducted and (2) you may contribute up to 100 percent of your business's net earnings—or up to 25 percent of all participants' compensation, to the same $41,000 limit as for the SEP-IRA.

Solo 401(k)s

These are like regular 401(k)s you might get from an employer—only much better. You have the same contribution limits as the SEP-IRA—$41,000 (plus the $3,000 catch-up). But the percentages are more generous. At lower levels of income, you may contribute 100 percent of your wages. The best part about these plans is that you may roll over your IRA funds into a solo 401(k) account. Then, you may borrow up to 50 percent of the account balance, or up to $50,000. This is the only account that lets you and your spouse (and even your children, if they are employees) get the maximum tax benefit—but still gives you access to your money. If each of them works for you and owns shares in the company, they may each have their own plan. That means, in a couple of years, you could have access to $100,000 or more easy capital. You may borrow the money without penalties or taxes, as long as you honor the payment plan—and don't shut down the business. Otherwise, you will face early withdrawal penalties and taxes if you don't pay it back.

Defined Benefit Plans

Defined benefit plans are a different animal and require some long-term planning. The concept is to provide you with a specific monthly payout when you retire. To get that payout later, how much do you have to put away now? The older you are, the more you get to put away. The computation is predicated on the three highest consecutive earnings years based on income or wages from your business. The annual benefit limit for 2004 is $165,000. You may contribute as much as 100 percent of those wages to achieve the benefit limit. The plan must be opened before December 31, but it may be funded until you file your tax return, including extensions.

This is an excellent option for anyone wanting to build up plan assets quickly. The biggest objection to these plans is that once you set them up, you are obligated to make the annual payment, even if your business doesn't have the money to cover the costs. So, what do you do in lean years? Suspend the plan. But be very careful how you handle this. If you get your timing wrong, the whole plan is invalid and may be subject to penalties. So work with a tax planning professional who really understands this area well. Not all do.

A good tax professional, whether it's an attorney, an enrolled agent, or a certified public accountant, can help you devise the best way to set aside money for the future by letting Uncle Sam give you tax breaks. This will cut the financial pinch so you can live well now—and when you're age 77.

Two last notes:

1. Various tax provisions are designed to sunset (disappear) on December 31, 2010.
2. Your legislature may change all the rules at any time, without warning.

So, if you build a retirement plan, be sure to get your professional or trade organization, your friends, contacts, chamber colleagues, and family to lobby Congress to keep the provisions intact.

Using the IRS to Your Advantage

Clearly, with the right kind of planning, you can practically wipe out your present tax obligation or at least move much of it to your retirement years, when your earnings are likely to be lower; although I'm finding that many of my clients' earnings are higher during their nonworking years than they were when they were struggling. A nice surprise.

One of the nice surprises they've gotten is Social Security. They didn't really expect it to still be there for them. So, let's just address that for a moment. In all of our efforts, we've done our best to reduce or eliminate the self-employment taxes paid in. You may want to rethink that strategy.

For those of you who have not built up your Social Security account, you may want to pay in for a while. This may be especially important to immigrants who don't have their forty quarters paid in through jobs. Have your tax professional help you develop a balanced strategy that cuts your taxes, increases your retirement income—and also ensures that you get the most out of Social Security when you retire.

Benefits Resources

- **Section 105 Medical Reimbursement Plan document.** www.smbiz.com /sbfrm002.html
- **Agri-BizPlan.** www.tasconline.com/html/frameset.html?agriplan_biz plan.html, (800) 422-4661
- **Explanation of Health Savings Accounts (HSAs).** www.taxmama.com /Articles/HSA1.html
- **eHealthInsurance.com.** www.ehealthinsurance.com: Look at their special section for Health Savings Accounts.
- **Employer-Provided Child Care Facilities Credit.** www.irs.gov/pub/irs-pdf/f8882.pdf
- **IRS Publication 970, Tax Benefits for Education.** www.irs.gov/publica tions/p970/ch11.html: For education fringe benefit.
- **Pioneer Funds.** www.pioneerfunds.com/uni_k/contributions.jhtml: The Pioneer Funds' chart compares contribution limits to various plans for self-employed and incorporated businesses.
- **MFS Investments Retirement Calculator.** www.mfs.com/retirement /index.jhtml
- **Merrill Lynch.** www.businesscenter.ml.com: Click on "Retirement and Benefits" for current information on a variety of plans.

11

ESTIMATED PAYMENTS

I have long contended that, however many zillion dollars the federal government costs us, we get it all back and more in the form of quality entertainment.

—Dave Barry

Estimated Payments Overview

You're in business now. Cool, isn't it? But your safety net is gone. If you're not on payroll, you don't get any W-2s. For the first time, you have to make your own tax deposits. Your mind is filled with questions.

- When do you make them?
- What forms do you use?
- Where do you send them?
- How much should you pay?
- What's the big deal if you don't make the payments?

Not making payments can cost you big-time! That's one of the two ways to destroy your business and drain your cash flow. (The other way is to skip paying payroll taxes. See Chapter 9 to learn about this important topic.) While it may hurt your wallet a little to make the payments each quarter, it might wipe you out, or worse, to try to pay all the taxes on April 15.

If you want to succeed in business set the money aside and pay the tax.

What's in It for You?

When you have a system to guide you, life is much less stressful. There's a comfort to knowing how much to budget each month for each of your expenses. Taxes are no different.

If you're a numbers freak, like me, you like to see a nice, steady monthly cash flow statement, with all the numbers being consistent. Knowing how much you'll need to pay the IRS each quarter, you can put a fixed dollar amount aside each month. You won't have to panic, wondering if you must make up for last quarter and pay a large amount all at once.

Best of all, if you do come up short, the IRS will go out of its way to help you because you've established a consistent history with them. It's like a credit history. The IRS is used to dealing with people who are contentious and belligerent. You'll be a breath of fresh air.

Think how easy it will be to get bank or venture capital financing once they see how responsibly you've handled your tax obligations. Lenders and investors get skittish when business owners come to them after having gotten themselves into tax trouble. Naturally, if you're totally brilliant and have a killer product, the "angels" might overlook your financial failings. Of course, they'll charge you more for the money.

Then again, not everyone needs to be paying estimates. After all, if you don't have a profit, you don't need to pay taxes, estimated or otherwise.

Who Should Be Paying Estimated Payments?

These are four categories of people who should be paying estimated payments:

1. People who are self-employed
2. People whose nonwage income is increasing (or expected to increase) in the current year
3. People who have done well on the stock market
4. People who have gotten a healthy inheritance (or other windfall), with assets that produce income

Anyone else? For business owners receiving wages, if you expect to owe extra taxes, simply have your tax professional manipulate your payroll tax withholding before year-end. That way, you never have to make estimated payments.

TABLE 11.1 Estimated Payment Schedule

When the 15th falls on a weekend or holiday, it's due on the following business day.

Quarter	Date	Number of Months
1st (Q1)	April 15	3
2nd (Q2)	June 15	2
3rd (Q3)	September 15	3
4th (Q4)	January 15 of following year	4

When Should You Be Making Those Payments?

When we talked about payroll quarterlies in Chapter 9, you learned that "quarterly" means every three months, right? Not when it comes to estimated payments. We're dealing with the tax code here. Some extremely clever lawmakers decided that *quarterly*, for tax purposes, breaks down as indicated in Table 11.1.

Notice that sometimes you've got to pay within two months; other times, the quarter is four months long.

How Much Must You Pay?

Before we get into any payment specifics, let's start with some fundamental tips about making estimated tax payments. Keep handy the link found at the end of this chapter to the online version of IRS Publication 505, which is about withholding and estimated tax payments. Changes in the rules will appear in there.

You will be using Form 1040-ES (and your state's equivalent) as seen in Figure 11.1. For the current year, you must only pay estimates if:

You expect to owe $1,000 or more beyond any payroll withholding.
and
1. Your withholding or other tax credits (education, children, and so on) will be less than 90 percent of the tax you expect to owe on your current year tax return

or
2. Your withholding or other tax credits (education, children, etc.) will be less than 100 percent of the tax shown on your prior year tax return. If you

FIGURE 11.1 Form 1040-ES, Estimated Tax Payment Voucher

Record of Estimated Tax Payments (Farmers, fishermen, and fiscal year taxpayers, see page 2 for payment due dates.)

Payment number	Payment due date	(a) Date paid	(b) Check or money order number or credit card confirmation number	(c) Amount paid (**do not** include any credit card convenience fee)	(d) 2003 overpayment credit applied	(e) Total amount paid and credited (add (c) and (d))
1	4/15/2004					
2	6/15/2004					
3	9/15/2004					
4	1/18/2005*					
Total	. . . . ▶					

*You do not have to make this payment if you file your 2004 tax return by January 31, 2005, **and** pay the entire balance due with your return.

Where To File Your Payment Voucher if Paying by Check or Money Order

Mail your payment voucher and check or money order to the Internal Revenue Service at the address shown below for the place where you live. **Do not** mail your tax return to this address **or** send an estimated tax payment without a payment voucher. Also, do not mail your estimated tax payments to the address shown in the Form 1040 or 1040A instructions. If you need more payment vouchers, use another Form 1040-ES package.

Note: *For proper delivery of your estimated tax payment to a P.O. box, you must include the box number in the address. Also, note that only the U.S. Postal Service can deliver to P.O. boxes.*

IF you live in . . . ▼	THEN use . . . ▼
Maine, Massachusetts, New Hampshire, New York, Vermont	P.O. Box 37001 Hartford, CT 06176-0001
Connecticut, District of Columbia, Maryland, New Jersey, Pennsylvania	P.O. Box 80102 Cincinnati, OH 45280-0002

Alabama, Florida, Georgia, Mississippi, North Carolina, Rhode Island, South Carolina, West Virginia	P.O. Box 105900 Atlanta, GA 30348-5900
Ohio, Virginia	P.O. Box 105225 Atlanta, GA 30348-5225
Delaware, Illinois, Indiana, Iowa, Kansas, Michigan, Minnesota, Missouri, Nebraska, North Dakota, South Dakota, Wisconsin	P.O. Box 970006 St. Louis, MO 63197-0006
Arizona, Utah	P.O. Box 1219 Charlotte, NC 28201-1219
Alaska, California, Hawaii, Idaho, Montana, Nevada, Oregon, Washington, Wyoming	P.O. Box 510000 San Francisco, CA 94151-5100
Arkansas, Colorado, Kentucky, Louisiana, New Mexico, Oklahoma, Tennessee, Texas	P.O. Box 660406 Dallas, TX 75266-0406

All APO and FPO addresses, American Samoa, the Commonwealth of the Northern Mariana Islands, nonpermanent residents of Guam or the Virgin Islands, Puerto Rico (*or if excluding income under Internal Revenue Code section 933*), dual-status aliens, a foreign country: U.S. citizens and those filing Form 2555, 2555-EZ, or 4563	P.O. Box 80102 Cincinnati, OH 45280-0002
Permanent residents of Guam*	Department of Revenue and Taxation Government of Guam P.O. Box 23607 GMF, GU 96921
Permanent residents of the Virgin Islands*	V.I. Bureau of Internal Revenue 9601 Estate Thomas Charlotte Amalie St. Thomas, VI 00802

* Permanent residents must prepare separate vouchers for estimated income tax and self-employment tax payments. Send the income tax vouchers to the address for permanent residents and the self-employment tax vouchers to the address for nonpermanent residents.

-------------------------- Tear off here --------------------------

Form **1040-ES** Department of the Treasury Internal Revenue Service	**2004** Payment Voucher **4**	OMB No. 1545-0087

	Calendar year—Due Jan. 18, 2005
File only if you are making a payment of estimated tax by check or money order. Mail this voucher with your check or money order payable to the **"United States Treasury."** Write your social security number and "2004 Form 1040-ES" on your check or money order. Do not send cash. Enclose, but do not staple or attach, your payment with this voucher.	Amount of estimated tax you are paying by check or money order. — Dollars / Cents

Type or print

Your first name and initial	Your last name	Your social security number

If joint payment, complete for spouse

Spouse's first name and initial	Spouse's last name	Spouse's social security number

Address (number, street, and apt. no.)

City, state, and ZIP code. (If a foreign address, enter city, province or state, postal code, and country.)

For Privacy Act and Paperwork Reduction Act Notice, see instructions on page 5.

FIGURE 11.1 *continued*

Form **1040-ES**	**2004** Payment Voucher **3**	
Department of the Treasury Internal Revenue Service		OMB No. 1545-0087

File only if you are making a payment of estimated tax by check or money order. Mail this voucher with your check or money order payable to the **"United States Treasury."** Write your social security number and "2004 Form 1040-ES" on your check or money order. Do not send cash. Enclose, but do not staple or attach, your payment with this voucher.

Calendar year—Due Sept. 15, 2004

Amount of estimated tax you are paying by check or money order.

	Dollars	Cents

Type or print

Your first name and initial	Your last name	Your social security number
If joint payment, complete for spouse		
Spouse's first name and initial	Spouse's last name	Spouse's social security number
Address (number, street, and apt. no.)		
City, state, and ZIP code. (If a foreign address, enter city, province or state, postal code, and country.)		

For Privacy Act and Paperwork Reduction Act Notice, see instructions on page 5.

- **Tear off here** -

Form **1040-ES**	**2004** Payment Voucher **2**	
Department of the Treasury Internal Revenue Service		OMB No. 1545-0087

File only if you are making a payment of estimated tax by check or money order. Mail this voucher with your check or money order payable to the **"United States Treasury."** Write your social security number and "2004 Form 1040-ES" on your check or money order. Do not send cash. Enclose, but do not staple or attach, your payment with this voucher.

Calendar year—Due June 15, 2004

Amount of estimated tax you are paying by check or money order.

	Dollars	Cents

Type or print

Your first name and initial	Your last name	Your social security number
If joint payment, complete for spouse		
Spouse's first name and initial	Spouse's last name	Spouse's social security number
Address (number, street, and apt. no.)		
City, state, and ZIP code. (If a foreign address, enter city, province or state, postal code, and country.)		

For Privacy Act and Paperwork Reduction Act Notice, see instructions on page 5.

- **Tear off here** -

Form **1040-ES**	**2004** Payment Voucher **1**	
Department of the Treasury Internal Revenue Service		OMB No. 1545-0087

File only if you are making a payment of estimated tax by check or money order. Mail this voucher with your check or money order payable to the **"United States Treasury."** Write your social security number and "2004 Form 1040-ES" on your check or money order. Do not send cash. Enclose, but do not staple or attach, your payment with this voucher.

Calendar year—Due April 15, 2004

Amount of estimated tax you are paying by check or money order.

	Dollars	Cents

Type or print

Your first name and initial	Your last name	Your social security number
If joint payment, complete for spouse		
Spouse's first name and initial	Spouse's last name	Spouse's social security number
Address (number, street, and apt. no.)		
City, state, and ZIP code. (If a foreign address, enter city, province or state, postal code, and country.)		

For Privacy Act and Paperwork Reduction Act Notice, see instructions on page 5.

Page 7

expect to have losses from the business, don't worry about making estimated tax payments on the business.

Wise heads feel that it is best to pay the minimum required taxes in advance.
You can put your money to better uses than the IRS can.

My Short Method

Use this shortcut if your expected taxable income will be the same as or higher
than it was last year. It's so simple. Everyone loves using it.

Start with your last year's return.

Look at page 2 of your 1040,	
Line 56—Total Tax. Let's say it was	$10,000
From that, deduct any withholding you	
have from any sources (wages, interest,	
dividends, unemployment). Let's say,	$3,000
Deduct the withholding you expect to have	
from last year's taxes	$7,000
Divide the result by four quarters ($7,000 ÷ 4)	$1,750

Ta daaa! That's how much you should be paying each quarter.

That's it. That's all there is to it. Read no further.

That Makes You Nervous? You Want to Pay More?

You'd rather pay just enough to owe nothing next April? OK, increase each of those
payments by a couple of hundred dollars.

You don't have to. All you have to do to avoid the penalties is to pay the min-
imums. Some people prefer to have a small refund. That's fine. Uncle Sam can
surely use your money.

You're well within your rights to open a savings account or investment
account to hold those funds until it's time to pay. But in today's economic climate
it may not be worth going to all that trouble. Earning 1.5 percent interest on my
money doesn't excite me. On $5,000, that's $75 of interest for the whole year. Of
course, when interest rates rise—or if your additional tax due is much larger—
you may have an incentive to hold on to that money.

Cash Flow Strategy: Yes or No?

Some businesses feel they can make better use of this money to grow their operations, so not making estimated payments is part of their strategy. This is not a good idea.

Take the example of the Klaus Company (not the real name), which had a steady stream of work. Klaus's bids were generally accepted for large-ticket jobs. He was able to subcontract some of the work, so he didn't need a payroll. He worked more than fifteen-hour days on the jobs, usually hundreds or thousands of miles from home. He'd be gone for months at a time. It's not that he didn't want to make the estimated payments. He wasn't home long enough to take care of bookkeeping or administration, or to cut the checks. Besides, every time he'd get a job little disasters beyond his control would occur, wiping out most of the profit on the job. (In one case, he and his crew were not permitted to work during office hours. No one mentioned that when he bid the job.) Often, he'd be working for nothing. While he felt there was no profit at all, the rent and family expenses were being paid. That means, he always had lots of self-employment taxes due. Since he didn't set it aside each quarter, in April there'd be no money. As time went on, he didn't pay the estimates, so he didn't get the bookkeeping done and he hasn't filed tax returns. He's behind for the last three years, and the IRS is about to attach his bank accounts.

In another example, Matt and Jamie Garrison of Aluria Software LLC, considering what it would cost them to borrow money, decided to hold back much of the money from their estimated taxes as their business grew. That money could be better used for payroll, payroll taxes, or advertising. As part of their strategy, they knew at the end of each year they had to save money, quickly, to cover the tax debt by April. They didn't always make it. By filing an extension, the Garrisons were able to keep the late payment penalties to 0.5 percent per month. With IRS interest rates at the lowest in my lifetime, the penalties and interest paid to the IRS were lower than interest rates charged by traditional lenders.

I bring you the story of Aluria Software LLC because Matt and Jamie successfully built it into a million-dollar business. Their strategy did not get them into big trouble. Aluria is one of the few companies who managed its funds successfully using this strategy.

Generally, when companies start tapping into the tax coffers, they're signing the death knell for their business. They end up like Klaus, whose business and marriage are both in jeopardy.

Worst-Case Scenario

Did I forget to tell you? Getting behind on your estimated taxes may destroy your marriage.

There's this whole snowball effect. First last year's estimates. Then, this year's taxes. Then, the IRS is attaching your bank account or levying your spouse's wages. Then, your children start noticing that you're afraid to answer the phone or get the mail. You start losing sleep, Then, you start quarreling with your spouse—usually over nothing. I cringe when I get calls from certain clients. I know they're into this loop. They're depressed. They can't work through their problem. They won't follow my advice, and their business starts going down the tubes. Then, the spouse calls.

While people are most afraid of going to jail over their tax troubles, that's not the worst thing that can happen to you. After all, in jail you get room and board, plenty of exercise, and a library to use. You won't work any harder than you do now—probably fewer hours, even. The worst thing isn't going to jail. No, the worst thing is staying home—watching your home, family, and reputation fall apart.

Am I scaring you? Well, I'm trying to.

Sorry, my friends, I've been doing this for a long time, working with people who think the rules don't apply to them. Your tax professional probably isn't dealing with this—he or she is sending those failures to people like me. There are a few of us in each town who work with taxpayers in trouble. We're not the ones running those ads on the radio or television, collecting huge fees. But the pros know who we are. People only come to us by word of mouth. It's a gut-wrenching business. I hate this part of my practice, and all of us in it want to do less of it. The only way for that to happen is to convince you not to get into trouble. So . . . don't monkey with your tax obligations.

If you can't afford your estimated payments now, what makes you think you'll be able to pay them in April? It's time to look at your budget and see what's wrong.

The only solid reason to delay those payments is when your business is cyclical. If much of your income comes in over the Christmas shopping season, for instance, or during the first quarter—you know you'll have the money in time.

Computing Your Estimated Installment Payments

Ideally, at this point in the book, you should sit down with the tax advisor on your team (see Chapter 1 to review). Figure out your payments, project your income, and estimate your profits, from all sources. Prepare for the meeting by making a list of your investments and how much income you expect. Do a realistic projection of your business profits. Your business plan from Chapter 2 and your accounting records from Chapter 4 should come in handy now. Run those numbers through one of the free handy online income tax estimator tools. The estimator at TaxBrain.com is straightforward. The estimator at TurboTax.com is more involved, but it will let you enter more detail.

Have your tax professional review the results to determine whether to revise your tax projections.

The main reason to use an electronic brain like TaxBrain and TurboTax is to compute self-employment taxes, Schedule SE (which you learned about in Chapter 9), and alternative minimum taxes Form 6251. Whenever I see people guesstimating their tax liability, those are the two big surprises they get on April 15. You think you have no taxable income because your mortgage, property taxes, and child tax credit swallowed up your taxes. Then, these two taxes rear their ugly heads.

Self-employment taxes amount to 15.3 percent of your business profits from Schedule C or your Schedule 1065 K-1.

The alternative minimum tax limits and rules have changed several times during the Bush administration, and they are talking about changing them again.[1] All you need to know is that if your itemized deductions are too high or your income reaches $58,000 (couples) or $40,250 (single, or head of household), you will owe taxes you didn't anticipate.

The original concept of the alternative minimum tax was to ensure rich people didn't get away without paying taxes. Instead, it's hitting the folks struggling to make ends meet.

There is one bright note about the alternative minimum tax. If you pay it this year, next year it generates an alternative minimum tax *credit* (Form 8801). That might reduce next year's tax—unless you have another alternative minimum tax. Chapter 32 of IRS Publication 17 can tell you more.

These are the kinds of questions and issues to submit to the Taxpayers Advocate. If you have a solution, or a viable suggestion, Nina Olsen, the Advocate, is open to your input. She writes an annual report to Congress, outlining problems taxpayers have had with the IRS and the tax system. She proposes fixes, which

---

1. HR 4131 Alternative Minimum Tax Repeal Act of 2004, April 2, 2004, to amend the Internal Revenue Code of 1986 to limit the increase in the number of individuals affected by the alternative minimum tax and to repeal the alternative minimum tax for individuals in 2014, available at http://thomas.loc.gov/cgi-bin/query/D?c108:1:./temp/~c108YtjKO4.

sometimes become legislation. The submission form is on the IRS website at www .irs.gov/advocate/article/0,,id=117703,00.html.

Paying the Tax

Naturally, if you have the money, make the payment. Always put the form number, the tax year, and your Social Security number (and your spouse's) on each check. (See the section on FYTIN in Chapter 13.)

The IRS is pushing their electronic payment system, Electronic Federal Tax Payment System (EFTPS). Once registered, you can make all your estimated payments online. It's actually a great idea. You can make your payments at the last minute, and you'll get proof that you paid it. The input form asks you all the pertinent questions. You're likely to get the payment applied to the correct tax year and for the correct account.

Is that important? You bet. If you don't put the correct information on the check, the IRS doesn't know to which form or year to credit the payment. This comes back to haunt you. It's such fun having the IRS locate your payment and apply it to the right account and year. You'll learn the IRS coded it wrong when you get a CP23 notice of underpayment (discussed in Chapter 13) for a year you thought you'd paid. So, yes, if you have access—pay online.

If you didn't set up EFTPS, you may pay by credit card. Chapter 13 tells you how. Since the information about how and where to pay changes so rapidly, it needs to be maintained online.

Tips to Reduce Underpayment of Estimated Tax Penalties

The IRS bases their penalty computation on the date and amount of your payments. Here's a way to make a December payment look like it was paid on time. Change it from an estimated payment to withholding.

Withholding

Did you know that when your taxes are taken out of your paycheck, the IRS treats all the withholding as if it had been paid in evenly throughout the year? Even if you had a total of $1,000 withheld from January through November and then paid in $20,000 in December, the IRS doesn't blink. This is something doctors and lawyers have been doing for decades. But it's not the greatest idea. It means scrambling during the most expensive gift-giving time of the year to come up with big chunks of cash to cover taxes.

While I really don't recommend that you handle your payments that way, it does give you a way to avoid late payment penalties when you get behind in your estimated payment schedule. After all, if you're reading this book late in the year, there's a chance you haven't kept up with estimated payments until now. You didn't realize how important they were. Now, you want to catch up and avoid the penalties.

How does this help when you're in business? If you have a spouse with a job, arrange to increase the withholding for his or her last paychecks of the year. You may even need to deduct everything except one dollar, so your spouse still gets a check. Will he or she be angry? Not if you hand over the money you would have mailed in for withholding.

When your spouse has a job, it's much easier just to increase his or her withholding all year long. We did that with my husband's paycheck when I operated as a partnership. I didn't need to pay as much each quarter. Now that I am an S-corporation, I am on payroll—and taking withholding out.

Another Withholding Option

When being paid as an independent contractor by your own company or a customer's, you have the option of requesting withholding from your fee. There's even a box on the Form 1099-MISC to allow for this. (See Chapter 9.) Take advantage of this option and deduct withholding from each remittance, if it can make your life easier.

Annualized Payments Method

When you file your tax return, use the worksheet on page 4 of Form 2210, Underpayment of Estimated Taxes by Individuals. (See Figure 11.2.) With good bookkeeping software, getting the information you need is easy. You must be able to compute your net profits from January through the end of these months: April, June, September, and December. Armed with this information, you or your tax pro will have to allocate your deductions to each period. You'll need to know when you paid big medical bills, made large charitable donations, or bought the expensive employee tool. Apply all the deductions to the appropriate time frame. Then follow the computations. Better yet, have a computer do it.

I'll tell you right now, unless you owe tens of thousands of dollars worth of tax, the time investment to fill in this page is prohibitive. Remember, you might

FIGURE 11.2 Form 2210, Underpayment of Estimated Tax

Form 2210 (2003)   Page **4**

Schedule AI—Annualized Income Installment Method (See pages 4 and 5 of the instructions.)

Estates and trusts, **do not** use the period ending dates shown to the right.
Instead, use the following: 2/28/03, 4/30/03, 7/31/03, and 11/30/03.

		(a) 1/1/03–3/31/03	**(b)** 1/1/03–5/31/03	**(c)** 1/1/03–8/31/03	**(d)** 1/1/03–12/31/03

Part I   Annualized Income Installments

		(a)	(b)	(c)	(d)
1	Enter your adjusted gross income for each period (see instructions). (Estates and trusts, enter your taxable income without your exemption for each period.) **1**				
2	Annualization amounts. (Estates and trusts, see instructions.) . . **2**	4	2.4	1.5	1
3	Annualized income. Multiply line 1 by line 2 . . . . **3**				
4	Enter your itemized deductions for the period shown in each column. If you do not itemize, enter -0- and skip to line 7. (Estates and trusts, enter -0-, skip to line 9, and enter the amount from line 3 on line 9.) **4**				
5	Annualization amounts **5**	4	2.4	1.5	1
6	Multiply line 4 by line 5 (see instructions if line 3 is more than $69,750) **6**				
7	In each column, enter the full amount of your standard deduction from Form 1040, line 37, or Form 1040A, line 24 (Form 1040NR or 1040NR-EZ filers, enter -0-. **Exception:** Indian students and business apprentices, enter standard deduction from Form 1040NR, line 35, or Form 1040NR-EZ, line 11.) **7**				
8	Enter the **larger** of line 6 or line 7 . . . . **8**				
9	Subtract line 8 from line 3 . . . . **9**				
10	In each column, multiply $3,050 by the total number of exemptions claimed (see instructions if line 3 is more than $104,625). (Estates and trusts and Form 1040NR or 1040NR-EZ filers, enter the exemption amount shown on your tax return.) **10**				
11	Subtract line 10 from line 9 . . . . **11**				
12	Figure your tax on the amount on line 11 (see instructions) . . . **12**				
13	Self-employment tax from line 34 below (complete Part II) . . **13**				
14	Enter other taxes for each payment period (see instructions) . . **14**				
15	Total tax. Add lines 12, 13, and 14 . . . . **15**				
16	For each period, enter the same type of credits as allowed on Form 2210, lines 1 and 3 (see instructions) **16**				
17	Subtract line 16 from line 15. If zero or less, enter -0- **17**				
18	Applicable percentage **18**	22.5%	45%	67.5%	90%
19	Multiply line 17 by line 18 . . . . **19**				
	Complete lines 20–25 of one column before going to the next column.				
20	Add the amounts in all previous columns of line 25 . . . . **20**				
21	Subtract line 20 from line 19. If zero or less, enter -0- **21**				
22	Enter 25% (.25) of line 9 on page 1 of Form 2210 in each column **22**				
23	Subtract line 25 of the previous column from line 24 of that column **23**				
24	Add lines 22 and 23 . . . . **24**				
25	Enter the **smaller** of line 21 or line 24 here and on Form 2210, line 18 . . . . ▶ **25**				

Part II   Annualized Self-Employment Tax (Form 1040 filers only)

		(a)	(b)	(c)	(d)
26	Net earnings from self-employment for the period (see instructions) **26**				
27	Prorated social security tax limit **27**	$21,750	$36,250	$58,000	$87,000
28	Enter actual wages for the period subject to social security tax or the 6.2% portion of the 7.65% railroad retirement (tier 1) tax . . **28**				
29	Subtract line 28 from line 27. If zero or less, enter -0-. **29**				
30	Annualization amounts **30**	0.496	0.2976	0.186	0.124
31	Multiply line 30 by the **smaller** of line 26 or line 29. . . . . **31**				
32	Annualization amounts **32**	0.116	0.0696	0.0435	0.029
33	Multiply line 26 by line 32 . . . . **33**				
34	Add lines 31 and 33. Enter here and on line 13 above . . . ▶ **34**				

Form **2210** (2003)

save $100 in penalties and pay your tax pro $150 to work out the numbers. (It's not that bad, but it should be.)

This is only worth doing if the substantial part of your income was received in the last three months of the year—or your big expenses happened in the beginning of the year. Otherwise, it won't save you much.

Don't Overpay Your Estimates if You're in Trouble

Perhaps in the past you got into trouble with the IRS or a state. Perhaps you have a former spouse chasing after you for support. Or suppose you've defaulted on your student loan or ignored traffic tickets. Until you clear up those problems, the IRS will be grabbing your refunds. In your case, you're better off owing a little bit, rather than shooting for a big refund. You won't get it.

The best idea, however, is to clear up those old debts, or get on a payment plan (which we'll discuss in Chapter 13) so they don't embarrass you in your business. The last thing you need is for your employees or vendors to get wind of your tax woes.

Basically, though, if you just follow the guidelines at the beginning of this chapter, the whole process is easy.

Estimated Payment Resources

- **Form 1040-ES, Estimated Tax For Individuals.** www.irs.gov/pub/irs-pdf/f1040es.pdf
- **Form 2210, Underpayment of Estimated Taxes by Individuals.** www.irs.gov/pub/irs-pdf/f2210.pdf
- **Form 6251, Alternative Minimum Tax—Individuals, Estates, and Trusts.** www.irs.gov/pub/irs-pdf/f6251.pdf
- **Form 8801, Credit for Prior Year Alternative Minimum Tax—Individuals.** www.irs.gov/pub/irs-pdf/f8801.pdf
- **IRS Publication 17, Chapter 32.** www.irs.gov/publications/p17/ch32.html#d0e76237
- **IRS Publication 505, Withholding and Estimated Payments.** www.irs.gov/publications/p505/ch02.html
- **Links to all states' tax forms.** www.taxadmin.org/fta/link/forms.html
- **TaxBrain Income Tax Liability Estimator and other tools.** http://taxbrain.com/taxcenter/estimator1.asp

- **TaxMama's Payment and Installment Agreement Information.** http: //taxmama.com/month/taxblues.html
- **The Taxpayer Advocate's Suggestion Page.** www.irs.gov/advocate /article/0,,id=117703,00.html
- **Thomas, The Library of Congress's Searchable Legislation Database.** http://thomas.loc.gov
- **TurboTax Income Tax Liability Estimator and other tools.** www.turbo tax.com/ts/t_and_r/calculators.html

12

SPECIAL CONSIDERATIONS FOR ONLINE BUSINESSES

The reasonable man adapts himself to the world; the unreasonable one persists in trying to adapt the world to himself. Therefore all progress depends on the unreasonable man.

—George Bernard Shaw

WWW = Who, What, Where?

In 1996, when talking to radio and television talk show hosts about an Internet site I had created, I had to devote most of that precious on-air time to explaining what the Internet was, how to get on it, and how to use the site's address to find it.

We've come a long way, baby! We've learned the jargon. We can find websites, with or without their www's. Today, no business is complete without a website. Even if you sell nothing, it's vitally important to establish a Web presence. You certainly want to secure ownership of the uniform resource locator (URL) that is your business's name.

Your website provides information about your business for your clients or customers to access when you're not available. We are all faced with questions our customers ask over and over again. You can easily provide the information online. With the right software and security, even a small company can arrange for clients, vendors, and customers to look up their own accounts, make corrections, and find information.

The Web offers many time-saving tools. It's easy to set up an online database with your clients' contact information. In fact, many accounting programs integrate with MS Word or Symantec's ACT! You can e-mail all your clients instantly when something important happens. Or you can target just a few—just those with children, for example. You simply write the message and click—and they have it. And they can respond instantly.

Compare that to the time and cost of writing to one hundred people. You print out all the letters, stuff the envelopes, add postage, and get everything to the post office before the last pick-up. The Internet offers so many time-saving applications that you can kill a lot of time, saving time.

All kidding aside, once you stick your toe into the Internet's web, you're stuck forever. And all kinds of new tax issues and questions surface.

What? I Thought There Was No Internet Tax

You're so right. For now, no one may assess you taxes for your use of the Internet.[1] In fact, the Internet Tax Nondiscrimination Act—Senate Bill 150—passed on April 29, 2004, extending the moratorium on Internet taxes.[2]

Unfortunately, though, that doesn't mean you don't have to pay taxes on the Internet. Senate Bill 150 only refers to communications activities—being connected to the Internet—access, online services, and hosting services. You can't pay a separate Internet tax for that. But you are paying taxes, nonetheless.

Have you looked at your phone bill lately? You know, the bill for the phone line you use to be connected—even if it's a DSL line or cable.

One of my recent phone bills shows:

Federal Subscriber Line Charge	$8.98	
9-1-1 Emergency System	.29	
CA High Cost Fund Surcharge—A	.08	
CA High Cost Fund Surcharge—B	.98	
Universal Lifeline Telephone Surcharge	.48	
Rate Surcharge Credit	−.54	(no explanation)
State Regulatory Fee	.05	
CA Relay Service and Communications Devices Fund	.13	(No one asked if I wanted to donate this!)

---

1. The Internet Tax Freedom Act, available at www.ecommercecommission.org/ITFA.html.

2. The Internet Tax Nondiscrimination Act (Senate Bill 150), available at www.congress.gov/cgi-bin /bdquery/z?d108:SN00150:@@@L&summ2=m&.

Federal Universal Services Fee	.78
Federal Taxes at 3.00 percent	1.49
Local Taxes at 10.00 percent	4.96
Total Taxes and Surcharges	$17.68

Holy baloney! That adds 17 percent to each of my phone bills. Are you telling me there are no Internet taxes?

Also, nowhere does Senate Bill 150, or any other law, say anything about not taxing income earned online or the sales of products and services.

The question is, of course, where will you be taxed? To answer that, you must know your nexus.

Nexus

What an odd word—*nexus*. What is it? A car? A telephone company? A quickie photo shop? No! *Nexus* means a place where you have a business presence. It sounds pretty simple, doesn't it?

Not according to Diana DiBello, Director of Tax at Vertex Inc. in Berwyn, Pennsylvania (www.vertexinc.com). She used nearly eighty PowerPoint slides to explain the complexity of this question to an audience of tax professionals. While the average small business owner doesn't need to know *that* much information, you do need to understand the information that typically affects small businesses like yours.

Start by answering this question correctly: Where is your business located?

- Is it in your home?
- Is it at your office?
- Is it where your website's server is located?
- Is it where your webmaster is located?
- Is it where your post office box is located?
- Is it where you've incorporated?
- Is it where you're drop-shipping your products?
- Is it where your salespeople are?
- Is it where your affiliates (commissioned sales force) are?
- Is it where your related companies are?
- Is it where your merchant account receives your money?
- Is it where your virtual assistant is located?

- Is it where your online shopping cart is hosted?
- Is it where your mailing list is hosted?
- Is it where your advertising agency or public relations agency is?
- Is it where you're running your ads?
- Is it where your shoppers or customers are located?

Are you starting to get the picture? A business's nexus can be widespread. But the good news is that with the advent of the Internet, home-based businesses can have customers all over the globe. Literally.

Why Do We Care About Nexus?

Nexus costs money. Even when you don't think you have a physical presence in a state, that state might believe it has the right to your money. State governments are hungry. With the slump in the economy after the wild ride in the 1990s, state revenues have dropped dramatically. With more people shopping over the Internet, states are also losing the sales taxes they used to count on.

Having to make up the money somewhere, states have tapped into anyone they feel is operating within their reach. And they've won. There are solid legal precedents for states to assess income and sales taxes from people and companies who lightly brush the boundaries of their domain.

You undoubtedly remember that infamous day in 1991 when Michael Jordan, playing for the Chicago Bulls, was hit by the State of California for a share of his earnings. David Hoffman, Tax Foundation economist and author of the "Jock Tax" report, explains: "The jock tax began with California trying to get back at Michael Jordan for beating the Lakers in 1991 and Illinois fought back with a retaliatory tax the next year. Ironically, if Jordan rejoined the Bulls in any capacity, he would find himself paying double taxes."[3]

Once other states learned that California had succeeded in taxing a transient, they too started to see this as a lucrative new means to replenish their depleted treasuries. The "jock tax" now affects all performers traveling across state lines, traveling sales folks, even Internet businesses. Many of my clients are affected. These days, their employers routinely provide W-2s with all the states' incomes

---

3. Tax Foundation report—Washington, D.C., July 14, 2003: " 'Jock Taxes' Spread as State and City Governments Try to Maximize Revenue from Nonresidents," available at www.taxfoundation.org /jocktax.html.

Where Is My Nexus?

I sit here in my living room; it is my principal office. I have several websites. One of the servers is in Colorado. I don't even know where the other one is. One of my mailing list servers is in Minnesota, or at least the company I pay is. He may be hosting his server in China, for all I know. My web designer is in Arizona. One of my corporations is in Nevada; the other is in California. My partners for various ventures are in India, New York, and Portugal. I have mailing addresses in Nevada and California, but my sites' shopping carts are in England and Missouri. The payment-processing center is in Utah. My tax returns are electronically transmitted to the IRS from a company in Maine. My tax clients are in Africa, Asia, South America, North America, Europe, Australia, New Zealand. . . . My affiliates, those people who get a commission for selling my products or referring clients to me, are all over the world.

With all this information, where is my nexus? And what part of it is affected by tax laws?

You're beginning to see how unclear this can be, even for a small home-based business, once you take it online.

---

and withholdings. Some of my film industry clients get three or four W-2s from the same employer for the same show.

Once you start making a lot of money online, if you're not aware of how the nexus rules and definitions affect your business, you might find yourself paying taxes to a state you've never visited.

For now, most likely, state income taxes on your earnings won't be your big problem. But sales taxes will be. You'll also face a problem with those 1099s we discussed in Chapter 9. We'll talk about both of these issues now.

Internet Sales Tax Issues

Many people believe because the Internet is so new—and the topic of online taxes is so new—that new ground will have to be broken to establish guidelines for when and how taxes are paid.

Actually, that's not really true. It's only new to you, because, suddenly, your local business is selling nationwide, or even internationally.

The sales tax issues involved with online transactions are the same ones the mail-order industry has been facing for decades. Presently, domestic sales tax issues are governed by your state's sales tax department. But what will happen in the long run? The states are getting together to create a system and software that collects sales tax from shoppers, remits it to the correct state automatically, and doesn't require the vendor to file forms in those other states. For more information on how states are working together, take a look at the Streamlined Sales Tax Project (http://streamlinedsalestax.org). It's still a long way from being implemented. Actually, what the states really want is for the federal government to mandate that companies charge sales taxes based on the destination state, nationwide. DiBello suggests that even if a law like this passes, it's only practical for the large national companies. There will be thresholds designed to exclude small businesses.

I have no faith in that threshold level. These are the same legislators who think a luxury auto is any car that costs more than $15,300—and that $100,000 is high income.

What do you do now? DiBello recommends that you stay tuned in to the status of the legislation so that when it does affect you, you're prepared.

In the meantime, should you simply ignore sales taxes for out-of-state shoppers?

Sales Tax Case Law

DiBello recently cited interesting situations where states went after companies who have no business presence in a state. Connecticut, for instance, sued Dell Computer for unpaid sales taxes because Dell contracted with a company to provide local service on customers' computers. The Connecticut Superior Court ruled against the state only because of the low volume of service calls. If the volume of repairs were higher, Dell would be paying sales tax in Connecticut.

Dell got hit because they simply had a contract with a local company.

What about your business?

Perhaps you're using an affiliate program or agents to sell your products on their own websites, or locally. You might just have created an "agency nexus" in their state. An agency nexus occurs when you have a representative in a state. Exactly what constitutes an agent depends on how aggressive the state is.

In another instance, the Scholastic Corporation was hit by California. You're familiar with their products. The *Junior Scholastic* magazines are in every dentist's office. We all got Scholastic books and publications in school, even preschool. That's how they got into trouble. Scholastic sold books to students by having their teachers give them order forms and collecting the money. The California Supreme Court held that because the teachers in California schools sell Scholastic's products, Scholastic does have nexus.

Think about how your business and sales avenues are structured. Will agency nexus affect you?

Sales Tax Nexus and Your Business

Because online sales tax is such a hot issue, I want to make sure you receive the best information possible. Until speaking with DiBello from Vertex Inc., I took a conservative approach to sales tax collections. I had been advising clients and readers that if they started shipping a high volume of sales to a state, it would be wise to register with that state's sales tax authority.

After all, you don't really pay the sales taxes. You collect it from your customers and pass it along to the state. It only comes out of your pocket if you don't collect, but should have.

DiBello clarifies a common misconception about your nexus. Just because you ship a lot of merchandise into any state does not mean you have to collect their sales tax. Under the present status of United States sales tax laws, to be required to collect sales tax, you must have "physical nexus" in that state. What do the physical nexus rules mean?

1. You must have a physical presence in the state.
2. There must be sufficient benefit to the merchant from the taxes.
3. The taxes can't interfere with interstate commerce or give the merchant unfair advantage.

This basically means that unless you have an office or store in that state, you don't need to worry about collecting sales taxes on your out-of-state sales.

But hiring a contractor or agent in another state to represent you, along with the agent's other companies, falls under the rules of agency nexus. Of course, if you place your own agent in a state and that person represents you exclusively, you've just established a physical presence in that state. For instance, the State of California has a tax collections office in Florida, where many former Californians have retired. California has nexus in Florida. Do you think the State of Florida should be taxing California on the taxes it collects?

You do have to comply with your own state's rules, but you already know that. You registered with your state's sales tax department for in-state sales when you went through your checklist in Chapter 1.

You have nothing more to worry about, right?

Not so fast. There are still those services you're using. What about them?

Rents and Services Domestically and Abroad

Operating on the Internet since 1995, it became clear that federal tax issues were going to emerge. As early as 1998, IRS spokesman Ed Mieszerski ruefully admitted, "Some of these questions [dealing with online taxes] will only be dealt with when they come before us as a result of an examination or court case."[4]

To date, I haven't seen a case addressing these issues head-on. But we will, and you need to make sure you have protection in place when these issues start to arise. To avoid problems, you need to be aware of the issues. Following are some real-life scenarios and some points to ponder.

Incorporated in Nevada (no state income tax), Starry-Eyed, Inc., is based at home in California and receives money from sales of products. Their inventory is stored and shipped from a fulfillment house located in Pennsylvania. The website is hosted on a server in New York. They encountered the following questions—the answers should help you stay legal, too.

Q: *As a corporation, can they deduct office-in-home costs? (As a proprietor they can, so . . .)*

A: Treat your office at home the way you would if you weren't doing business online. Chapter 7 explains the rules.

Q: *In which state are they conducting business? All work, including design, artwork, search engine placement, etc., is often done by people working from their homes, often across the country. Under what circumstances would those workers be employees? Will the company have to file income, sales, or property tax forms in each (or any) state?*

A: Consider your business nexus to be only those states where you have a physical presence. Comply with all local rules.

Q: *Should they be sending a 1099-MISC to the web hosts (those hosting their actual site) for rent?*

A: The web server rent is unclear. If you want to be safe, send the 1099-MISC for rent.

---

4. In a memo to the author, in response to Internet-related tax questions, for use in the 1998 Insiders Series Workshops for tax professionals in Burbank, California.

Q: *Some work is being done by foreign nationals in their own country. Since payment is being made for services rendered, how do they 1099 a foreigner? Must they issue a 1099? Must they take any backup withholding?*

A: Don't send 1099s to foreign individuals or companies outside the country that do work for you. If you knowingly hire a U.S. citizen or someone who holds a green card who works overseas, issue the 1099-MISC. Don't withhold taxes, unless the IRS sends you a withholding order on that person. Review the 1099 instructions in Chapter 9 for guidance.

Let's look at another company with some different issues.

I Can Sell Anything To Anyone (ICSATA) is based in the United States and their website also is hosted here. They operate an associate or affiliate program. Other websites link to their site—and ICSATA pays the linked companies a commission on whatever sales arise from those links (this is similar to how Amazon.com operates). Many of the companies that are linked are overseas businesses.

Q: *Is this a commission, referral fee, royalty . . . what?*

A: When someone is a contributor to the design, content, or substance of your product or services, and they are contractually entitled to a share of the sales, it's royalty. Otherwise, you're paying commissions. Chapter 5 explains why we care about the distinction.

Q: *Is any of this subject to self-employment tax?*

A: When regular salespeople receive commissions, it's self-employment income. Why shouldn't this be? Chapter 11 explains self-employment taxes.

Q: *Are 1099s issued to all parties (inside and outside of the United States)?*

A: No need to issue 1099s outside the country—unless they are U.S. citizens or green card holders.

Frequently, when you ask the IRS these types of questions, you'll receive a vague answer. The above answers provide the most sensible approach for you to use until the IRS issues formal guidelines.

Legal Issues on the Internet

Once your business touches the Internet, you're going to be hit with some powerful legal issues, and you won't realize it until you get into trouble. The best guide to this topic is attorney Jonathan I. Ezor's book *Clicking Through: A Survival Guide for Bringing Your Company Online.*

So many things can affect you, even if you're just minding your own business.

- **You face copyright issues.** For instance, did your web designer give you a written release for all the graphics and design? Or does he or she own your site?
- **You face liability issues.** You have affiliates marketing your product or service. They say something that isn't true, without your permission. You're the one getting sued.
- **You face spam issues.** You think you're sending out a simple newsletter. But one person gets his or her nose bent out of shape and decides he or she never subscribed. What do you do?
- **You have liability issues.** You are running someone's ads on your site. Perhaps you have banners through an affiliate program. You might be using Google's Adsense service. Someone clicks on an ad and is unhappy with the product. Are you liable?
- **You face privacy issues.** Issues with privacy can become very nasty. Suppose someone hacks your site or telephone book and steals client information? Or you do something with a sponsor? Your members can get really unpleasant if they feel invaded.

Overall, we're just scratching the surface of Internet issues. But don't let the worries get to you. Resources like Ezor's book and the HelpDesk (see the Resources section at the end of the chapter) will keep you safe.

The World Wide Web is an exciting environment. It can make your dreams come true. It did for me, and many of the people I know. The streets are virtually paved with gold. As I've said before, the Internet has the pioneering spirit and excitement of the Old West—law just hasn't been established yet. Getting there is lots of fun.

In the End

Most issues related to Internet taxation are unclear and apt to change. You now know you don't have to worry about sales taxes across borders. For all the other areas, when questions arise, treat them the way you would if you were not doing business online. If you're not sure, check with your advisory team for guidance. If they can't give you reliable guidance, you can always try TaxMama or the HelpDesk (see resources below). One of our tax professional members will either have an answer or be able to point you to a resource that can help you.

Online Business Resources

- **Vertex Inc.** http://vertexinc.com: This authority on all sales tax issues—and other business tax issues—publishes software and reference materials for companies engaged in interstate commerce. Sign up for their free newsletter.
- **The Tax Foundation.** www.taxfoundation.org: Find tax facts, statistics, and in-depth analyses of federal and state governments.
- **Streamlined Sales Tax Project.** http://streamlinedsalestax.org: This is a cooperative effort by most U.S. states to create a universal sales tax system to allow them to collect sales taxes on Internet sales.
- **Senate Finance Committee.** www.senate.gov/~finance: See it before it becomes law.
- **TaxMama.com.** http://taxmama.com: The Ask TaxMama feature is free. Pose your question. If it hasn't been asked dozens of times before, you'll get an answer.
- **The Internet's HelpDesk.** www.ihelpmate.com: The I-HelpDesk & WebReview Digest is a free weekly digest with members worldwide. This is the place to come if you have any questions at all about operating a website or doing business on the Internet. The members answer your questions and help each other repair or improve their websites. Resources, services, providers, and products are discussed and reviewed.
- **The Internet Affiliate Marketing Association.** http://iafma.org: If you have a product or service to sell, increase the size of your sales force by establishing an affiliate program. Using specialized software that keeps track of the source of sales, you can pay commissions to people who carry your logo or your advertisements. It's less of a risk than paying for ads. You only pay them when they make a sale. But your logo or product is visible all the time. An excellent way to spread brand awareness, this method turned Amazon.com into a household name. iAfma has lots of free tools to educate you about how affiliate programs work and what tools to use to establish your own. Basic membership is free. Other levels are paid.
- **Google's Adsense.** http://google.com/Adsense: If your website provides useful information, Google can provide advertising revenues for your site. Once

accepted, you simply paste their code on your site and Google sells the advertising. The software reads the content on your page and serves advertisements related to the content. People are excited, saying it adds value to their articles or information. The income is terrific—and you never have to sell an ad or give out information about your demographics.

- **Google's AdWords.** https://adwords.google.com/select: Use this to advertise and to test your advertising campaigns.

All of these sites have advice for a low fee, but you should note that satisfaction is guaranteed—expertise is not.

- **Google Answers.** http://answers.google.com/answers: You set the price—from $2 to $200. Researchers will provide remarkably good information, with links to the sources of the data.
- **Keen.com.** www.keen.com: Seek out a tax professional, based on their area of expertise and their satisfaction rating. There are more than a hundred tax professionals with all levels of expertise. Keen allows you to call them and pay only for your time online.
- **The National Association of Tax Professionals.** www.natptax.com, (800) 839-0001: They will provide written responses to your tax questions, with citations supporting their answers.
- **Jest for Pun.** www.workinghumor.com/jfp/index.htm: The source of most of the humorous quotations used in this book.

13

TAX NOTICES, AUDITS, AND COLLECTION NOTES

Blood's not thicker than money.
—GROUCHO MARX

This chapter will walk you through some of the routine or terrifying interactions you will have with the IRS. Whenever you get notices about audits or owing money, don't just ignore the notices. Always address them. If you are afraid or uncomfortable about dealing with the IRS alone, engage the services of a good local tax professional who understands how to handle audit or collections issues. Not all tax pros do. Ask them to tell you how much experience they have—and if they're successful. If they complain about all their problems with the IRS, move on. The real pros know how to get right to the key people who can help you.

Dealing with Basic Tax Notices for Individual Returns

When you file a tax return—or don't file—sometimes, there may be errors or you will have a balance due. The IRS has a series of standard notices they send you. Each notice has a little CP code on the top right-hand corner of the first page of the letter. *CP* stands for "computer paragraph."

The notices are issued in a particular timed sequence by the IRS computer. If you don't respond in time for someone to receive your response and key it into the computer, it will automatically spit out the next one. If you are mailing a response right at the end of the response period, call the IRS immediately. Ask them to put a hold on any collections actions until they receive your information. Let me repeat—*call the IRS*. Don't just hope they'll get your response in time. And when you call, always be sure to write down the name of the person you speak with, their IRS employee number, and the date and time of the conversation. (They give you that information at the beginning of each conversation. But they say it quickly, so don't overlook it. If necessary, ask them to repeat it slowly—and to spell it for you.) Follow up with a written note to the IRS and/or that employee, summarizing your conversation.

Incidentally, if you get the right person, or the right group, they may be able to accept your information over the phone and the fax. If they have helped you, it's always nice if you send a thank-you letter. Remember, even though the agency is the big, bad IRS, you are dealing with real live people who have jobs and families. A nice letter in their file does two things. First, it could help them get a raise or a promotion. Second, a copy stays with your file, too, and alerts the IRS that you are a nice person. In the future, that could work in your favor.

A Key to IRS Notices

- **CP 12—Math Error—Overpayment of $1 or More.** You still have a refund coming, but it may be lower than you expected. Look for child tax credit adjustments or disallowed dependents because of a Social Security number mismatch. *You have sixty days to respond or pay.* Compare the numbers on the notice to your tax return. The IRS's adjustment may be wrong. Or you may never have gotten a check from them. Respond in writing before the deadline, with your explanation.
- **CP 14—Balance Due, No Math Error.** This is the computation of the underpayment penalties and interest to your tax return. It may also include late filing or payment penalties. *You have twenty-one days to respond or pay.* You can reduce the underpayment of estimated tax penalty if most of your income was received toward the end of the year. Use the annualized income installment method of computing your penalties, found on page 4 of the Form 2210, Underpayment of Estimated Tax by Individuals, Estates, and Trusts as seen in Figure 13.1.
- **CP 23—We Changed Your Estimated Tax Total, You Have an Amount Due.** Perhaps one or more of the checks you thought were estimated payments were something else (perhaps payments for last year's tax). It's also possible that you sent a check but didn't write the correct year, form number, and/or Social Security number on it. The IRS may have your money but

FIGURE 13.1 Form 2210, Underpayment of Estimated Tax by Individuals, Estates, and Trusts

Form **2210**	**Underpayment of Estimated Tax by Individuals, Estates, and Trusts**	OMB No. 1545-0140
Department of the Treasury Internal Revenue Service	▶ See separate instructions. ▶ **Attach to Form 1040, 1040A, 1040NR, 1040NR-EZ, or 1041.**	20**03** Attachment Sequence No. **06**
Name(s) shown on tax return		Identifying number

Do You Have To File Form 2210?

	Yes	
Complete lines 1 through 7 below. Is line 7 less than $1,000?	▶	**Do not file Form 2210.** You do not owe a penalty.

No ↓

	Yes	
Complete lines 8 and 9 below. Is line 6 equal to or more than line 9?	▶	You do not owe a penalty. **Do not file Form 2210** (but if box **E** below applies, you must file page 1 of Form 2210 below).

No ↓

	Yes	
You may owe a penalty. Does any box in Part II below apply?	▶	You **must** file Form 2210. Does box **B, C,** or **D** apply?

No	**Yes**
	▶ You must figure your penalty.

No ↓ / ↓

Do not file Form 2210. You are not required to figure your penalty because the IRS will figure it and send you a bill for any unpaid amount. If you want to figure it, you may use Part III or Part IV as a worksheet and enter your penalty amount on your tax return (see page 2 of the instructions), but **do not file Form 2210.**	You are **not** required to figure your penalty because the IRS will figure it and send you a bill for any unpaid amount. If you want to figure it, you may use Part III or Part IV as a worksheet and enter your penalty amount on your tax return (see page 2 of the instructions), but **file only page 1 of Form 2210.**

Part I	**Required Annual Payment** (see page 2 of the instructions)		
1	Enter your 2003 tax after credits from Form 1040, line 54 (or comparable line of your return) .	**1**	
2	Other taxes, including self-employment tax (see page 2 of the instructions)	**2**	
3	Refundable credits. Enter the total of your earned income credit, additional child tax credit, credit for Federal tax paid on fuels, and health coverage tax credit for eligible individuals	**3** (	)
4	Current year tax. Combine lines 1, 2, and 3	**4**	
5	Multiply line 4 by 90% (.90) **5**		
6	Withholding taxes. **Do not** include estimated tax payments. See page 2 of the instructions . .	**6**	
7	Subtract line 6 from line 4. If less than $1,000, you do not owe a penalty; **do not file Form 2210**	**7**	
8	Maximum required annual payment based on prior year's tax (see page 2 of the instructions) .	**8**	
9	**Required annual payment.** Enter the **smaller** of line 5 or line 8	**9**	

Next: Is line 9 more than line 6?

☐ **No.** You **do not** owe a penalty. **Do not file Form 2210** unless box **E** below applies.

☐ **Yes.** You may owe a penalty, but **do not file Form 2210** unless one or more boxes in Part II below applies.

• If box **B, C,** or **D** applies, you must figure your penalty and file Form 2210.

• If only box **A** or **E** (or both) applies, file only page 1 of Form 2210. You are **not** required to figure your penalty; the IRS will figure it and send you a bill for any unpaid amount. If you want to figure your penalty, you may use Part III or IV as a worksheet and enter your penalty on your tax return (see page 2 of the instructions), but **file only page 1 of Form 2210.**

Part II	**Reasons for Filing.** Check applicable boxes. If none apply, **do not file Form 2210.**

A ☐ You request a **waiver** (see page 1 of the instructions) of your entire penalty. You must check this box and file page 1 of Form 2210, but you are not required to figure your penalty.

B ☐ You request a waiver (see page 1 of the instructions) of part of your penalty. You must figure your penalty and waiver amount and file Form 2210.

C ☐ Your income varied during the year and your penalty is reduced or eliminated when figured using the **annualized income installment method.** You must figure the penalty using Schedule AI and file Form 2210.

D ☐ Your penalty is lower when figured by treating the Federal income tax withheld from your wages as paid on the dates it was actually withheld, instead of in equal amounts on the payment due dates. You must figure your penalty and file Form 2210.

E ☐ You filed or are filing a joint return for either 2002 or 2003, but not for both years, and line 8 above is smaller than line 5 above. You must file page 1 of Form 2210, but you are **not** required to figure your penalty (unless box **B, C,** or **D** applies).

For Paperwork Reduction Act Notice, see page 5 of separate instructions.   Cat. No. 11744P   Form **2210** (2003)

continued

FIGURE 13.1 *continued*

Form 2210 (2003)   Page **4**

Schedule AI—Annualized Income Installment Method (See pages 4 and 5 of the instructions.)

Estates and trusts, **do not** use the period ending dates shown to the right. Instead, use the following: 2/28/03, 4/30/03, 7/31/03, and 11/30/03.

		(a) 1/1/03–3/31/03	(b) 1/1/03–5/31/03	(c) 1/1/03–8/31/03	(d) 1/1/03–12/31/03

Part I Annualized Income Installments

1	Enter your adjusted gross income for each period (see instructions). (Estates and trusts, enter your taxable income without your exemption for each period.) **1**				
2	Annualization amounts. (Estates and trusts, see instructions.) . . **2**	4	2.4	1.5	1
3	Annualized income. Multiply line 1 by line 2 . . . . **3**				
4	Enter your itemized deductions for the period shown in each column. If you do not itemize, enter -0- and skip to line 7. (Estates and trusts, enter -0-, skip to line 9, and enter the amount from line 3 on line 9.) **4**				
5	Annualization amounts **5**	4	2.4	1.5	1
6	Multiply line 4 by line 5 (see instructions if line 3 is more than $69,750) **6**				
7	In each column, enter the full amount of your standard deduction from Form 1040, line 37, or Form 1040A, line 24 (Form 1040NR or 1040NR-EZ filers, enter -0-. **Exception:** Indian students and business apprentices, enter standard deduction from Form 1040NR, line 35, or Form 1040NR-EZ, line 11.) **7**				
8	Enter the **larger** of line 6 or line 7 . . . . **8**				
9	Subtract line 8 from line 3 . . . . **9**				
10	In each column, multiply $3,050 by the total number of exemptions claimed (see instructions if line 3 is more than $104,625). (Estates and trusts and Form 1040NR or 1040NR-EZ filers, enter the exemption amount shown on your tax return.) **10**				
11	Subtract line 10 from line 9 . . . . **11**				
12	Figure your tax on the amount on line 11 (see instructions) . . . **12**				
13	Self-employment tax from line 34 below (complete Part II) . . . **13**				
14	Enter other taxes for each payment period (see instructions) . . **14**				
15	Total tax. Add lines 12, 13, and 14 . . . . **15**				
16	For each period, enter the same type of credits as allowed on Form 2210, lines 1 and 3 (see instructions) **16**				
17	Subtract line 16 from line 15. If zero or less, enter -0- **17**				
18	Applicable percentage **18**	22.5%	45%	67.5%	90%
19	Multiply line 17 by line 18 . . . . **19**				
	Complete lines 20–25 of one column before going to the next column.				
20	Add the amounts in all previous columns of line 25 . . . . . **20**	▨			
21	Subtract line 20 from line 19. If zero or less, enter -0- **21**				
22	Enter 25% (.25) of line 9 on page 1 of Form 2210 in each column **22**				
23	Subtract line 25 of the previous column from line 24 of that column **23**	▨			
24	Add lines 22 and 23 . . . . **24**				
25	Enter the **smaller** of line 21 or line 24 here and on Form 2210, line 18 . . . . ▶ **25**				

Part II Annualized Self-Employment Tax (Form 1040 filers only)

26	Net earnings from self-employment for the period (see instructions) **26**				
27	Prorated social security tax limit **27**	$21,750	$36,250	$58,000	$87,000
28	Enter actual wages for the period subject to social security tax or the 6.2% portion of the 7.65% railroad retirement (tier 1) tax . . **28**				
29	Subtract line 28 from line 27. If zero or less, enter -0-. **29**				
30	Annualization amounts **30**	0.496	0.2976	0.186	0.124
31	Multiply line 30 by the **smaller** of line 26 or line 29 . . . . . **31**				
32	Annualization amounts **32**	0.116	0.0696	0.0435	0.029
33	Multiply line 26 by line 32 . . . . **33**				
34	Add lines 31 and 33. Enter here and on line 13 above . . . ▶ **34**				

Form **2210** (2003)

hasn't applied it to any specific year. Find your cancelled check and make very clean photocopies of both the front and back. Send the check to the IRS with the notice and your explanation. *You have twenty-one days to respond or pay.*

- **CP 24—We Changed Your Estimated Tax Total, You Are Due a Refund.** Quite often, you have either not recorded a payment to the IRS or didn't remember that you applied last year's refund to this return. The second page of the notice will show a list of the payments and dates the checks were received by the IRS. *There is no need to reply.* By the time you get the notice, the IRS will already have sent the check. However, they may be giving you credit for a payment you intended for a different year. Since you're getting the money back, you might not care. But it may involve an estimated payment that you had made on time for the current year—and now you'll get hit with underpayment of estimated penalties. To avoid this problem in the future, make sure you always write the following three pieces of information on each check you send to any government agency. TaxMama's acronym **FYTIN** may help you remember:

  - **F.** The form number.
  - **Y.** The tax year you're paying (use a separate check for each year).
  - **TIN.** The taxpayer identification number (TIN)—your Social Security number (SSN) or employer identification number (EIN)—to credit with this payment. If you are paying money in toward a married filing joint return, list both SSNs.

  If the IRS sends you a refund for a payment that was intended as an estimate and you shouldn't have gotten the refund, do this: (1) Write "VOID" on it. (2) Make a copy. (3) Send it back with a letter explaining that you want that money applied to your account. Define the tax form and year. This will prevent penalties for a tax you did mean to pay.

- **CP 49—Overpaid Tax Applied to Other Taxes You Owe.** The IRS will send you this notice if you owe money for prior years. You might also get one of these if you owe back child or spousal support, state income taxes, or motor vehicle fines. The IRS will also grab your refund if you've defaulted on student loans or owe money to the Social Security Administration. The notice will spell out which years or debts are being paid. Often, the money isn't staying with the IRS. When the money is sent to another agency, you'll have to get a release from them. When that's the case, don't even waste your time trying to get more information about the outstanding debt from the IRS.

They won't have it. You'll have to go to the source, for instance, the motor vehicle department, the district attorney's office, and so on. You'll need to contact the agency that initiated the lien on your refund. Sometimes you get an unpleasant surprise, learning about an old IRS balance you didn't know about or forgot. Track down the details. While the IRS may have only grabbed $39 this year, don't just shrug it off as being too small to matter. They might take $3,000 next year.

- **CP 80—Reminder—We Have Not Received Your Tax Return.** The IRS's records show payments or credits for this year. Prepare and file the return. (See CP 515 below.)
- **CP 90/CP 297—Final Notice—Notice of Intent to Levy and Notice of Your Right to a Hearing.** You will only get this notice if you have ignored all the other notices. *You have thirty days to respond or pay.* If you know you owe the money, call the IRS to work out a payment plan or an offer in compromise (OIC). Ask them to put a hold on the collections activity until you either file the OIC or start the payment plan. Once you're on the plan, they will hold off as long as you're current on your payments.
- **CP 91/CP 298—Final Notice Before Levy on Social Security Benefits.** (See CP 90/CP 297 above.)
- **CP 161—No Math Error—Balance Due.** This is the business version of CP 14.
- **CP 501—Reminder Notice—Balance Due.** *You have ten days to respond or pay.*
- **CP 504—Urgent Notice—We Intend to Levy on Certain Assets.** Respond within ten days or lose your bank account, wages, or other funds the IRS knows where to find. (If you have a government contract or 1099s have been filed under your Social Security number—watch out.) Note: If your bank or employer calls to tell you your wages or bank account have been levied or garnished, don't panic. The bank and your employer must hold those funds for twenty days to give you time to fix the problem. How can you solve this problem? First, get a copy of the levy notice they received. Then, call the IRS *immediately*. If you can set up a payment plan or get them to agree to give you some time (typically thirty to forty-five days), you'll be able to get them to release the levy.

  - **Good News.** The bank levy only lets them grab the money in the account on the day it receives the levy. Any money deposited afterward is safe— until the next levy.

- **Bad News.** If wages are garnished, that deduction continues until you get the IRS to release it or until you pay the balance in full.

- **CP 515—Request for Tax Return.** They don't have it. If you sent it in—do it again. Be sure to stamp it as a copy (or write "Copy" over it). Sign it, dating it the same date that you originally filed it. If you never filed a return—prepare one and file it now.

- **CP 523—Notice of Default on Installment Agreement (IA).** When you signed the IA, you gave the IRS your bank account numbers and gave them permission to levy if you didn't make your payments. Now they will. *Call immediately.* (See CP 90/CP 297 above.)

- **CP 2000—Notice of Proposed Adjustment for Underpayment/Overpayment.** This results from the IRS's computers matching up all the W-2s, 1099s, 1098s, and K-1s issued under your SSN. Quite often, the notices are wrong. Or it is reporting stock sales, on which you had losses anyway. The information is reported somewhere on your tax return. Review the notice carefully. If the IRS is wrong, call the phone number on the form immediately and ask for another thirty days to respond. That way, if it takes a while for your response to reach them, they won't already be billing you. When they are right, it's because you left off employment income (perhaps a brief job early in the year) or dividends you forgot about. If the IRS is correct, just pay the bill. You don't need to file an amended return. *You have thirty days to respond or pay.*

If the notice has a number that isn't listed above, the IRS recommends you call the phone number listed on the letter within the deadline shown on the letter. And yes, sometimes you only have a few days because the notice was mailed late. The IRS computer doesn't know when it was mailed, so it will take the next action on schedule. Don't argue with the IRS staff person who answers the phone. They aren't at fault. Be pleasant and polite and they'll be more apt to help you.

IRS Audits

Sooner or later, just about all businesses get audited. Not that often though. The IRS does happen to be behind on their audits. But they released an announcement in April 2004 about rolling out their new, more aggressive audits of businesses.

During the IRS's fiscal year 2002 (covering your 2001 tax return), the IRS audited less than half a percent of all tax returns filed.[1] That makes you feel great, right? Think again. Of those 827,000 audits, more than 21 percent were business returns. Business returns include all returns with Schedule Cs, corporations, S-corporations, and partnerships. I didn't include farm returns. In effect, more than 1 percent of all business returns were audited.

Nearly 3 percent of all personal tax returns with Schedule Cs showing less than $25,000 of income were examined. That means your Schedule C with a low profit gives you three times the chance of any other business return of being audited—and six times the chance of anyone without a business.

On the other hand, if you had any corporation or partnership with assets of less than $250,000, your chances of being audited were less than a third of a percent (0.31 percent) of all partnership, corporation, and S-corporation returns filed. And it was barely 2.5 percent of all audits.

That was then.

Today, the IRS is more aggressive. They've hired five thousand more people to start doing more audits and collecting more money. Their targets are small businesses, Schedule Cs, and especially S-corporations. They know that's where the real errors can be found.

Why am I boring you with these statistics? Because it will help you with two areas of your business. First of all, it will help you determine what business format you want to adopt. Second, it will help you understand just how much risk there is of your transactions being scrutinized. So, if you're thinking of doing something questionable—you know the risk.

Anticipating an Audit: Laying the Groundwork

Knowing you're being audited is usually simple. You get an audit notice. If you've moved frequently and haven't updated your address with the IRS by filing Form 8822 (see Figure 13.2), you might not have gotten their notices. If this happens, some nice Fed in a dark suit will come knocking on your front door. And you'll go running out the back door to call your tax professional. (Yes, one client of mine really did that. And it's not a good idea.)

---

1. IRS Statistical Reports—Table 10. Examination Coverage: Recommended and Average Recommended Additional Tax after Examination, by Size and Type of Return, Fiscal 2002, available at www .irs.gov/pub/irs-soi/02db10ex.xls.

FIGURE 13.2 Form 8822, Change of Address

Form **8822**	**Change of Address**	OMB No. 1545-1163

Form **8822**
(Rev. December 2003)
Department of the Treasury
Internal Revenue Service

Change of Address

▶ Please type or print.

▶ See instructions on back. ▶ Do not attach this form to your return.

OMB No. 1545-1163

Part I   **Complete This Part To Change Your Home Mailing Address**

Check **all** boxes this change affects:

1 ☐ Individual income tax returns (Forms 1040, 1040A, 1040EZ, TeleFile, 1040NR, etc.)

     ▶ If your last return was a joint return and you are now establishing a residence separate
from the spouse with whom you filed that return, check here . . . . ▶ ☐

2 ☐ Gift, estate, or generation-skipping transfer tax returns (Forms 706, 709, etc.)

     ▶ For Forms 706 and 706-NA, enter the decedent's name and social security number below.

   ▶ Decedent's name   ▶ Social security number

3a Your name (first name, initial, and last name)	**3b** Your social security number
4a Spouse's name (first name, initial, and last name)	**4b** Spouse's social security number

5   Prior name(s). See instructions.

6a Old address (no., street, city or town, state, and ZIP code). If a P.O. box or foreign address, see instructions.	Apt. no.
6b Spouse's old address, if different from line 6a (no., street, city or town, state, and ZIP code). If a P.O. box or foreign address, see instructions.	Apt. no.
7 New address (no., street, city or town, state, and ZIP code). If a P.O. box or foreign address, see instructions.	Apt. no.

Part II   **Complete This Part To Change Your Business Mailing Address or Business Location**

Check **all** boxes this change affects:

8 ☐ Employment, excise, income, and other business returns (Forms 720, 940, 940-EZ, 941, 990, 1041, 1065, 1120, etc.)
9 ☐ Employee plan returns (Forms 5500, 5500-EZ, etc.).
10 ☐ Business location

11a Business name	**11b** Employer identification number
12 Old mailing address (no., street, city or town, state, and ZIP code). If a P.O. box or foreign address, see instructions.	Room or suite no.
13 New mailing address (no., street, city or town, state, and ZIP code). If a P.O. box or foreign address, see instructions.	Room or suite no.
14 New business location (no., street, city or town, state, and ZIP code). If a foreign address, see instructions.	Room or suite no.

Part III   **Signature**

Daytime telephone number of person to contact (optional) ▶ ( )

**Sign
Here** ▶

Your signature	Date	▶ If Part II completed, signature of owner, officer, or representative	Date

▶

If joint return, spouse's signature	Date	Title

For Privacy Act and Paperwork Reduction Act Notice, see back of form.   Cat. No. 12081V   Form **8822** (Rev. 12-2003)

continued

FIGURE 13.2 *continued*

Purpose of Form

You may use Form 8822 to notify the Internal Revenue Service if you changed your home or business mailing address or your business location. If this change also affects the mailing address for your children who filed income tax returns, complete and file a separate Form 8822 for each child. If you are a representative signing for the taxpayer, attach to Form 8822 a copy of your power of attorney.

Changing Both Home and Business Addresses? If you are, use a separate Form 8822 to show each change.

Prior Name(s)

If you or your spouse changed your name because of marriage, divorce, etc., complete line 5. Also, be sure to notify the **Social Security Administration** of your new name so that it has the same name in its records that you have on your tax return. This prevents delays in processing your return and issuing refunds. It also safeguards your future social security benefits.

Addresses

Be sure to include any apartment, room, or suite number in the space provided.

P.O. Box

Enter your box number instead of your street address **only** if your post office does not deliver mail to your street address.

Foreign Address

Enter the information in the following order: city, province or state, and country. Follow the country's practice for entering the postal code. Please **do not** abbreviate the country name.

Signature

If you are completing Part II, the owner, an officer, or a representative must sign. An officer is the president, vice president, treasurer, chief accounting officer, etc. A representative is a person who has a valid power of attorney to handle tax matters or is otherwise authorized to sign tax returns for the business.

Where To File

Send this form to the **Internal Revenue Service Center** shown next that applies to you.

 If you checked the box on line 2, see **Filers Who Checked the Box on Line 2 or Completed Part II** for where to file this form.

Filers Who Checked the Box on Line 1 and Completed Part I

IF your old home mailing address was in . . .	THEN use this address . . .
Alabama, Florida, Georgia, Mississippi, North Carolina, Rhode Island, South Carolina, West Virginia	Atlanta, GA 39901
Arkansas, Colorado, Kentucky, Louisiana, New Mexico, Oklahoma, Tennessee, Texas	Austin, TX 73301
Alaska, Arizona, California, Hawaii, Idaho, Montana, Nevada, Oregon, Utah, Washington, Wyoming	Fresno, CA 93888
Maine, Massachusetts, New Hampshire, New York, Vermont	Andover, MA 05501
Delaware, Illinois, Indiana, Iowa, Kansas, Michigan, Minnesota, Missouri, Nebraska, North Dakota, South Dakota, Wisconsin	Kansas City, MO 64999
Ohio, Virginia	Memphis, TN 37501
Connecticut, District of Columbia, Maryland, New Jersey, Pennsylvania	Philadelphia, PA 19255
American Samoa	Philadelphia, PA 19255
Guam: Permanent residents	Department of Revenue and Taxation Government of Guam P.O. Box 23607 GMF, GU 96921
Guam: Nonpermanent residents Puerto Rico (or if excluding income under Internal Revenue Code section 933) Virgin Islands: Nonpermanent residents	Philadelphia, PA 19255
Virgin Islands: Permanent residents	V. I. Bureau of Internal Revenue 9601 Estate Thomas Charlotte Amalie St. Thomas, VI 00802
Foreign country: U.S. citizens and those filing Form 2555, Form 2555-EZ, or Form 4563 Dual-status aliens All APO and FPO addresses	Philadelphia, PA 19255

Filers Who Checked the Box on Line 2 or Completed Part II

IF your old business address was in . . .	THEN use this address . . .
Connecticut, Delaware, District of Columbia, Illinois, Indiana, Kentucky, Maine, Maryland, Massachusetts, Michigan, New Hampshire, New Jersey, New York, North Carolina, Ohio, Pennsylvania, Rhode Island, South Carolina, Vermont, Virginia, West Virginia, Wisconsin	Cincinnati, OH 45999

Alabama, Alaska, Arizona, Arkansas, California, Colorado, Florida, Georgia, Hawaii, Idaho, Iowa, Kansas, Louisiana, Minnesota, Mississippi, Missouri, Montana, Nebraska, Nevada, New Mexico, North Dakota, Oklahoma, Oregon, South Dakota, Tennessee, Texas, Utah, Washington, Wyoming	Ogden, UT 84201
Outside the United States	Philadelphia, PA 19255

Privacy Act and Paperwork Reduction Act Notice. We ask for the information on this form to carry out the Internal Revenue laws of the United States. We may give the information to the Department of Justice and to other Federal agencies, as provided by law. We may give it to cities, states, the District of Columbia, and U.S. commonwealths or possessions to carry out their tax laws. We may give it to foreign governments because of tax treaties they have with the United States. We may also give this information to Federal and state agencies to enforce Federal nontax criminal laws and to combat terrorism.

Our legal right to ask for information is Internal Revenue Code sections 6001 and 6011, which require you to file a statement with us for any tax for which you are liable. Section 6109 requires that you provide your social security number on what you file. This is so we know who you are, and can process your form and other papers.

You are not required to provide the information requested on a form that is subject to the Paperwork Reduction Act unless the form displays a valid OMB control number. Books or records relating to a form or its instructions must be retained as long as their contents may become material in the administration of any Internal Revenue law. Generally, tax returns and return information are confidential, as required by section 6103.

The use of this form is voluntary. However, if you fail to provide the Internal Revenue Service with your current mailing address, you may not receive a notice of deficiency or a notice and demand for tax. Despite the failure to receive such notices, penalties and interest will continue to accrue on the tax deficiencies.

The time needed to complete and file this form will vary depending on individual circumstances. The estimated average time is 16 minutes.

If you have comments concerning the accuracy of this time estimate or suggestions for making this form simpler, we would be happy to hear from you. You can write to the Tax Products Coordinating Committee, Western Area Distribution Center, Rancho Cordova, CA 95743-0001. **Do not** send the form to this address. Instead, see **Where To File** on this page.

Whether you deal with the audit yourself or turn it over to a pro, you need to understand the process. After all, you'll be gathering all the documents. Following the guidelines here will save you hundreds of dollars off your professional's invoice.

Your Return Is About to Be Scrutinized

What will the IRS want to know? Their primary goal is not to see if you have receipts for the expenses you reported on your tax return. What they're really looking for is unreported income. You're about to get some insider information on how to handle audits.

Unless you have a simple tax return, don't handle the audit yourself. Send a seasoned tax professional to the audit instead. In addition to the paperwork, the auditor will be looking you over during the audit. They will focus on five fundamental audit issues:

1. Your financial lifestyle
2. Your standard of living and reasonableness of business operations costs
3. Your spending habits and new purchases (conspicuous consumption)
4. All your bank deposits
5. Whether you reported all income from 1099 or W-2 reports

If these factors don't match your tax return (or industry practices), the IRS will suspect unreported income, inflated expenses, or worse, though your source of funds may simply be nontaxable income. When you've done nothing wrong, you don't want your intermingled accounts to get you into trouble.

Remember, the IRS is the nation's tax collectors. It knows that people will do anything to reduce their taxes—even something illegal. The IRS's main focus is no longer on substantiating expenses. The IRS is serious about identifying unreported income and making the audits profitable.

With so many electronic tools and information-sorting technology, it has become easy to pinpoint the right tax returns for audit. Before they see you, or your representative, the IRS can run a search of your name or your company name on the Internet.

The IRS can find your press releases or newsletters, puffing your company's successes. They can find your marriage, engagement, birth, and death notices. If you throw a really big confirmation, bar mitzvah, or wedding, chances are your pictures and announcements are online. You may even have a website. Consider this: you're probably giving the IRS the information yourself. So make sure that

FIGURE 13.3 How the IRS Knows More About You Than Your Return Shows

Inside Info: Within IRS Records

W-2s	IRP (Information Returns Program)
1099s	Market Segment Spec Program (MSSP)
Audits of other people's returns	National Research Program (NRP)
Audits of related or pass-through entities	Prior audit(s)
Collections	Prior examiners
Currency and Banking Retrieval System (CBRS)	Tax returns
Casinos	
CTRs (Currency Transaction Reports)	
Customs	
F-Bar (report—foreign bank accounts)	
Form 8300	

Data from Everywhere Else

Agencies	Law enforcement
Bankruptcies	Liens
Better Business Bureau (BBB)	Mortgages
Bureau of Labor Statistics (BLS)	OSHA
Court records (amount/holder)	Permits
Department of Agriculture (DOA)	Probate
Department of Motor Vehicles (DMV)	Property records
Department of Social Services (DSS)	Small Business Administration (SBA)
Department of Transportation (DOT)	Social Security Administration (SSA)
Divorces	U.S. Post Office (USPS)
Fictitious Name Register	

City and State Information

Employment/unemployment	Permits
Licenses	Sales tax

Other Sources

Banks/S&Ls/Credit unions	Former personal contacts/relationships
City directory	Informants
Corporations (charters, etc.)	Insurance providers
Credit applications/reports suppliers	Internet searches
Dun & Bradstreet	Landlord
Employer	Legal databases
Employees/contractors	Newspaper articles
Ex-spouse/children	Public utilities
Neighbors	Third-party contacts—various
Employer's personnel records	Trade associations

the information you've put into the public arena matches what the IRS sees on your tax return.

Don't believe me? Google your name. Now, Google your business name. See?

Where Else Will the IRS Look for Information About You?

Take a look at Figure 13.3. You'll find a whole list of sources the IRS can use to find out about you and your industry if they are uncomfortable with your audit. Typically, before an audit, the examiner will pull all the information the IRS has on you internally. (See the first section of Figure 13.3.) Sometimes, they don't have time to get it all, so they ask you to bring things—like prior year returns. If you notice errors, don't fix them. Sooner or later the examiner will pull the actual return that was filed—and you want them to match. Right?

The IRS will only dig into the sources in the second section if they feel you're holding back information. If the examiner doesn't believe your story about that $10,000 deposit being a loan from Dad, they'll start digging into city, state, or credit resources to see if there is evidence of a business you're not reporting.

Remember, the IRS is the arm of the U.S. government that caught Al Capone, Darryl Strawberry, and Heidi Fleiss. They have access to substantial internal and external resources about people—especially in today's computer age.

How Do You Overcome the IRS's Advantage?

In order to be the most successful in an audit, make sure your representative knows as much about you as the IRS knows. You never want your representative going to an audit only to have him or her learn that the IRS has communications from you that your pro is ignorant of, or that the IRS knows about income or bank accounts that your tax pro doesn't know about.

Be sure to disclose all income sources to your pro. Pull a copy of your own credit report to see what the IRS will find.

If you have unexplained or suspicious transactions, you may want to consider hiring an attorney instead of hiring an enrolled agent or certified public accountant.

Keep in mind: Your reputation and credibility with the IRS are your best assets if you want to minimize audit damage. If you're caught in a lie, the IRS won't help you reduce the impact of your errors.

If you have inadvertently not reported income, there may be a good reason for your oversight. If the IRS understands it wasn't intentional, they may help you avoid fraud and other penalties.

What Will Happen During the Audit?

First, you should have received a letter telling you what items on your tax return will be examined.

Look carefully at the pages that outline what the IRS wants to see. If you don't understand the letter, you may call the IRS office before you get there and ask for clarification. That ought to shock them. Few people ever do that besides tax professionals.

During the audit, your examiner will ask a series of questions about you, your past audits, your personal circumstances, and so on. Answer the questions as honestly as you can. Never lie and don't argue or evade their questions. They're just filling out their form. If you don't know an answer, say so.

Once finished with the general questions, they will focus on the tax return. Their first concern is how much income you received. After that number makes sense, they'll look at your expenses or the other areas under consideration.

The auditor will have a printout of the 1099s issued to you. Those 1099s show interest-bearing bank accounts and money-market accounts, with account numbers. The IRS will already know about your accounts, so bring all the bank statements requested to the audit.

The Most Important Item to Prepare—Proof of Cash

The auditor will look at your income first. To see what the auditor will see, prepare your own proof of cash. When overlooked by taxpayers or tax professionals, this one step can cause more trouble in audits than any other.

When the IRS takes all your bank statements, from all your accounts, and adds up the deposits, what will they find? If you're as casual about what goes into your bank accounts as most people, the IRS will find much more money showing up as deposits than you ever earned.

The total deposits will include loans, gifts, cash advances, inheritances, repayments of loans by family or friends, insurance proceeds. . . . Are you getting the picture? In fact, one of the biggest sources of bank statement inflation is transfers from one account to another. If you leave it up to the auditor, it will look as if you didn't report income.

What happens if you leave it up to the IRS? Let me tell you about George.

George owned about twenty-five low-income residential buildings when he got audited one year. He went to the audit without any real preparation. When the auditor did the proof of cash, she discovered more than half a million dollars of unreported income. The tax, with penalties and interest, was more than $300,000. His tax preparer went back to the IRS and requested an audit reconsideration. While the tax preparer didn't do a great job preparing his second audit, he did get the balance cut by $20,000. That still left $280,000 due. Worse, the State of California would probably add another $100,000 when they were notified about the audit results.

George got lucky. He ran into a sympathetic IRS collections officer—Marta—who had audit background, too, and listened to George when he insisted that he never had that kind of income. Marta helped us to find the obvious transfers and nonincome items. We found several, including proceeds from mortgages, when he refinanced two buildings and pulled cash out. Unfortunately, there was still $300,000 to identify. George was adamant it wasn't income. We found the answer when George remembered that he had borrowed money from the bank using his certificates of deposit as security. We couldn't provide records of the transactions. He had none. George's bank had burned down in the Rodney King riots in April of 1992.[2]

How did we convince the IRS that the $300,000 wasn't income? We located his old bank manager and had her write a letter saying that she knew he made a regular practice of borrowing against those certificates of deposit. The IRS dropped the rest of their assessment.

In George's case, if he or his tax pro had simply done the proof of cash, they'd have known about the large discrepancy before the audit. They could have rescheduled the audit until he tracked down all the nonincome items. It would have saved him thousands of dollars of professional fees. More important, George would have avoided the stress and fear that comes when the IRS keeps trying to attach your bank accounts, wages, and investment accounts for a year or two.

So, how do you prepare this nifty proof of cash? It's really easy. See Figure 13.4 for step-by-step instructions.

Now, take a look at an example in Figure 13.5. Prepare it yourself on paper or using spreadsheet software. It makes no difference. Just do it neatly.

Looking at the total column, the IRS would have determined that your income was $141,960 based on adding up all the deposits to all the accounts. Look at the actual income in the total column. You can see that the net paycheck amounted to $40,140.

---

2. Los Angeles reporter Stan Chambers of television station KTLA writes about the Rodney King and Watts riots, available at www.citivu.com/ktla/sc-ch1.html.

FIGURE 13.4 Proof of Cash

Add all the deposits on all the bank statements for all twelve months. Use a spreadsheet like the one in Figure 13.5. Make a separate column for each bank account and a TOTAL column.

Deduct the following items from the TOTAL column:
- ☐ All personal loans
- ☐ Gifts or inheritances deposited to the account (get paperwork to prove it's a gift)
- ☐ Credit card cash advances deposited to the account
- ☐ Bank loans
- ☐ Refinancing proceeds deposited to the account
- ☐ Social Security or disability income
- ☐ Other nontaxable income (IRS tax refunds, certain lawsuit settlements, certain scholarships, etc.)
- ☐ Transfers between accounts
- ☐ Loans repaid to you by family or friends
- ☐ Refunds from stores for personal purchases
- ☐ Reimbursements from employers for your expense reports (be prepared to produce the reports)

Now you understand how the IRS can think you have $100,000 more income than you really do. That's why it's so important to be prepared.

Okay. You've established that you didn't deposit more money than you reported on your tax return. What's next during your audit?

Time to Work on Expenses

In ideal situations, when you have a business, you have a profit and loss statement and a balance sheet, along with a detailed general ledger printout. Or you could go in with an accordion file with all the receipts neatly arranged into categories—with each batch of expenses totaled with adding machine tapes attached. You can probably do this when you have receipts that only belong in one expense category. But if the receipt or check needs to be split among several categories, what are you going to do? Think of credit cards. Each statement has auto expenses, office supplies, meals, travel, and/or entertainment. Unless you can make several photocopies of each statement to attach to each batch, you have a problem.

That's why it's important for you to do your bookkeeping *before* you go to an audit. Do it, even if you never bothered doing it before. (See Chapter 4 for more

FIGURE 13.5 Proof of Cash Spreadsheet

	Note	Checking	Savings	Money Market	Total
			Deposits to All Accounts		
Jan		3,345	250	650	4,245
Feb		3,345	50	650	4,045
Mar	1	3,845	250	150	4,245
Apr	2	5,345	250	1,950	7,545
May	3	3,545	250	1,115	4,910
June		3,345	250	1,115	4,710
July	4	45,345	250	41,115	86,710
Aug		3,345	250	1,115	4,710
Sept		3,345	250	1,115	4,710
Oct		3,345	250	1,115	4,710
Nov		3,345	250	1,115	4,710
Dec	5	4,345	250	2,115	6,710
(1) Total Deposits		85,840	2,800	53,320	141,960

Less: Deduct all deposits that are not income

	Note	Checking	Savings	Money Market	Total	
Advances	1	500				From credit card
Transfer	2	2,000				From money market
Advances	3	200				From credit card
Refinance	4	42,000				Mortgage loan proceeds
Gift	5	1,000				From family
Transfers			2,800	53,320		From checking
Total nonincome		45,700	2,800	53,320	101,820	
(2) Actual income [(1) − (2)]		40,140	0	0	40,140	

Explanation of my cash flow:

All wages are deposited to the checking account.

Transfers are made each month to savings and money-market accounts.

The house was refinanced and the credit cards paid off in escrow.

The rest of the money from the refinance was transferred to the money-market account.

on recordkeeping.) Sure, your expenses might come out differently than they appear on the tax return. Don't worry. If your total expenses are the same, or similar, you'll be fine.

What if, After the Bookkeeping, Your Expenses Are Still Way Off?

You'll need to find the ways to come up with additional expenses—legally. Look here:

- **Credit Cards.** Did you enter all the business expenses from each statement? From each credit card? Do you have a personal card that you sometimes used for business? Remember to include those business expenses. Did you skip December's bill because it has a January date on it? Grab that bill. If the charges were in December, you may use them.

  Did you have bad credit and have to use someone else's card? Get their statements—and some of the receipts that show you signing for the charges. You may need some proof, but if you show the IRS examiner your really bad credit report, he or she might just smile and understand.
- **Cash.** Did you pay for things using cash in the normal course of the day but there are no receipts? Make reasonable estimates. Look back through your appointment book. If you traveled, make a list of the dates and places. List all the tips you gave out each day. List the cab fares, tolls, public transportation costs, and so on. Did you pay for parking, meters, pay phones? Using a spreadsheet—just list all the different out-of-pocket expenses. Be sure they don't add up to more than the cash you drew from your ATM or bank account.

For expenses where the IRS permits you to use standard amounts (auto/mileage, meals, and travel per diems), compare the actual costs with the standard rates. Often, I have been able to bypass a detailed scrutiny of the expenses via one of these methods. Tables with allowances for several years are available on the Internet. Chapter 6 will tell you where to find them.

If you've pulled everything together and you still find discrepancies—call a tax professional. Find a tax pro with experience in audits, bookkeeping, and your industry. A professional may be able to read your mind and help you remember what you were thinking when you originally came up with the numbers on your tax return.

Unless, of course, you either simply made them up—or lied.

Still coming up short? You'll know before you go into the audit what you will lose. It won't be so intimidating when you already know the worst case.

What if You Don't Have Any Receipts?

The tax code operates on the "ordinary and necessary" principle. IRC §162 allows the deduction of ordinary and necessary expenses paid or incurred in carrying on a trade or business.[3] If it appears that an activity was entered into for profit, the rules of Section 162 are applied to each expense.

While the IRS is not always excited about the application of this principle, the courts have ensured that we taxpayers get the benefit of it. There's the old Cohan rule from 1930, when the appeals court decided in favor of entertainer George M. Cohan.[4] Cohan had deducted all his travel, meals, and business expenses without producing receipts. Can't you just see George M. riding around the country on rickety cars, buses, and trains, with his trunks full of vaudeville gear, costumes, props, and all, *and* dragging around another bag just for receipts and accounting records? Well, neither could the court. They determined that if the expenses make sense for your line of work, profession, or trade, you should be entitled to reasonable deductions in line with your industry—even if you don't have receipts.

I tested the theory with a client who also happened to be an entertainer. Barry was audited a couple of years ago for his $50,000 worth of business expenses. Well, like good old George M., Barry had nary a receipt for all his travel, meals, and so on. Using various outside documents, like *TV Guide* and the postcards he sent me from the road each week, I was able to prove his travels. IRS accepted all the expenses, with no receipts and better yet, no conflict. It was resolved at the auditor level, right in the office. Of course, it did take a little negotiating.

Negotiating

During an audit, you can negotiate, to some extent, on all levels. You must have a basis for your request. In George's case, discussed earlier, we were able to get the

---

3. IRC §162, available at http://uscode.house.gov/uscode-cgi/fastweb.exe?getdoc+uscview+t26t28 +180+1++%28%29%20%20AN.

4. *Cohan v. Commissioner*, 39 F.2d 540 (1930)

IRS to believe that $300,000 wasn't income because we were able to prove a pattern of behavior. In exchange for a letter from a banker, I was able to negotiate away $300,000.

Having a basis for your request may involve doing research on similar issues and being able to bring copies of those cases to the auditor. It may involve getting statements from objective third parties. It may involve agreeing to give up one set of expenses, so you can keep others that are more important to you in the future. For instance, I had a client whose tax return included an in-home office, while he was an employee, and $15,000 worth of garments he'd bought as samples. Alex was willing to give up the in-home office for that year, as long as the full amount of the garments was accepted. He needed those garments to support a tax court case. But we didn't care about the employee-office-in-home, because the following year he was a full-time independent contractor.

They won't do it just because you ask. Not even if you're really cute.

TaxMama's Three Basic Rules of Tax Negotiating

1. **Know.** Before you start negotiating know exactly what you want to accomplish. (The IRS doesn't need to know that—but it's critical that you have it defined in your own mind.)
2. **Give up.** Have something to give up. (Do your audit preparation so thoroughly that you find the expenses you overlooked. Look at missed itemized deductions— always a good source of errors in your favor!)
3. **Have backup.** Give the auditor/appeals officer something tangible to put into the file to support your position. It saves them time and makes them look good to their superiors on review.

In George's audit, we weren't able to prove the last $133,000 of deposits were transfers or loans. Since I was able to prove that there was a consistent pattern of behavior, however, I could negotiate with the IRS about the rest. They would accept the logic and conclude it was not income in exchange for my preparing a worksheet with an explanation to provide the auditor for his file. It gave him an excuse to accept my position that the deposits probably were not income.

Office auditors have the discretion to decide what documentation is acceptable. They have to believe the information they see is adequate. Be sure to make an extra set of copies of all the schedules and workpapers for the auditor's file. It provides documentation and makes him or her look better when superiors review the auditor's determination.

Audit Reconsiderations, Appeals, and Tax Court: Some Brief Words

An audit reconsideration[5] is when the IRS agrees to reopen an audit that has already been completed and is past all the deadlines for protest on the local level. It is *not* an appeal. The audit goes back to the same level of examination, often the same office, which conducted the original audit. They will not give you reconsideration if you have already signed off, agreeing to the original audit. You must have additional information that wasn't presented at the first audit. They will also give you this opportunity if you didn't appear for the original audit. When you ask for the reconsideration, you'd better have at least 80 percent of your material ready. You generally get one shot to present your case. So prepare it well. While the IRS rarely agrees, you *can* get audit reconsiderations. First, you must have the audit report, which is either on a Form 4549 or Form 1092-B. If you were working with an examiner, ask him or her for help. If you no longer have that contact information, call the IRS's main phone number at (800) 829-1040 and make the request. If you still have a contact name, ask the auditor's group manager for the reconsideration. If that doesn't work, here are your other options:

- Write to the branch chief.
- Have your tax professional contact the Practitioner Priority Service (PPS). (It's a special hotline for the tax pro community.) PPS has a Form 3410, Request for Audit Reconsideration. Also request Forms 3411 and 3412.
- Contact the Taxpayers Advocate at (877) 777-4778.
- Make an appointment for an IRS Problem-Solving Day.
- Contact the Small Business/Self-Employed Operating Division.
- Contact the Deputy Director, Compliance Field Operations.
- Contact the Director of the IRS.

Don't ever give up. There's always somewhere to go when you disagree with an audit. Decide if the cost to fight your battle is worth what you will win. Sometimes, it's cheaper just to give in to the IRS. But, if it's really a matter of principle and all avenues fail, you may want to look for an advocacy group to take your case on. Sometimes, what's happening to you is happening to enough other people that it's worth setting up a class action suit or rewriting legislation.

---

5. Internal Revenue Manual, Part 4, Chapter 13 Audit Reconsideration—Read the IRS's internal instructions, available at www.irs.gov/irm/part4/ch12s01.html.

Should You Use Appeals Only as a Last Resort?

Some tax professionals find the appeals process is sometimes easier to deal with than auditors. While all auditors must have college degrees, the degree does not necessarily have to be in accounting or taxation. Sometimes they are not as well trained as we would like. With the IRS hiring five thousand new employees between 2004 and 2005, expect to see a lot of people new to auditing.

By the time the IRS agents get promoted to the appeals level, they have extensive field experience, education, training, and the ability to use and understand tax research and research tools. You are dealing with a seasoned professional who has more decision authority than the office auditor and many field auditors.

Appeals' goal is to settle cases without litigation. They evaluate your case's strengths and weaknesses with an eye to how your case will stand up in court. Appeals officers will pull the relevant court cases, decisions, and precedents (or at least the items the officer thinks are relevant). Ask them for their citations when you meet. Most important, have your own research ready. Give them a copy of your cases (not just the citations to cases) with your points highlighted. It will enhance their willingness to cooperate with you. You've done a big part of their job and they have objective documentation, in your favor, to put into your IRS file.

Remember, generally, an appeal is not about supporting expenses. It is about tax law and precedents. If deductions were not substantiated during audit, expect the appeals officer to require supporting documents.

Most tax professionals use the appeals process to their advantage. So can you. When confronted with a particularly troublesome auditor and a group manager who will not intervene, a tax pro would simply call a halt to the whole process. I'd tell the IRS to post their adjustments and walk away.

Then, I'd wait for the audit determination letter (thirty-day letter). When it comes, it tells you right on it that you can request an appeals hearing. If you haven't already, get a good tax professional involved. They'll do a more efficient job at this level.

When writing the letter requesting the hearing, briefly include specific areas where the auditor is incorrect and outline the documentation you have to add for this hearing. *Do not* include a harangue of the auditor's bad qualities or what's wrong with the IRS or the system.

Meanwhile, get all your documentation together. This will include all the support for the unresolved income/expense issues. It will require that you do in-depth research on the tax law issues involved. This is where all that work you did on your business plan will pay off. If you have losses, the business plan will prove that wasn't your intention. But things do go wrong.

Getting Your Case to Tax Court

If you've missed your opportunity to go to appeals after the thirty-day letter, wait for the ninety-day letter (Notice of Deficiency). Owing less than $50,000 means you're eligible to file your petition as a small case. You'll find a Small Case Tax Petition Kit online at the U.S. Tax Court's website, www.ustaxcourt.gov/forms/Petition _Kit.pdf.

You may use an attorney, a CPA, or an enrolled agent (EA) to represent you. With a CPA or EA, you'll need to sign the petition. Once the case gets kicked back to appeals, they will handle the meeting for you. Tax court cases usually get resolved at this level. I've resolved all my clients' tax court cases without ever going beyond appeals. In fact, reading many tax court decisions, it's clear some cases only went to tax court because the taxpayers were really rude or unpleasant to appeals— or their representative wanted to make some extra money. There are also those cases that look simple but were pushed up to tax court to establish a precedent.

Strategy: Use as much of the ninety days to get your records as ready as possible. Send your petition in at least ten days before the end of the ninety days. Enclose the $60 filing fee and mail to:

> The United States Tax Court
> 400 Second Street, NW
> Washington, DC 20217

Owing Taxes

All right, you've exhausted all logical ways to reduce your audit assessment. Or you filed a tax return and owe money. How do you go about paying it?

Naturally, if you have the money, send the check and get it over with. If you're not liquid right now, here are some ways to pay.

Credit Card

The first two companies listed below have contracts with the IRS and other government agencies. They have been processing millions of dollars worth of government credit card payments for about a decade. (The EFTPS program is a part of the IRS.) There are two advantages to using credit cards. The first is that you will have immediate proof of payment. The second is the bonus or mileage points you earn for those charges.

- **www.OfficialPayments.com.** Pay IRS, state, and local taxes online.
- **www.pay1040.com.** Make federal tax payments online.
- **www.eftps.gov.** Pay quarterly estimates, payroll taxes, and business taxes online.

When using these services, the tax agency doesn't pay the merchant fees—you do. (Merchant fees are the costs the merchants normally pay for accepting your credit card.) These fees will cost about 2.5 to 5 percent of the taxes you pay. (They call it a "convenience" fee—that's for the convenience of the tax agency, not you.)

Suppose you'd like to use your credit cards but don't want to pay online. Here are two other ways to use your credit cards.

- **Alternative number one.** Use your credit card checks (you get all those things in the mail, daily, right?). Read the fine print. See what they are going to charge you. See if you can get a no-transaction-fee check. Remember to ask for reduced interest or 0 percent interest on the charge. You might still get your mileage points.
- **Alternative number two.** Call your credit card company and request a cash advance to be deposited into your account. It will take a week or ten days, so do it now. If you cajole sweetly, you might get it without transaction fees— otherwise, expect to pay 2 to 3 percent of the amount charged. Look for a card that has a maximum fee. Beware. Some don't. Be sure to request low or 0 percent interest, and ask about the mileage points.

You Can't Afford to Pay Now, But Will Ultimately

If this is the case, there are three ways to go.

1. **File Form 9465, Installment Agreement Request.** This is the method the IRS suggests. Think twice before requesting an installment agreement (IA). There is a $43 fee for an IA, which you will have to pay again and again if you default on the agreement. In addition, you give the IRS your bank account numbers and the right to attach your funds if you're late or miss a payment. In the past, the IRS levied the bank account immediately when you were late. These days, the kinder, friendlier IRS gives you a chance to make good. Anyone may get an installment agreement, as long as you're not in default on another balance.
2. **Don't file the Installment Agreement Request.** Send the IRS whatever you can afford with the first balance due letter. Save up and send money every

time the IRS sends you a balance due notice. If you expect to have enough money to pay the balance off in about six to nine months, this may be a little cheaper and less invasive than requesting the IA. You'll still be paying interest on the penalties and taxes, but the interest is in the 5 percent range these days—that's probably less than many credit cards.

3. **Borrow the money from family or friends.** If they love you and trust you—and you're really reliable about paying them back—it's the best option. When you're a few days late, they won't be attaching your bank account. If you're going to flake out on the loan, though, don't borrow the money in the first place. You will destroy valuable relationships and trust. There are still other options.

When the Balance Is Too Large to Pay Off

The balance is so large that you're just never going to have the money. You're elderly and are living on a fixed income. You're insolvent. You can't even afford a bankruptcy attorney. You're not hiding any assets or money. If this is the case, call the IRS and tell them the truth. The IRS can put a special collections hold on your balance due for six months or a year and will contact you to review the situation for the next ten years. If, during that time, you can never pay it, you're off the hook.

There is a ten-year limit for the IRS to collect money from you after a tax debt is recorded. Your state may have different limits, or no limits at all.

Some actions can stop that clock, but it's best if you get a good tax professional to help you determine where you stand when you're in that situation. I always have a tax attorney perform those computations.

Request an Offer in Compromise (OIC)

Suppose you aren't really insolvent, but the balance is just so unbearable that you feel beaten down by it. Perhaps you have a job or some sort of steady income from your business, but you'll never earn enough to pay all the taxes due.

You do have a way out. The Offer in Compromise (OIC) Program might be able to help you. When you file an offer in compromise, you're asking the IRS to accept a fraction of what you owe on your taxes—and to write off the rest of your debt. But don't get carried away. There is no promise that your tax debt of $50,000 will get cut to $3,000.

The OIC Myth. "WASHINGTON—The Internal Revenue Service today issued a consumer alert, advising taxpayers to beware of promoters' claims that tax debts can be settled for 'pennies on the dollar' through the Offer in Compromise Program. Some promoters are inappropriately advising indebted taxpayers to file an Offer in Compromise (OIC) application with the IRS. This bad advice costs taxpayers money and time. An Offer in Compromise is an agreement between a taxpayer and the IRS that resolves the taxpayer's tax debt. The IRS has the authority to settle, or 'compromise,' federal tax liabilities by accepting less than full payment under certain circumstances."[6]

Qualifying for an Offer in Compromise

Late-night television, radio, and even some daytime television commercials fill your ears with promises of tax miracles. You're probably getting lots of e-mail, too. Since the IRS filed a tax lien against you, your mailbox is being filled with solicitations from certain tax firms promising you quick resolution of your problem. The truth is they'll take far too much of your money—and not help you nearly as much as you'd expect. One promoter even offered a discounted price of $1,500 to give you a do-it-yourself kit, with instructions. That firm was shut down by the IRS and some members did jail time. Only use firms when you can get a recommendation from someone you know who has used them successfully. Otherwise, go to your own tax professional to have them help you—or to ask them for a recommendation.

The IRS also offers a do-it-yourself kit. It's free. There's a Form 656 kit that can be downloaded from the IRS's website. The IRS even provides workshops on filling in these forms. Check the IRS website at www.irs.gov or call them at (800) 829-1040 to see if they are offering a workshop near you. Before you do all that, let's see if you qualify.

What if you don't qualify for an OIC? Don't waste your time applying if you don't meet the IRS standards for applying. Here are some general parameters—not the ones the IRS posts—but the reality they use when considering your offers:

- Are you young, healthy, and able to work?
- Do you have a college education but are choosing not to pursue work in your own field because you'd rather follow your dream?
- Do you have a steady income?
- Do you have equity in your home? Or an IRA or other retirement account?

---

6. IRS Notice 2004-17, dated February 3, 2004, available at www.irs.gov/newsroom/article/0,,id= 120169,00.html.

- Are you expecting a windfall? An inheritance? Or a great job about to start pouring money your way? Don't lie. That's tax fraud. It's one of the few reasons the IRS will send you to jail.

Look at your own earning capability over the next five years. Even though it may be tight, if there's enough left over, by living within your means, the IRS will reject your offer. They won't wait while you pursue your dreams and live as a starving artist. They'll simply reject your offer in compromise.

Suppose you do qualify and are ready to prepare an OIC. Be thorough. Attach legible copies of all forms, bank statements, and bills requested by the IRS. Enclose three months' worth. If you're not willing to provide the IRS with this much information, don't even start the process. The IRS now requires a fee of $150 be sent in with the application. So, you're wasting your money if you don't follow through.

The IRS reports that more than 80 percent of applications for offers in compromise are rejected as incomplete. Another 10 percent are rejected because people don't respond. If you simply attach everything and enclose anything else they want, you're already in that small minority that might get accepted.

While I warn you away from unscrupulous representatives, I do recommend that you work with a competent tax professional who has a track record of getting OICs for their clients. It is a long, complicated process and having a pro who has gone through it can help. Since you must provide all the documents anyway, you can save yourself dozens of hours of billable time if you gather them all and organize them yourself. I won't go into any more detail. The application packet is remarkably self-explanatory.

Presently, the IRS is overloaded on offers in compromise applications. Expect the process to take about a year to a year and a half. Really. It's slow and nerve-wracking.

The costs? Even if you hire an ethical tax professional to deal with the IRS on your behalf, expect to pay for at least ten to fifteen hours, if you're organized and cooperative. If you must be chased down and hounded to get documents or if you just dump all your records on them and expect them to do all the work, you're back up to twenty to forty hours.

How About Filing Bankruptcy?

Perhaps you don't want to go through the misery of an OIC. You may not want to subject yourself to remarkable levels of stress and frustration, feeling you're at the mercy of an arbitrary system. You have one last alternative.

Look into tax bankruptcy. It's not easy to qualify, but it is faster than an OIC. It's less intrusive—and it's much cheaper. Attorneys handling this will typically charge about $3,000.

To discharge your taxes in bankruptcy, you must qualify.

- All your returns have been filed.
- If filed, the taxes due were not based on fraud.
- If filed late, the return was filed two years or more before the bankruptcy petition.
- The tax return, with extensions, was due three years or more before filing of the bankruptcy petition.
- Tax liability was assessed more than 240 days before filing of the petition.

All of those requirements must be met in order to qualify.

There are several complications about how the 240 days are counted, or what stops the clock. As with all benefits, this one won't come too easily.

The biggest hurdle for many to overcome is the emotional one. There is an intense feeling of failure, of self-denigration when you're reduced to this. But, if this is your only—or your best—option, take it. Trust me. I've seen the transformation in people who did. Many people spend years trying to resolve their tax debt through the IRS's channels and simply end up wasting five or ten years feeling worthless, unable to sleep, and unable to maintain their relationships. Yes, taxes do destroy relationships.

Sometimes, it's best to just clean the slate and start fresh. But if you do, make sure you don't get into trouble again. Please, don't use tax bankruptcy as part of your regular tax plan.

Summary of IRS Interactions

The information in this one chapter took me more than twenty years to learn. Much of it came through sheer stubbornness and the refusal to back down to my fear of the IRS. The rest of the information came through lots of audits and thousands of responses to notices. It helped that in the past few years, we really did get a kinder, gentler IRS.

Using the guidelines in this chapter, you'll never have to be afraid of the IRS, or mystified by their confusing notices. You have everything you need to know how to respond to the usual notices—and audits.

Tax Notices, Audits, and Collection Notes Resources

Important Acronyms
- **FYTIN—Form, Year, TIN.** What you write on all checks to government agencies.
- **KGB—Audit Negotiating Tool.** Know, give up, backup.

Web Resources
- **Form 433-A, Collection Information Statement for Wage Earners and Self-Employed Individuals.** www.irs.gov/pub/irs-pdf/f433a.pdf
- **Form 433-B, Collection Information Statement for Business.** www.irs.gov/pub/irs-pdf/f433b.pdf
- **Form 656, Offer in Compromise Application and Instruction Packet.** www.irs.gov/pub/irs-pdf/f656.pdf
- **Form 2210, Underpayment of Estimated Taxes.** www.irs.gov/pub/irs-pdf/f2210.pdf
- **Form 8822, Change of Address.** www.irs.gov/pub/irs-pdf/f8822.pdf

Online Credit Card Payment Resources
- **www.OfficialPayments.com.** Lets you pay IRS, state, and local taxes online.
- **www.pay1040.com.** Make federal tax payments online.
- **www.eftps.gov.** Pay quarterly estimates, payroll taxes, and business taxes online.

General Bankruptcy and Tax Bankruptcy Resources
- **TaxMama.** http://taxmama.com/AskTaxMama/169/bk.html
- **U.S. Tax Court.** www.ustaxcourt.gov/forms/Petition_Kit.pdf: U.S. Tax Court Small Case Petition Kit.

EPILOGUE

Some Final Words of Advice— and Resources to Rely On

If a man empties his purse into his head, no man can take it away from him. An investment in knowledge always pays the best interest.

—BENJAMIN FRANKLIN

All Good Things Must End

We've been together for so long now, I'm going to miss you. I have great confidence in your success. You've done everything right along the way. Your business plan is smashing. You worked out some of the kinks in the first few months of operations, so it's been rebalanced. Your tax pro has reviewed your accounting records, to high praise. Your customers love you.

Most of all, your home and family life has been enriched, through your family's enthusiastic participation in shaping your legacy.

Let me leave you with this comment from my favorite writer and egotist, Isaac Asimov: "I am at least as intelligent as my tax advisor. So, I should have no trouble understanding the tax laws. But if I were to concentrate my energies towards learning everything I needed to know, the world would be deprived of many of my books."[1]

Follow Asimov's advice. Learn enough about taxes to build a strong foundation. Keep your trusted tax advisor handy. Then concentrate your energies on what you do best—running your business.

---

1. For a history on the good doctor, his writings, his films, and his life, go to www.asimovonline.com.

Resources

You've been immersed in tax and business information throughout this book. You've learned so much more than you ever expected. There's so much to learn, to know, about tax law and strategy. This book was designed to be your guide— to lead you to more information. It was designed to open your mind to creative ways of thinking—to bring you perspectives you didn't have before and won't find anywhere else.

You've got power you never had. (Have I said this before? A dozen times perhaps? Oh my goodness, I've become my mother!) But, please, you're in business. Don't prepare your own tax returns. You have an advisory team. Use it. The team and the resources listed throughout the book will help keep you all up to date. Most of the resources in these pages are available quickly and freely on the Internet.

Hang On to These Important Phone Numbers

- **IRS main phone number.** (800) TAX-1040 or (800) 829-1040
- **IRS Forms and Publications Order Line.** (800) TAX-FORM or (800) 829-3676
- **IRS E-Help for EFTPS, Telefile and e-Services.** National toll-free number: (866) 255-0654
- **Social Security Administration.** (800) 772-1213

For more resources, please check the end of each chapter and the wonderful index in this book. Thanks for letting me join you on your new business adventure!

Always leave them laughing when you say goodbye!

—George M. Cohan of Cohan Rule fame[2]

---

2. Stacy A. Teicher, "No, your husband is not deductible . . . and other IRS tales," *Christian Science Monitor*, April 15, 2004: www.csmonitor.com/2004/0415/p01s04-wmgn.htm.

INDEX

ABOUT THE AUTHOR

Taking her first tax class in college, Eva Rosenberg declared she was avoiding this subject—for good. The information changes too much, too often. Who could ever keep up?

Intending to grow up to be Vice President of International Marketing for IBM, Eva took a brief detour spending a couple of years with national CPA firms. Doing taxes temporarily, to earn a living while completing her M.B.A. in international business, Eva kept running into companies and people with tax problems needing solving. Looking up, more than twenty years later, she finds herself the go-to-girl for the tax community. CPAs, attorneys, and enrolled agents call her when their clients get audited—or have tax problems that can't be resolved. Eva finds solutions that surprise even her—or she negotiates a fair resolution.

Eva Rosenberg has written books, articles, tax columns, and even chapters of tax textbooks. An Internet pioneer and mentor to many, Eva founded the Internet's HelpDesk & WebReview in 1997 to provide a safe place to ask dumb questions about your business website. Still going strong with thousands of readers worldwide, the HelpDesk is now in a blog format at www.ihelpmate.com. Join. It's free.

Those years and experiences make Eva a popular resource for journalists. You'll find her quoted in publications as diverse as the *Wall Street Journal, Christian Science Monitor, Chicago Tribune, New York Times, Los Angeles Times, USA Today, Glamour, Woman's Day,* and the *National Enquirer.* Her tips appear regularly in banking publications, including those of Wells Fargo, Guaranty Bank, and BankRate.com. Eva is still awed each time she sees her name in print.

An immigrant to America who has seen life as both a charity recipient and a donor, Eva has the refreshing ability to understand and address the needs of the rich and the poor, as well as the ESL and non-English-speaking community— and to cut through the sob stories. She recognizes just how easy it is, in America, to move your address from the back seat of your semidemolished car to the deck of your 100-foot yacht, with your GPS and satellite-based Internet connection— and to lose it all. Or, to live for free on the kindness of strangers.

Eva's frankness, sense of humor, and casual, stand-up tax delivery make her a popular talk show guest and speaker around the country. Her CBS.MarketWatch.com tax columns are eagerly anticipated by readers, wondering just what IRS button she's going to push next. Eva proudly displays a framed copy of IRS Notice 2004-27 issued as a result of one of her CBS.MarketWatch.com articles.

Known as TaxMama for both her warmth and her nagging, Eva, an enrolled agent, is the publisher of TaxMama.com and author of the weekly, syndicated Ask TaxMama column. The TaxMama.com site is a free resource, warmly welcoming all taxpayers and tax professionals. Through the site, Eva provides articles, IRS news, links to tax forms for the IRS and all states, and free answers to visitors' tax questions . . . along with her own twist on pending and current legislation. Of course, Eva knows that people really come for the Money Funnies—the jokes pages.

Go to TaxMama.com for your free subscription and access to a continuing stream of tax advice, news, and tips—where taxes are fun.

Use this special sign-up address just for *Small Business Taxes Made Easy* readers, http://taxmama.com/subscribeEASY, to get an autographed e-gift from your TaxMama.